Representing Shakespeare

Representing Shakespeare

England, History and the RSC

Robert Shaughnessy

Lecturer in Literary Studies
University of the West of England

HARVESTER
WHEATSHEAF

New York   London   Toronto   Sydney   Tokyo   Singapore

First published 1994 by
Harvester Wheatsheaf,
Campus 400, Maylands Avenue,
Hemel Hempstead,
Hertfordshire, HP2 7EZ
A division of
Simon & Schuster International Group

Front cover photograph of Kenneth Branagh reproduced
by kind permission of the Shakespeare Birthplace Trust,
Stratford-upon-Avon.

Typeset in 10½/12pt Times by Photoprint, Torquay,
Devon

Printed and bound in Great Britain by
Biddles Limited, Guilford and King's Lynn

British Library Cataloguing in Publication Data

A catalogue record for this book is available
from the British Library

ISBN 0–7450–1560–3

1 2 3 4 5 98 97 96 95 94

For Nicola,
and in memory of
Patrick Shaughnessy, 1929–93

Contents

List of Illustrations   ix

Acknowledgements   x

Introduction   1

Part I   Performing Histories

Chapter One
Representing Shakespeare   11

Chapter Two
Production criticism, critical production   22

Part II   Cycles

Chapter Three
We'll meet again   37

Chapter Four
Masters of War: *The War of the Roses* (1963–4)   41

Chapter Five
Anarchy in the UK: *Henry IV* (1975) and
Henry VI (1977)   59

Chapter Six
Victorian values: *Henry IV* (1982) and
The Plantagenets (1988)   72

Part III   Heroes and Villains

Chapter Seven
Shakespeare through the looking-glass:
Richard II (1973)   91

Chapter Eight
Playing soldiers: *Henry V* (1975 and 1984)   105

Chapter Nine
Murder in the cathedral: *Richard III* (1984)   122

Part IV: Shakespeare Bastardised

Chapter Ten
Barton's Bard: the 1974 *King John*   133

Chapter Eleven
All is True? the Davies–Edgar *Henry VIII* (1983)   149

Chapter Twelve
A bastard to the time:
King John at The Other Place, 1988   163

Conclusion   176

Notes   182

Bibliography   205

Index   219

List of Illustrations

1. *The Wars of the Roses* (1963): Richard III (Ian Holm) confronts Richmond (Derek Waring).
2. *Henry VI* (1977): Anton Lesser as Richard, Alfred Lynch as Edward, Jack Klaff as George and Anthony Naylor as Clifford.
3. *The Plantagenets* (1988): Joan of Arc (Julia Ford) is burnt at the stake.
4. *Richard II* (1973): The coronation sequence, with Ian Richardson as King Richard.
5. *Henry V* (1975): Alan Howard as King Henry, Philip Brack as Exeter, Derek Smith as the Archbishop of Canterbury, Oliver Ford-Davies as the Ambassador, Anthony Naylor as Clarence.
6. *Richard III* (1984): Antony Sher as Richard.
7. *King John* (1974): Emrys James as King John, Jeffrey Dench as Pandulph.
8. *King John* (1988): Robert Demeger as Hubert, Nicholas Woodeson as King John.

Acknowledgements

The photographs between pages 102 and 103 are reprinted by kind permission of the Shakespeare Birthplace Trust.

I am grateful to those colleagues and friends who have at various times commented upon earlier drafts of this book, offered advice, assisted me with my research, and engaged in dialogue with me about its subject matter: in particular, Jacqueline Aldridge, Kate Fullbrook, Liam Harte, Nick Otty, Derek Paget, Tim Rhodes and John Turner. I am deeply indebted to Christopher McCullough for his patience, sound advice and good humour as the supervisor of the doctoral thesis upon which this book is based; thanks are also due to Gerry Harris for urging me to think about publishing it, and to Graham Holderness and John Russell Brown for helping me to rework the material into its present form. I am also grateful to Jackie Jones and Janet Clayton of Harvester Wheatsheaf for their impeccable editorial guidance.

Above all, I want to thank Nicola Shaughnessy for her keen eye and critical wit, for her continuing support, and for her hand in all of this.

Introduction

In June 1992 the drama critic of the *Observer* newspaper, Michael Coveney, chaired a discussion between past and present Artistic Directors of the Royal Shakespeare Company (Sir Peter Hall, Terry Hands and Adrian Noble) on the state of the contemporary classical theatre in Britain. Amidst a number of questions on current trends in Shakespearean performance, Coveney put it to the three directors that the history plays might well be seen as 'the cornerstone of the canon for a Shakespeare company'. Sir Peter's reply to this suggestion was immediately and emphatically positive: not only were the histories 'the epic of England', representing 'the full range of Shakespeare', but they also involved the actor in 'a social reflection of the minute in which that actor is speaking to his audience'. Adrian Noble's response was to reveal that he had directed a production of *Henry V* in 1984 'because suddenly I was in this country that had gone to war in the Falklands and I think Shakespeare writes better about soldiers than any other playwright'.[1] Both directors voiced the belief that the histories have (or can be made to have) a recurrent topicality that is perhaps unique among Shakespeare's plays. Moreover, they thought that a primary task of any modern theatre company committed to the production of Shakespeare is (or should be) to exploit and develop this potential as far as it can.

This book is an exploration of the implications of that belief, tracing the fortunes of Shakespeare's history plays at the hands of the RSC during the twenty-five years between *The Wars of the Roses*, directed by Peter Hall and John Barton in 1963, and *The Plantagenets*, directed by Adrian Noble in 1988. The period between these monumental stage adaptations of Shakespeare's first historical tetralogy marks a profound transformation in the critical and theatrical perception of Shakespeare's plays, as literature, as theatre, and as a cultural force; it also marks a period of rapid and far-reaching social and political change in Britain. In 1963, *The Wars of the Roses* inaugurated what seemed to be a new relationship between the practices of Shakespearean criticism, the theatre and its audiences, and contemporary society, placing the work at Stratford-upon-Avon at the centre of Shakespeare studies and, it was hoped, of liberal cultural life. The cycle promised a new way of producing Shakespeare, not least in its success in refashioning some of the most reviled and neglected plays in the canon into one of the key events in the history of the post-war British theatre. Two and a half decades later, *The Plantagenets* addressed a very different theatrical, critical and political world: with the RSC and its claims upon (and for) Shakespeare open to question, and with the Shakespearean canon itself now the focus of highly charged political debate.

Between these two major cycles lies the subject matter of this book. It is a selective, or rather symptomatic, performance history of the first and second tetralogies, of *King John* and *Henry VIII*. It examines the ways in which the history plays have been transferred from page to stage in a specific institutional setting, and the contribution they have made to the development of the RSC. In order to maintain the institutional focus, the study is confined to the work of this company, rather than broadened to consider the variety of forms that history play production has taken in other theatres and under the auspices of other companies during the post-war period. My aim is to place these performance events within their cultural contexts, in order to explore the variety of ways in which the staging of Shakespeare is a means of negotiating, confronting or evading the pressures of the present. Throughout this history, changing techniques of – and attitudes to – perform-ance and *mise-en-scène* (in terms of set design and costume, styles of delivery, characterisation, performer–audience rela-tions) are seen not only as representative of artistic and economic shifts within the RSC, but also as reflections of broader historical and ideological movement and conflict. My concern, then, is with the performance of Shakespeare as cultural production, as a social practice; above all, as a political (if not overtly politicised) activity. This book examines some of the ways in which Shakespeare's plays have been made to address and intervene in the present, in the context of the disintegration of welfare capitalism and post-war national and economic decline; it also examines the ways in which Shakespeare (as both a body of work and a cultural myth) has acted as a conduit for current aspirations and anxieties, and as an arena wherein ideologies of nation, state and selfhood are legitimated, negotiated and occasionally contested. In places this means teasing out the parallels which have been deliberately inscribed in the productions by their directors. Equally often, however, it involves reading productions against the grain, in order to expose their contradictions, silences and evasions, their covert political implications – in short, their hidden history. I shall also be considering the extent to which the RSC has set itself up as a uniquely privileged organisation, speaking authoritatively through, for and on behalf of Shakespeare, in the modern theatre.

My discussion is underpinned by the conviction that the centrality of the histories to the RSC's cultural project (and hence, in terms of the company's institutional position, to the political culture of post-war Britain) has origins, and implications, which extend well beyond the literary and theatrical. It is well established that the history of these plays' reproduction since the seventeenth century has shown them to be particularly prone to overtly political appropriation, providing the basis for hierarchical and nationalist ideologies of England and Englishness extending far beyond criticism and the theatre. Although my primary focus is upon the impact of contemporary history upon performance, rather than vice versa, this sense of mythical cultural significance is one of the wider concerns of this book. Of particular interest to me are the ways in which the continued reanimation of Shakespeare's histories, and hence of 'Shakespeare's England', has contributed to the persistence of a myth of 'England' itself, coexisting as a fiction of unity and national destiny alongside the reality of the socially divided political and geographical entity known variously as Britain, Great Britain and the United Kingdom.

There is more at stake here than the quotation of jingoistic rhetoric or the invocation of pastoral nostalgia; of highly visible forms of nationalistic, patriotic or royalist appropriation such as productions of *Henry V* and *King John* during wartime, or of *Henry VIII* alongside royal coronations. There is also the question of how far the cultural reproduction of Shakespeare's history – in the theatre as in criticism – promotes the transformation of 'real' history into Shakespeare or Shakespeare into history, refashioning not only the medieval centuries but perhaps the whole of British (or English) history into a Shakespearean fiction. Such fictions tend to be more compelling than the other 'factual' versions of history (especially medieval history) that may be in circulation. As Peter Saccio points out in his 1978 study, *Shakespeare's English Kings*:

> Indeed, far more than any professional historian, and despite the fact that the professionals have improved upon him in historical accuracy, Shakespeare is responsible for whatever notions most of us possess about the period and its political leaders. It is he who has etched upon the common memory the graceful fecklessness of Richard II, the exuberant heroism of Henry V, the dazzling villainy of Richard III.[2]

Ever since Victorian producers established the practice of illusionist, archaeological reconstruction in the presentation of the histories (beginning with Kemble and Planché's *King John* in 1823) – making them a medium for instruction by deliberately obliterating the differences between Shakespearean and contemporary historical representations – theatrical tradition has played a major part in the promotion of the plays, and the myths that surround them, to the status of quasi-factual historiography.[3] This elevation of Shakespeare has important cultural and political implications; for by making this Renaissance dramatic historiographer into a primary mediator of the medieval to the modern period, the theatre has facilitated the induction of the values of liberal humanism into the general historical consciousness. Thus history is seen to take on the characteristics of Shakespearean drama: heroic-individualist, male-dominated, cyclical, driven by an essentialised, transcendent notion of human character. Taking the histories seriously, each era models history, via Shakespeare, in its own ideological image.

Concentrating on aspects of the work of the RSC, each part this book offers a different perspective upon Shakespeare's history in performance. Part I offers a sketch of the theatrical and critical contexts of the more detailed discussions that follow, tracing first the institutional history of the RSC, and then moving to a consideration of the practice of theatre criticism itself. This is in part because throughout its history the RSC has had a uniquely close relationship with academic Shakespearean criticism. Sometimes fraught, occasionally symbiotic, and frequently contradictory, the RSC's work has been instrumental in the turn towards performance in modern Shakespeare criticism, while a reputation for scholarship (based on an amalgamation of the criticisms of Tillyard, Leavis and Kott) has been a defining aspect of its institutional identity. But there are also questions of a theoretical and methodological nature to be considered: it hardly needs emphasising here that an openly political approach may well be at odds with many existing protocols of Shakespearean performance and criticism. Such an approach runs directly counter to the philosophy of the majority of theatre practitioners, the expectations of most spectators, the stated institutional objectives of the RSC and, most importantly for my present argument, the dominant traditions of reviewing and criticism. A great deal has been written about Shakespeare's plays in performance, and a substantial amount about the RSC; but, until recently, rather less attention has been paid to the cultural politics of Shakespearean theatre production, still less to the politics of theatre criticism itself. In order to open up the practices of theatre history, performance and stage-centred criticism to such scrutiny, I examine briefly some of the particular theoretical and methodological issues arising from the practice of writing about Shakespearean performance. There are significant implications here for my own project, and it seems only fair to be clear about what kind of theatre history this book aims to provide.

The second part concentrates on the RSC's stagings of play cycles as one of its most distinctive contributions to the history of modern Shakespearean production. It offers detailed readings of the 1963–4 *Wars of the Roses* cycle, the 1975 cycle, consisting of *Henry V*, the two parts of *Henry IV* and *The*

Merry Wives of Windsor, the 1977 cycle of the *Henry VI* plays, the 1982 production of the *Henry IV* that inaugurated the Barbican Theatre in London, and the 1988 *The Plantagenets*. Presented at key moments in the RSC's history, each cycle provided the opportunity for both company and national self-examination and self-definition. Developing the idea of the Shakespearean hero as cultural role model, Part III moves from the cycle to the single play, examining various permutations of Shakespearean heroism and villainy in key productions of the 1970s and 1980s, particularly in terms of the ideologies of selfhood, individualism and political leadership that they can be seen to promote. The productions under consideration are: John Barton's 1973 *Richard II*, which alternated Richard Pasco and Ian Richardson in the roles of Richard and Bolingbroke; the Terry Hands–Alan Howard *Henry V* (1975), which while nominally part of a cycle was celebrated as a production very much on its own; the 1984 'post-Falklands' *Henry V*, starring Kenneth Branagh and directed by Adrian Noble; and the legendary 1984 production of *Richard III*, directed by Bill Alexander and with Antony Sher in the title role. Part IV takes a detour into the more marginal areas of both the Shakespearean canon and RSC history-play production, examining some of the company's more radical, adventurous and controversial interventions, from John Barton's bizarre reconstitution of *King John* in 1974 to Howard Davies's determinedly Brechtian *Henry VIII* in 1983, and also Deborah Warner's production of *King John* in The Other Place in 1988.

Perhaps it needs to be emphasised here that although much of what I have to say about the RSC and its work is critical on both ideological and theatrical grounds (and the two are inseparable), this book is not intended to offer an account of the rights and wrongs of contemporary Shakespearean production, as evaluated against the plays' authoritative or definitive theatrical identity. In relation to this point, rather than attempting to advance a particular reading of Shakespeare's histories as performance texts, I have limited the scope of my enquiry to the appropriation and reconstruction of a body of literary works within a specific political and institutional context. Here, and throughout this book, 'appropriation' is not used in a pejorative or judgemental sense: it is the inevitable process through which the literary work is reproduced as a theatrical script. Of course the RSC has reinvented Shakespeare in its own image: it could not be otherwise. What is at issue is not the principle of Shakespearean theatrical appropriation, but the nature and implications of the practice. I evaluate the productions discussed not on the grounds of what they allegedly do to Shakespeare, but on what they do to (and for) us.

I do not see the project of this book as being to define what the RSC should, or should not do to, with and for Shakespeare's plays, either politically or theatrically. It is important here to place the political arguments in perspective. Considering the RSC's institutional status as a bourgeois arts corporation in a market economy, funded through a combination of state subsidy, corporate sponsorship and box-office receipts, and its identity as both the theatrical guardian of Shakespeare and an organisation that has been driven by a degree of middle-class cultural radicalism, it would be naive (to say the least) to expect its dominant modes of Shakespearean production to be revolutionary rather than liberal or conservative. And yet there remain sufficient contradictions and ambiguities within the RSC, both institutionally and in terms of artistic policy, for its work to become something more interesting, and more amenable to radical intervention, than a simple rehearsal or reflection of the ideologies of the British state. As we shall see, the productions themselves – sometimes despite the best efforts of directors, performers and critics – retain enough contradictory elements for them to escape their official function. Finally, and in relation to this emphasis on contradiction and instability, it is also worth stressing here that certain distinctive, irreproducible and fundamentally extratextual characteristics of the theatre medium radically differentiate live Shakespearean performance from other modes of appropriation and reproduction; and that these differences have crucial political as well as artistic implications. These characteristics are the immediacy and ephemerality of live theatre, the fact that it is centred upon bodily presence of the performer, and its public and collective nature as a mode of communication. Performance, in other words, may always be in excess of the textualisations it generates and from which it originates. If throughout this book

I attempt to trace the shapes of ideology in the production and reception of Shakespeare in the theatre, it must be remembered that the disruptive, indeterminate and unpredictable elements of the medium itself are always ready to throw the workings of ideology into disarray.

Part I

Performing Histories

Chapter One

Representing Shakespeare

Shakespeare's history plays have always been at the centre of the RSC's work. In the period covered by this book, the main stage at Stratford hosted productions of all ten plays in the group: three monumental productions each of the *Henry IV* and *Henry VI* cycles, as well as stagings of the rarely performed *King John* and *Henry VIII*. Even considering that the RSC's entire mode of operation is geared towards the constant recycling of the thirty-seven plays in the Shakespeare canon, the frequency of recurrence is striking. As a generic group, the histories have proved consistently successful with audiences and critics, while individual productions have become landmarks in the RSC's own history: *The Wars of the Roses* in 1963, John Barton's *Richard II* in 1973, Terry Hands's *Henry V* in 1975 and, in 1984, the Sher–Alexander *Richard III*. More than any other Shakespearean group, the histories have created a sense of continuity and connectedness within and between seasons: as in 1963–4, when *The Wars of the Roses* combined the entire First and Second Tetralogies; and in 1974, when Barton's *King John* quoted elements of his own previous season's *Richard II*; and also in 1980, when Terry Hands's productions of *Richard II* and *Richard III* placed Alan Howard (who had played both Henry V and Henry VI in Hands's productions of the late 1970s) in both lead roles. In its continuing engagement with the histories, the RSC's work has been at its most distinctive; and it is where the original aims and aspirations of the RSC, as originally formulated by Peter Hall in the early 1960s, have been most clearly articulated.

The unique aspect of the RSC, as it was originally constituted, was that it took the tradition of modelling Shakespeare for the present, and visibly institutionalised it, making it a

conscious, conspicuous artistic policy. The organisational
changes engineered by Peter Hall when he assumed directorship of the Stratford Festival in 1959 have been well documented: these included the adoption of the Royal Charter; the
renaming of the Shakespeare Memorial Theatre as the Royal
Shakespeare Theatre; obtaining a London base in the Aldwych
Theatre which would take transfers from Stratford as well as
providing a platform for new playwriting; and establishing a
system of actor training and instituting three-year artists'
contracts in the hope of building a permanent company along
the lines of the Berliner Ensemble.[1] Behind all these modernising initiatives was a desire to stimulate a new cultural invest-
ment in Shakespearean theatre production: as well as being the
repository of tradition and authority, Shakespeare was, in the
hands of Hall and his associates, to become *relevant*. As Alan
Sinfield has demonstrated, this impetus derived from the wider
demographic and cultural shifts that were, in the late 1950s and
early 1960s, beginning to propel the class fraction of which Hall
was so representative – the university-educated bourgeoisie –
towards key positions of cultural power and influence.[2]

Hall's policy exemplified this shift: on the one hand, his reign
at Stratford maintained continuity with established traditions of
high art; on the other, the tradition was revitalised by an
incursion of apparent cultural radicalism. The latter aspect was
manifest in the RSC's new metropolitanism, which linked
pastoral Stratford with soon-to-be-swinging London; in the
practice of playing classical alongside contemporary drama; in
determined attempts to dress Shakespeare in modernist
clothes; in avowed populism; and in its enthusiastic courting of
the 'youth' audience. All this added up, to use Sinfield's
phrase, to 'Shakespeare-plus-relevance', or 'the combination of
traditional authority and urgent contemporaneity' which was –
at least for the 1960s and 1970s – to become the RSC's
unofficial *raison d'être*.[3] It was within the terms of this formula-
tion that the histories would become so important to the RSC,
for it was in these plays that relevance could be explored
directly and with the greatest conviction. In 1963, before
beginning rehearsals for *The Wars of the Roses*, Hall spoke of
how Shakespeare's comprehensiveness enabled modern directors to find 'Samuel Becket [sic] in *Lear*, or the Cuban crisis in

Troilus;[4] yet the histories brought the parallels even closer to home, to 'man's deep instinctive lusts',[5] but also (as he put it nearly thirty years later) to 'the Macmillan crisis and Quintin Hogg throwing his hat into the ring . . . and Professor Jan Kott'.[6] Relevance could be timeless and universal, and it could also be local and particular; the secret of the RSC's success lay in its suppleness in manoeuvring between the two positions. The histories were to allow plenty of scope for manoeuvre. Staging a recurring dream of medieval England, the RSC can be seen not simply to reflect but to play with, to re-present, the history of our times; as material events, they are also part of that history.

Hall's recruitment in 1960 of ex-Cambridge don John Barton as a director established the RSC's reputation for scholarship and academic responsibility; while the appointment in 1962 of the reputed *enfant terrible* Peter Brook to the Artistic Directorate (shared with Hall and Michel Saint-Denis) signalled a commitment to avant-garde radicalism. Under Hall's overall direction the RSC mounted the productions which were to typify this dual identity, and which were to have a decisive impact on twentieth-century Shakespearean production and criticism: Hall and Barton's *Troilus and Cressida* in 1960, Brook's *King Lear* in 1962, *The Wars of the Roses* a year later, and Hall's 1965 *Hamlet*. In 1964, the year of the Shakespeare Quadricentenary and the election of Harold Wilson's first Labour government on a modernising, culturist agenda, the RSC secured its claim to substantial public subsidy. Its subsequent and continuing vexed relationship with the mechanisms of state funding has been a key artistic and political issue for the company, its supporters and its opponents ever since. During the Hall years, the RSC's campaign for political recognition in the form of public funding was matched by an overt concern with large-scale political issues in its Shakespeare productions, and in controversial experiments such as the LAMDA Theatre of Cruelty season in 1963 and Brook's anti-Vietnam War piece *US* in 1965.

Following Hall's resignation as Artistic Director in 1966, his protégé Trevor Nunn was appointed to replace him. With this change the RSC immediately began to move from political to more private and personal concerns – while the middle-class university students, whom Hall saw as the RSC's potential audience, were fast moving in the opposite direction. The liberal disaffection that had produced the demand for Hall-style relevance at the start of the decade had, by its end, assumed a more radically political character in the shape of the Civil Rights and Women's movements, and in opposition to the Vietnam War; in other quarters, it was dissipated in self-destructive drug-induced introversion. By 1970, Nunn could claim that in the RSC's work now 'the interest has been far less political . . . we are concerned with the human personalities of a king or queen rather than with their public roles.'[7] The RSC nonetheless retained a toehold on the alternative culture by embracing its more apolitical, mystical aspects. Nunn's 1969 production of *Henry VIII* (the RSC's first history play since 1964) appeared as part of a season of Late Plays, ending with 'a sonorous white hippie mass' as actors advanced on the audience chanting 'peace, plenty, love, truth' as a mantra.[8] The same season included a production of *The Winter's Tale* featuring the pastoral scenes presented 'as a free-ranging, *Hair*-type musical'.[9] It was Peter Brook, however, who most cannily caught the mood of the times. In 1968, he even went so far as to link Shakespeare (via his notion of 'Holy Theatre') with the drug scene: 'More than ever, we crave an experience that is beyond the humdrum. Some look for it in jazz, classical music, in marijuana and in LSD';[10] this resulted in 1970 in the hallucinogenic mysteries of his celebrated *A Midsummer Night's Dream*.

In 1972, the RSC reverted briefly to its commitment to public political relevance, and to the large-scale politics, large-scale spectacle style of *The Wars of the Roses*, in Nunn's quasi-cycle of Roman plays. This began with *Coriolanus*, progressed through *Julius Caesar* and *Antony and Cleopatra* and ended with *Titus Andronicus*: a four-play cycle of barbarism, civilisation and decadence which Nunn regarded as apocalyptically prophetic of imminent social collapse and, perhaps, nuclear catastrophe. Interviewed in 1971, he asserted that 'They are speaking directly to us now . . . At the end of that sequence of plays it is a world teetering on the edge of extinction.'[11] The critical response to *The Romans* was altogether less favourable than it had been to *The Wars of the Roses*: the enterprise seemed to many to illustrate the perils of a deadly mixture of hubristic directorial intervention, elaborate spectacle and technological sophistication. As the decade progressed, controversy was fuelled by accusations that the RSC's work (like that of the National Theatre, which moved to its new site on the South Bank in 1976) was characterised by conspicuous, wasteful consumption: from the Right, as a prelude to later Thatcherite onslaughts on the 'featherbedding' of state-subsidised industry; from the Left, as part of the campaign against the large theatrical institutions' massively disproportionate claim on funding, achieved at the expense of smaller, community-based and more overtly political theatre companies.[12] At the same time, partly as a way of resolving the contradictions between its establishment status and its more radical objectives, the RSC cultivated its own internal 'alternative' theatre for Shakespeare. In the late 1960s, the RSC latched on to developments in touring, fringe and underground theatre by launching a series of small-scale projects: notably the Theatre-in-Education group, Theatregoround, in 1966, and the seasons at The Place in the early 1970s. Combining elements of fringe philosophy, Brook's aesthetics of the empty space and a Grotowskian conception of poor theatre, this work led to the opening of two studio spaces, The Other Place in 1974 and The Warehouse in 1977. Initially, in the work of The Other Place's first Artistic Director, Buzz Goodbody, this small-scale venture had an explicitly (if imprecisely) political focus, but this was soon to be diluted into using the studio spaces for the production of 'chamber classics'.[13] Despite the RSC's privileged status, its financial position worsened as subsidy contracted in the face of the mounting economic and political crises of the 1970s. Amidst the rapid disintegration of the post-war welfarist consensus, an escalation of industrial militancy following the defeat of Edward Heath's Conservative government by the 1974 miners' strike, anti-colonial action in Ireland, Scotland and Wales, and the resurgence of the hard Right inside and outside the Conservative party, the RSC found itself adopting an increasingly minimalist and anti-scenic mode of production in its main-house productions as well as in its studio theatres. Critical and theatrical trends towards anti-illusion suited the economic austerity of the times, and the distinctive new style of RSC poor theatre, shaped in particular by the productions of Terry Hands, went along with an increasingly right-wing political stance. This was most notable in his 1975 *Henry V*, 'a reminder of national greatness . . . a gutsy, reviving production at a time of national adversity.'[14]

The collapse of Callaghan's Labour government at the end of the decade, and the election of the first Thatcher government, marked the beginning of the end for the Aldwych Theatre and The Warehouse, as the RSC moved its London base to the Barbican Centre, which opened in 1982 with Nunn's production of the two parts of *Henry IV*. If the 1960s had seen a shift from the public to the private in the RSC's work, the 1980s witnessed the company moving towards the privatised. As public subsidy was cut back in the course of the decade, the RSC came to rely increasingly upon business sponsorship (in a new twist to its royal status, it agreed to a special relationship with Royal Insurance in 1987) and from the self-subsidising initiatives of lucrative West End transfers. The Artistic Directorship passed from Nunn to Hands to Adrian Noble, but artistic policy remained consistent. In an era of commercial risk-reduction, productions became pictorially more elaborate and referentially more eclectic (in the popularly 'postmodern' style), and increasingly hierarchical, along traditionally star-centred lines. With the opening of the RSC's replica Jacobean playhouse The Swan in 1986, and its consistently successful productions of plays by Shakespeare's contemporaries, awkward questions began to surface about the continued centrality of the RSC's main-house work – indeed, about the centrality of Shakespeare in the repertoire. By the time of *The Plantagenets* in 1988, which is where this history closes, the RSC had surrendered a great deal of the cultural ground which had been staked out thirty years previously: in some ways, stylistically, economically and politically, it had returned to the conditions within which the company was formed.

Such is the broad economic and political framework within which the productions discussed in this book operated. It is also necessary here to examine the immediate physical context of these productions, the stage space as well as the cultural space which they inhabit. For the most part, the RSC has presented the histories in the Royal Shakespeare Theatre, the large

(1,600-seat), end-on, proscenium-arch playhouse which many still regard as the centre not only of the company's work but also of world Shakespearean production. In sheer physical terms, this is clearly not the type of theatre for which Shakespeare's plays were originally designed. Written for the open platform of the Elizabethan popular stage with its non-illusionist methods of representation, and its energetically participating audience stood and seated on three sides of the action, Shakespeare's histories could well be seen to be significantly at odds with a theatre geared towards the production of large-scale spectacle and scenic illusion. This disparity has long been noted, and can be traced back to the genesis of what was then the Shakespeare Memorial Theatre amidst the ashes of its Victorian predecessor, which was destroyed by fire in 1926. More than anything else, the Shakespeare Memorial Theatre/ Royal Shakespeare Theatre stands as a monument to a very English spirit of compromise, in that it is the architectural embodiment of the attempt to mediate between the forces of tradition and innovation in the twentieth-century Shakespearean theatre. The expedient (and widely celebrated) self-immolation of the 'particularly hideous and inconvenient'[15] old Shakespeare Memorial Theatre had provided the opportunity for a decisive break with the Victorian theatre. In particular, the Elizabethan revivalist movement, led by William Poel, urged the possibility that Shakespeare at Stratford could be rehoused in circumstances less obviously designed for the production of pictorial illusion: at the very least, in an arena or thrust-stage theatre, more radically, in the shape of a reconstructed Elizabethan playhouse.[16] Adopting a more conciliatory stance, the director of the Stratford Festival, William Bridges-Adams, spoke in 1928 of the principle of 'absolute flexibility'; the new theatre, he hoped, was to be:

> a box of tricks out of which the child-like mind of the producer may create whatever shape it pleases. It should be able to offer Mr Poel an Elizabethan stage after his heart's desire. It should be no less adequate to the requirements of Professor Reinhardt.[17]

This ideal theatre, a playground of the imagination and the site of reconciliation between the opposing factions in early twentieth-century Shakespearean production, was to remain an appealing fantasy. The actual result was far less exciting: when it opened in 1932, the new Shakespeare Memorial Theatre was revealed to be very much the same as the old. The building had the art deco functionalism of 1930s architecture, and had abolished the baroque ornamentation of the Victorian theatre, so that 'there was no red plush, and not a gilded cherub or caryatid in sight';[18] but it still centred upon a picture-frame stage which extended only nominally beyond the proscenium arch, and which decisively separated the spectator from the stage. The box of tricks was, in reality, a trap.

This, in its essentials, was the theatre which the RSC inherited when it began operations in 1961; it is the theatre which the company and its audiences have been stuck with ever since. Perhaps the most revolutionary gesture Hall could have made upon assuming the mantle of Artistic Director would have been to emulate the unknown arsonist of 1926; in the event, the new regime was marked by the introduction of a few minor reforms. David Addenbrooke summarises:

> The stage was raked, and the apron was cut away at both sides to allow two rows of angled seats to be added at the front of the stalls. The new stage extended 14 feet into the auditorium and was intended to bring the players into closer contact with the audience than had ever before been possible at Stratford.[19]

But even as he introduced the modifications aimed at mitigating the tyranny of the proscenium arch, Hall insisted upon the primacy of the end-on configuration for Shakespeare: 'try the explicit and still communication of "To be or not to be" with your back to half the audience . . .'[20] During the next thirty years, the RSC made repeated, sometimes controversial, attempts to reconstruct the relationship between audience, performers and stage space by placing rows of seating on stage, extending the forestage into the auditorium, and stripping the proscenium walls. In 1976, the company even went so far as to re-dress the stage in plain timber and to extend a circle of balcony seating behind the proscenium in a theatre-in-the-round approximation of the Elizabethan playhouse. Yet the theatre remains stubbornly resistant to change, retaining always the basic configuration of the picture-frame stage.

The practical implications of this set-up, in terms of its poor acoustics, restricted sightlines and discrepancies of scale between the performer and the stage space, have been repeatedly identified by both critics and practitioners, and need not be elaborated here. As Tyrone Guthrie succinctly put it in 1959, the Royal Shakespeare Theatre is 'an uneasy and unworkable compromise' whose architectural form compels 'the elaboration of spectacle'; as a result, 'a pageant is mounted to the accompaniment of a Shakespearean text'.[21] My interest is in how the stage of the Royal Shakespeare Theatre, in so far as it more or less enforces a predominantly pictorial mode of Shakespearean production, also sustains a relationship between spectators, performers, the performance event, and the text which is as much ideological as it is spatial and physical. It is a stage which is physically highly suited to the production of what Brecht has described as the 'Aristotelian' form of drama, which 'shows the structure of society (represented on the stage) as incapable of being influenced by society (in the auditorium)'.[22] At one level, the relationship between spectator and spectacle can be seen in economic terms: with its theatrical machinery arranged in order to naturalise the technology of illusion, the picture-frame stage is a near-perfect metaphor for the capitalist mode of production, subordinating the performers and the social relations between them to the setting. The carefully arranged and brightly lit space framed by the proscenium arch is an animated shop window display, redefining everything within it – props, costumes, scenery, actors' bodies – as merchandise, the sight of which can be hired by the attentive, desiring spectator. As Keir Elam points out, a semiotic approach to theatrical communication holds that any object, once placed on a stage, 'is in some sense transformed: it acquires, as it were, a set of quotation marks';[23] in the bourgeois pictorial theatre, this fundamental process of semiotisation marks the transformation of the elements of the *mise-en-scène* into fetishised commodities. Thus the stage space and its properties mimic the capitalist production process, wherein commodities (as Marx puts it) are 'changed into something transcendent'; they acquire a luminosity which ensures that 'a definite social relation between men . . . assumes, in their eyes, the fantastic form of a relation between things'.[24]

From the point of view of the spectator, the configuration of the stage and auditorium in the Royal Shakespeare Theatre is designed to position him or her in relation to this spectacle in what are also primarily economic terms. A typical picture-frame theatre, the Royal Shakespeare Theatre is a model of economic and social hierarchy defined in terms of distance from, and orientation to, the stage itself: the more expensive the seat, the better the view. In this, the Royal Shakespeare Theatre fulfils what Catherine Belsey has identified as the classic ideological function of the realist scenic theatre in constituting spectatorship in terms of power and subjection. Drawing upon a Lacanian conceptualisation of the gaze of the theatre spectator, Belsey notes that on the scenic stage 'certain coherences of social and spatial relationship are taken for granted':

> The actors portray concrete individuals who interact with each other as unified subjects . . . proportion is defined from the point of view of an optimum position in front of the stage, from which the fictional world is visible, recognizable and separate.[25]

The stage space presents itself to the spectator's gaze as a sight (or site) to be mastered, and it is this power relation which holds him or her in place, 'a disclosure which offers the spectator an absolute (and illusory) transcendence'.[26] Thus does the picture-frame stage foster in the spectator a sense of existential power and autonomy at the same time as it emphasises political powerlessness, the impossibility of altering or intervening in the social world depicted on stage.

In such a context, many of the political questions that might be asked of Shakespeare's history plays are definitively framed before a production even gets started. History is reduced to an ongoing conflict between the architectural and the personal, between the huge and impersonal environmental forces embodied in the magically mobile scenery, and the 'real' individuals impersonated by the actors as existentially and psychologically indistinguishable from the spectators. The discrepancies of scale between the actor and the semi-autonomous setting ensure that the theatrical representation of history and social reality is a contradictory combination of big pictures and small gestures, with no obvious or comprehensible social relationship between the individual and the political. As a result, history itself is presented as either deterministic or a matter of voluntary agency; and it is intelligible only in a pictorial form organised according to laws of proportion and perspective which confirm the spectator's secure position in the present. As a result, the multiple historical and theatrical perspectives of the plays themselves collapse into a single, determinate point of view: history emerges as an illustrative record of tableaux vivants, creating an illusion of verisimilitude through architectural pastiche, 'authentic' costumes and period detail.

In the chapters that follow, I shall trace the efforts of a variety of directors and performers to negotiate their own versions of Shakespeare's history within this framework. In the following chapter, the focus is upon their critical context, in particular the discourses which have mediated, shaped and defined not only the RSC's work, but also subsequent ways of commenting upon and contextualising that work. Like any other mode of critical or historical writing, the practices of theatre history and production criticism have their own institutional histories, their own theoretical dimensions, their own politics. It is to these that I now turn.

Chapter Two

Production criticism, critical production

In the previous chapter, the role of 'scholarship' in the formation of the RSC's distinctive institutional identity was briefly mentioned. Later chapters examine in more detail the specific constitution of the RSC's scholarly agenda, particularly during the 1960s, where a heady amalgam of Tillyard's historicism, Leavisite close reading and analysis, Kott's modernism and Barton's textual studies underpinned the company's reputation for radicalism and responsibility. Here I consider the ways in which the formation of the RSC inaugurated a new relationship between criticism and theatre practice, with significant implications for both. Of particular significance is the fact that the coalition between professional theatre and the academy legitimated contemporary theatre production as a subject for scholarly research, analysis and debate.

This growth of interest in the contemporary Shakespearean theatre during the 1960s was part of the broad movement in twentieth-century Shakespeare studies towards stage-centred or performance criticism. It included diverse critical positions and methodologies: historical research into the conditions of the Elizabethan theatre; studies of stage conventions, techniques and iconography; interpretative criticism; theatre history; studies of metadrama; the testimony of actors and directors; and combinations of some or all of these.[27] From William Poel onwards, moreover, performance criticism has exhibited an argumentative and polemical strain, acting (like so many 'revolutions' in critical history) both as a disruptive and as a conciliatory force within the broader field of literary Shakespearean criticism. It has been both radical and conservative, materialist and idealist, antagonistic to the dominant modes of literary criticism and deeply implicated within them.[28]

Shakespeare's theatrical dimensions, repeatedly redefined, have been subject to radically divergent appropriations: as the condition of the text's historical specificity and as the guarantee of its eternal afterlife; as both actuality and ideal; as a structure of oppression and as a force for liberation from academic elitism and interpretive rigidity; and as an argument both for and against character, history, theory and criticism. This fractured tradition provides another important formative context for the work for the RSC, particularly in the sense that the antagonisms and contradictions within stage-centred criticism, and in its relations with the broader field of Shakespeare studies, also inform the company's dialectic between 'Shakespeare' and 'relevance'.

My specific concern here, however, is with the way in which that work has been mediated through the growing body of writing which is concerned with documenting and discussing contemporary Shakespeare performance. Like other forms of performance criticism, production criticism (as David Samuelson has designated it[29]) has its own distinct history: it began to develop in a substantial form in the early 1960s and has gained ground ever since. Prior to this period, writing about contemporary Shakespearean production, aside from journalism, was largely confined to the autobiographies of actors and producers and to occasional articles in *Shakespeare Quarterly* or *Shakespeare Survey*. The few full-length studies that did appear tended to be wide-ranging and synoptic in form and elegiac, anecdotal and quasi-autobiographical in style, and often primarily concerned with the practicalities of recreating Elizabethan methods of staging in the modern theatre.[30] Often the tone of these accounts is a little diffident and apologetic, as if the subjective practice of writing about Shakespeare in performance were secondary to the more systematic and serious business of professional literary scholarship and criticism. Since the 1960s, however, the status of production criticism has changed, as marked by the publication of a number of key works: *The Masks of Othello*, the first of Marvin Rosenberg's encyclopaedic stage histories of the quartet of major tragedies, appeared in 1961;[31] followed by A. C. Sprague's *Shakespeare's Histories* in 1964;[32] and John Russell Brown's *Shakespeare's Plays in Performance* in 1966.[33] The last book, in particular, established the idea that the single, notable stage production could be documented in detail, critically analysed and subsequently revisited; that it could begin to be considered as a significant rather than merely anecdotal element in the history (and identity) of the play. During the 1960s and 1970s review articles dealing with contemporary production in *Shakespeare Quarterly*, *Shakespeare Survey* and *Shakespeare Jahrbuch* expanded and proliferated, becoming more detailed and reflective; as did articles discussing the theoretical and methodological issues arising from the practice of production criticism itself.[34]

The fact that production criticism appeared as a serious force as and when it did is, I would suggest, due to much the same educational, theatrical and political changes as led to the formation of the RSC. It is possible to attribute the emergence of production criticism as a response to the new seriousness and commitment of the RSC itself, so that academic legitimacy became one of the company's rewards for quality and intellectual complexity. In the context of the increasing legitimation of drama and theatre studies as academic subjects, with the establishment of a number of university drama departments in Britain throughout the 1960s, and with young, university-trained directors hopefully aiming productions at young, university-trained audiences, it seemed that Shakespearean production at Stratford, like the British theatre in general, had entered a renaissance, shifting from superficial entertainment and reverential or thoughtless reproduction to critical intervention. In this, the RSC's promotion of the director from the role of producer to intellectual guardian of the production was instrumental. In 1959, Richard David proposed that collaboration between academic criticism and the theatre might be achieved by a meeting of actors and scholars,[35] but Hall's revolution at Stratford in the 1960s was to ensure that it was the relationship between the director and the critic that would prove to be the focus of attention. Production criticism began to function as a system for the legitimation and regulation of directorial intervention. Following an author-centred model of literary criticism, production criticism geared itself towards close discussion of selected directorial works, to the merits of the interpretative decisions taken, and eventually to the formation of a 'canon' of productions. By repeatedly asserting its scholarly credentials, the RSC encouraged such attention; moreover, the relative durability of production criticism – as compared to the more ephemeral, disposable judgements of journalistic reviewing – fostered the sense that each Stratford Shakespeare production had a historical as well as immediate significance. From the outset, the RSC's identity involved a keen sense of its own history and traditions, a sense that was manifested in the public statements of its directors, in the presentation of its programmes and publicity materials, its commemorative volumes, and in the efforts it has made to preserve records of its productions. In practical terms, the RSC's proximity to the Shakespeare Birthplace Trust in Stratford-upon-Avon facilitated the archivisation of its own work, immediately transforming it into centralised and access-ible theatre history, encouraging scholarly interest and offering the conditions for ready-made doctoral research.[36] The RSC suited (perhaps needed) production criticism as much as the latter suited the RSC.

But there were also compelling political reasons for the growth of interest in contemporary Shakespearean perform-ance during this period; and in order to establish this it is necessary to consider the origins of production criticism in its cultural and critical context. Recent histories of post-war criticism have demonstrated that the political legacy of McCarthyism and the Cold War had left Shakespeare studies at the end of the 1950s, particularly in the United States, in the formalistic grip of New Criticism.[37] At the beginning of the 1960s it was becoming evident that – for all its previous excitement as a 'democratising' method – the practice of treating the Shakespeare text as the self-contained, fetishised cluster of image patterns was fast becoming a sterile and repetitive activity. Intensified, perhaps, by the approach of the Shakespeare Quadricentenary in 1964, this growing realisation provoked a number of Shakespearean critics to move from questions about the current state of criticism to broader issues of the history and philosophy of the discipline of Shakespeare studies.[38] Even by itself, such self-scrutiny was potentially embarrassing, since it questioned not only the present disposi-tion of Shakespearean scholarship and criticism but perhaps their very legitimacy; the disruptive potential of such awkward questions was further exacerbated by the changing academic climate. Considerably more significant (and dangerous) for the discipline was the transformation of the cultural and political base of university education in Britain and the United States during the 1950s and 1960s, the expansion which was instrumental in the formation and development of the RSC. As the newly educated, youthful lower-middle class became increasingly disaffected in the course of the 1960s, its disaffection was partly manifested in intensified and increasingly audible demands for relevance – demands which were heard even in the rarefied fields of Shakespearean criticism and pedagogy. It was this demand, operating within a rapidly mutating culturist framework, that provided the context for the pioneering works of Marxist Shakespeare criticism[39] and which created such propitious circumstances for Jan Kott's *Shakespeare Our Contemporary*;[40] but it was the academic legitimation of contemporary Shakespearean production that provided the safest opportunity for criticism to become relevant. By focusing upon the contemporary theatre and its controversies, foregrounding a tangible, challenging and immensely studiable Shakespeare, criticism found a way of appearing fashionably up to the minute without having to become political; and the apparent radicalism of the RSC's work naturally fitted the bill. Moreover, as an accessible form of criticism and history, studies of plays in production also partially satisfy the demand for theatrical engagement with the plays themselves without the risks of actually having to do practical work. With radical energies thus diverted, the more literary-based forms of Shakespeare criticism were free (for the time being) to get on with the business of tracing image patterns, producing character studies and avoiding questions of Shakespeare's relation to issues of gender inequality, racial conflict and class struggle.

By the beginning of the 1970s the lineaments of a canon of Shakespearean performances (dominated by RSC productions) were already in place. The landmark productions of the post-war Shakespearean theatre had become sufficiently distant to be treated as history; yet they were still recent enough to be considered as contemporary. In a further twist to the Shakespeare-plus-relevance formula, the RSC now had the authority of its own past productions to draw upon, emulate or react against. Throughout the decade, the major productions of the 1960s were critically reassessed, and key productions of the 1970s were checked over for admission into the canon. In 1970, Hall and Barton's script for *The Wars of the Roses* was published, providing a scholarly resource for 'those who are interested in studying our text and the theatrical potential of the *Henry VI's*'.[41] The 1975 production of *Henry V* was instantly commemorated in a volume which included the script, directorial statements and reprints of reviews.[42] In 1977, Stanley Wells's *Royal Shakespeare*, an account of four 'major' RSC productions, was published;[43] and in 1978 Richard David offered what seemed to be a definitive record of the RSC in the 1970s in his *Shakespeare in the Theatre*.[44] David Addenbrooke's sympathetic history *The Royal Shakespeare Company: The Peter Hall Years* appeared in 1974, followed by Sally Beaumann's *The Royal Shakespeare Company: A History of Ten Decades* in 1982 and by Colin Chambers's Marxist account of The Other Place and The Warehouse, *Other Spaces*, in 1980.

While the RSC's work was increasingly comprehensively documented, it also provided a stimulus for the discussion of the more contentious issues of Shakespearean performance – in particular, the power of the director, which the RSC had done so much to institute. The debate for and against directorial licence, which can be seen to encode conflicting political claims upon Shakespearean authority, had been running for some time; in the 1970s it came to assume a new prominence.[45] Much of the opposition came from conservative defenders of Shakespeare's integrity, but at times the critique could also assume a potentially radical edge. In 1974, John Russell Brown launched a polemic against scholars and directors, *Free Shakespeare*, in which he argued that both criticism and theatre practice – and this was particularly evident in the work of the RSC – conspired to produce a reductive, appropriative and authoritarian Shakespeare, geared towards commodity production rather than the immediacy and spontaneity of theatre art. Although the solution Brown proposed to counteract these tendencies was utopian in conception and ultimately idealist – he advocates a mode of pedagogy and performance which would 'forget "argument", "criticism" and "interpretation", in favour of exploration and encounter'[46] – the critique can be seen to have political implications of which Brown, perhaps, was unaware. Writing in 1972, David Selbourne focused upon Peter Brook's *A Midsummer Night's Dream*, to offer a more hard-hitting analysis. Brook's apparent libertarianism, as he saw it, masked a more fundamentally authoritarian, market-centred ideology: all the energy and technical accomplishment added up to was a 'director-shaped commodity'.[47] There is (as always) more at stake than a merely literary quarrel over the meaning of Shakespeare, or a dispute over the legitimacy of this or that mode of production: the issues are implicitly ones of academic, theatrical and institutional power. The academic critical response to all this was the politicisation of Shakespeare studies; the RSC's was to channel dissent into The Other Place, and to adopt the primary defensive tactic of the theatre professional: thus Nunn dismissed attacks on directors' theatre as 'essentially academic slogans'.[48]

Despite such antagonisms, many commentators seemed convinced at the end of the 1970s that scholarship and professional performance had established a newly beneficial relationship which was most vividly exemplified in the reciprocity between the RSC and academic criticism. In 1977 J. L. Styan published *The Shakespeare Revolution*, in which he traced what he regarded as an epochal shift in twentieth-century criticism and performance: in the former, the 'grand discovery' that 'Shakespeare knew his business as a playwright'; in the latter, the progression from 'the illusory realism of Henry Irving to the non-illusory statements of Peter Brook'.[49] For Styan the 'uneasy but passionate marriage of scholarship and the stage'[50] began with William Poel, was developed by Granville-Barker and Tyrone Guthrie, and culminated in Brook's *A Midsummer Night's Dream* and in Barton's 1973 *Richard II*, in which 'past traditions of realistic presentation are being stripped away and the spirit of Elizabethan ritual and role-playing reminds [the playgoer] of Shakespeare's essential theatricality in a way that Brecht would fully have endorsed'.[51] In retrospect, of course, Styan's rhetoric of radical transformation seems ironic, given the quite different critical forces (of Marxism, feminism and post-structuralism) gathering in the wings for the more directly political Shakespeare revolution of the 1980s. As Kiernan Ryan noted at the end of the decade, 'the new perspectives and alternative projects' defined by these new approaches 'have thrown the rationale, and hence the authority, of hitherto confident modes of criticism into serious question'.[52] In such a climate of crisis, the stage-centred approach, despite its claims, has been seen as ideologically complicit with humanist literary criticism.[53] I do not intend here to engage in a detailed discussion of the politics of performance criticism and its relation to its literary counterpart (institutionally and pedagogically, the situation, I would argue, is in any case more complex than straightforward complicity). However, I would point out that both Styan's manifesto for Shakespeare studies and his metacritical narrative tended to elide important differences, some potentially antagonistic, between various modes of stage-centredness: between Poel's fundamentalist revivalism, Granville-Barker's theatricalisation of Bradleian character-study, Bradbrook's historically based study of conventions and Brook's modernism. There is a further irony in the fact that the trend towards theatrical non-illusion – which by the time Styan was writing seemed irreversible, particularly in the work of the RSC – proved to be short-lived, as Shakespearean production in the 1980s moved rapidly back to a pictorially elaborate, illusionistic style. Terry Hands later confirmed this: 'In 1981 we took a policy decision to go into spectacle.'[54]

Yet although Styan's vision of the future of Shakespeare criticism and performance, in which 'actor and scholar will teach each other . . . the scholar will modify the actor's illumination, the actor will modify the scholar's, a process of infinite adjustment',[55] was inaccurate in certain key aspects, there was one respect (beyond the widespread lip-service paid in all modes of subsequent criticism to the notion that Shakespeare's plays ought to be treated as drama rather than, or at least as well as, literature) in which it proved more relevant. At the end of the 1970s, with the canon of significant twentieth-century theatre productions of Shakespeare's plays in place, performance history began to emerge from a fairly specialist interest into the mainstream of academic publishing. Richard David's *Shakespeare in the Theatre* found a ready market as an early example of this trend. Published in 1978, it was reprinted a year later, and remained in print for a decade. But David's was in some ways an old-fashioned type of production criticism, in that, although considerably more selective, exacting and judicious than the memoirs of the 1950s, it nonetheless followed their subjective form of the detailed eyewitness account, examining key productions in order to elaborate general principles of Shakespearean performance. Subsequent production criticism has relied less on first-hand experience and reminiscence and more on the records of productions, as it has increasingly treated performance in terms of documentary history. The RSC, as we have seen, was particularly well placed to serve this expanding critical industry, and in the 1980s its past came to seem more important to criticism than its present or future. Ralph Berry's *Changing Styles in Shakespeare*, published in 1981, indicated future developments: a selective twentieth-century performance history of five plays, it offered a symptomatic account of 'the ways in which we have fashioned Shakespeare after our own image' while retaining the sense that these refashionings nonetheless embodied 'the permanent truths that are coded into a Shakespeare text'.[56] Subsequent production histories have generally operated within this framework of textual authority combined with historic particularity; and as such have proved to be an accessible mode of introductory Shakespearean criticism. In the 1980s the format has been adopted by a variety of publishers and developed in numerous series of book-length stage histories of single plays, the most durable of which has been Manchester University Press's 'Shakespeare in Performance' series, which commenced in 1984 with J. L. Styan's study of *All's Well that Ends Well*.[57] There is, it would seem, a ready market for these types of study, which can often act as an introduction not only to the performance history of the play, but also to wider issues of criticism and interpretation. Acting as an increasingly widespread pedagogic corollary to the critical casebook and the single-play study guide, they are well suited to the market-led, modular structures of university education in Britain and the United States in the 1980s and 1990s. In the context of such critical accounts, the canonical production takes on a new and different life. Encapsulated in a couple of iconic production photographs and anything from five to fifty pages of exposition, it has been recycled as narrative.

Here, I would suggest, it is important to recognise what is

subjectively at stake in the writing and reading of these histories: that is, theatre history needs to be regarded as a narrative mode with a particular appeal of its own. Production criticism (and this is perhaps the key to its accessibility) often tends towards an almost novelistic realism and narrative flow in its efforts to restage the performance in the imagination of the reader. Especially when it is discussed alongside film and television productions, the stage production is recalled in primarily visual (perhaps cinematic) terms: the 'reality effect' of theatre history as prose narrative positions its reader as the sole spectator at a private screening of the performance. Sara Eaton's comments on the imaginative visions of the Elizabethan stage found in New Historicist writing have a direct relevance here. Drawing upon film theory (and in particular on Laura Mulvey's discussion of the relationship between illusionism and visual pleasure), she argues that, characteristically, 'a writer's critical gaze . . . reconstruct[s] the dramatic text as though the eyes were a camera, thus recreating a mental performance of the text in as voyeuristic a manner as any film director would'. Thus the imaginative licence of critical speculations and theatre history 'situates the spectator as a privileged "invisible guest" at a very subjective performance of the text'.[58]

In the case of production criticism, the illusion of voyeuristic mastery is all the more deceptive because its readers enact a 'mental performance', not of a text, but of a performance and its textual representations, in the form of reviews, promptbooks, photographs and video records. In these circumstances, the idea that production criticism provides anything other than a partial and selective record looks increasingly dubious; this may well be unavoidable (and I cannot exclude this book from these considerations), but it raises questions about what exactly it is that production criticism is trying to recover. Just as the theatre performance recurrently figures as a poignant metaphor for transience, ephemerality and mutability, so production criticism may be a fundamentally elegiac critical form. In its attempts to reconstruct an authoritative record through the sifting of the fragmentary and contradictory textual traces of dead productions, the stage history frequently reaches towards the imagined felt life of a vanished performance. Thus, like

Hamlet in pursuit of his father's ghost, Ralph Berry's *Changing Styles* is concerned with 'tracing that most transient of identities, the visible shape of Shakespeare as he moves across the stage'.[59] Similarly, as a preface to his study of *King Lear*, Alexander Leggatt casts the theatre historian in a Beckettian role reminiscent of the hapless protagonist of *Krapp's Last Tape*:

> As the play changes, so the productions vanish. Reviewers disagree; promptbooks are silent on the things we most want to know; archive videotapes show tiny figures moving in a badly lit space with nothing like the effect of a live performance; production photos show posed shots and give close-ups of makeup that was never designed for a camera. Memory cheats . . . I have been astonished by how often my memory is at odds with the evidence – much of which depends on other people's memories.[60]

Perhaps this is a useful reminder of the extent to which the narratives of production criticism are a form of realist fiction; but to me its tone suggests something further: that production criticism (which is structured around an absence) has at its heart a powerful, potentially debilitating nostalgia. As autobiography merges with documentary research in Leggatt's account, it becomes apparent that the representation of performance in writing may be part of humanist criticism's endless quest for order, meaning and origin, a doomed attempt to recover an irretrievable, idealised past. Thus production criticism adds its own distinctive voice to what Catherine Belsey has memorably described as 'a choric elegy for lost presence'.[61] This elegiac sense is heightened when, as so often it does, production criticism augments its narrative visualisations by incorporating photographs from productions into the critical text. Included as the index of authenticity and historical facticity, the posed and selective nature of the production photograph, as Leggatt notes, define it as a persuasive and poignant fiction. Susan Sontag's observations on photography seem particularly apt here: as she puts it, the affective force of the photograph lies in its 'irrefutable pathos as a message from time past', as it testifies to 'another person's (or thing's)

mortality, vulnerability, mutability'.[62] In the context of the
theatre, of course, that impression of transience and mutability
is doubly reinforced: photographs (and more recently video
records) remain as a haunting vestige of all that has melted into
air.

There is, then, an indeterminacy at the heart of production
criticism which undermines its repeated claims to an authenticity and validity which is more solidly, empirically grounded
than what Styan calls 'the irrelevancies of impressionistic [i.e.
literary] criticism for which the writer need consult no other
than himself'.[63] In this book I consider the documentary
evidence of performance – reviews, photographs, production
promptbooks, and so on – not as a means of access to the half-
glimpsed truth of the original production but as a body of texts
which are governed by their own narrative laws and conventions, and which have their own hidden histories and politics. It
is as much (if not more) a study of the texts which are generated
by the chosen performance events as it is a history of the events
themselves; in part because it is only as texts that the canonical
productions discussed here continue to produce significance in
the present, influencing theatre production, criticism and pedagogy, and demanding critical rereading. I aim to offer a
different kind of theatre history: one that is interested less in
what the RSC's methods, styles and traditions of production
reveal about Shakespeare's plays than in how these strategies
of representation and intervention intersect in reality with
ourselves, our own histories, and our own political struggles.

Part II

Cycles

Chapter Three

We'll meet again

By the end of the day, complete strangers were offering one another wine-gums.[1]

In its modest way, Bernard Levin's account of audience behaviour during an all-day performance of the three parts of *Henry VI* at the Aldwych Theatre in 1978 attests to the tendency for such events to play mild havoc with the protocols of English bourgeois theatre. As a feature of Shakespearean history cycles, the nine-hour event protracts and intensifies one of the key elements of drama in performance, the passage of time, into an acute experiential reality – sometimes it seems to miniaturise the movement of history itself. Attending a morning to midnight cycle of histories, which is a day's work rather than a good night out, means engaging in a cultural ritual fraught with considerable self-conscious import and prestige, while the arduous quality of the theatrical marathon fosters a slightly delirious sense of determination and *esprit de corps* among cast and audience alike – a camaraderie that is appropriate to patriotic narrative. When entertainment gives way to participation in the making of theatre history, audience psychology undergoes a curious sea change. The institutional and environmental pressures which conventionally work to privatise the individual spectator's enjoyment of the performance (isolating him or her in darkness, silence and polite indifference to neighbouring theatregoers) are temporarily alleviated, if not suspended. Stumbling back to one's seat after the third or fourth interval, it becomes increasingly difficult to maintain the sang-froid that normally ensures the avoidance of eye contact: sheepish grins and apologetic half-greetings begin to acknowledge mutual complicity in the unfolding theatrical epic. In a curious inversion of conventional theatregoing behaviour, high seriousness is subverted by spontaneity, as the performance of the cycle begins to liberate some of the spirit of carnival and play that is so frequently squashed in the institutionalised theatre. Once again, Shakespeare works his usual magic in a transformation of the business of theatregoing; perhaps there are stirrings of the communality that is fondly attributed to the Elizabethan theatre – a convivial organic society, and a dimly remembered playground world of childish pleasures, crystallised in the simple charitable gesture of a shared sweet.

It is in the context of such social transactions that Shakespearean theatrical production takes place. This experiential quality distinguishes the effects of performance from those of reading, while also accounting in part for its peculiarly unpredictable ideological potency. From the institutional point of view, though, the theatre has on the whole followed Shakespearean criticism in interpreting the history plays in conservative terms. When the school of literary historicism pioneered by E. M. W. Tillyard established the habit of conglomerating Shakespeare's previously disparate, underrated history plays as cycles, sequences and tetralogies, they offered readers a reconstructed whole that was far greater than the sum of its parts: epic dramas that aspired to the condition of the Victorian novel (and of nineteenth-century historical writing), transcending the episodic and picaresque through the unifying *telos* of the Tudor Myth.[2] Directors and producers of these plays, slowly following suit in the post-war British theatre, combined the pleasures of expansive narrative with those of theatrical and national celebration. Cycles were also events: taking drama which was larger than life and giving it a life larger than drama. The concept of the cycle, combining a sense of the sequential progression of moral and political causes and effects with that of an eternal recurrence which eradicates difference and change, generates its own meanings: in performance, significance accumulates diachronically, through repetition and parallelism, through the leitmotif and palimpsest. This is where history is transformed into epic ritual and myth; at the heart of these cycles is an endlessly replayed patriarchal narrative, a struggle between generations of fathers and sons projected on a national scale. The rehearsal of predominantly male concerns is a feature that the history cycles have in common with the majority of Shakespeare's perform-ances in the modern theatre, of course; and these seem particularly adaptable to the demands of patriarchy. The frequency with which the battlefield recurs as the site of significant action in the histories invokes a traditional arena for the celebration of masculine prowess; the tussles staged therein complement psychic conflicts, as the formation of national and personal identities interlink. In the modern theatre, as we shall see, the father–son relationship forms the central dynamic: not only does the law of the father find successive embodiments in figures such as John of Gaunt, Henry IV, Henry V and the Duke of Gloucester, but it is also manifested on a larger scale: as God, Shakespeare, or even history itself. The appeal of the cycle is that it frames this relationship in terms of inevitable and eternal recurrence, transforming masculine identity, and its epic struggles towards integrity and maturity, into universal truths.

The recurrence of cycles is itself cyclical. In 1951 Anthony Quayle (belatedly following F. R. Benson's one-off production of the *Henry VI* plays in 1906) reintroduced the large-scale Shakespearean cycle to the Stratford repertory in a production of the Second Tetralogy (*Richard II* to *Henry V*), as a patriotic contribution to the Festival of Britain;[3] in 1963 Peter Hall and John Barton established the reputation and identity of the fledgling RSC with their adaptation of *Henry VI* and *Richard III* as *The Wars of the Roses*. Rolling around at roughly twelve-year intervals ever since, history cycles have continued to perform for the RSC an economically and artistically regener-ative role, forging a sense of unity, clarity and purpose, acting as a reminder that the company exists for something more profound and far-reaching than the repertory production of single plays: to carry the national burden of Shakespeare, his, and our, supposed mythical history.

The experiential quality of theatrical myth-making is worth stressing: underpinning the following discussion is the belief that the manufacture of ideology in Shakespearean theatre practice operates at other levels than in directorial intellectual-isations of interpretative decisions and staging strategies. The politics of contemporary Shakespeare production are not just its overt critical agenda but – perhaps pre-eminently – a lived relation between spectators and performance, woven into the complex social and cultural practices of theatregoing. It is true, nonetheless, that directors of the plays and producers of cycles have often deployed literary criticism as an ideological legitimation of their practice. Anthony Quayle substantiated the 1951 cycle in critical terms by enlisting the support of John Dover Wilson, who applied to the productions a synopsis of Tillyard's and his own more overtly propagandist historicism; Peter Hall paraphrased Tillyard and cited Kott to legitimate *The Wars of the Roses*. As we shall see, such elucidations may be important in explaining the *intentions* behind a directorial interpretation, but are of more debatable relevance to the production's *effects*, which may be less ideologically rigorous than the scholarly rationale might suggest. In any case, the RSC's relation to developments in academic criticism has, over time, become less and less direct. In the early 1960s it was easy to trace the connection between the work at Stratford and the critical agendas defined by Leavis, Tillyard and Kott; during the 1970s, there was a fleeting convergence between the theatrical proponents of the (relatively) empty space and the energetic academic lobbyists for a free Shakespeare. By the 1980s, however, academic criticism had simply become another element among the debris and bric-à-brac of a postmodern production style, visible mainly in the continuing commitment to the concept of the cycle itself. Criticism turned, via post-structuralism, Marxism, feminism and New Historicism, to an examination of Shakespeare's plays as political discourse, tracing their hidden histories, their configurations of ideology, their inscriptions of power, their strategies of subversion and containment; above all, their radical historical and cultural *otherness*. Meanwhile the RSC maintained the view that Shakespeare continues to be our contemporary, not just for an age and all time, but particularly and emphatically for now. What this has meant in practice is the subject of the following pages.

Chapter Four

Masters of war:
The Wars of the Roses (1963–4)

The Wars of the Roses cycle will be pretty familiar territory to anyone with more than a passing interest in the history of Shakespeare in performance. Commencing in 1963 with the three *Henry VI* plays compressed into two and presented as a trilogy together with *Richard III*, and culminating in the following year (with the addition of the complete Second Tetralogy) in a monumental seven-play sequence, this Wagnerian opus, fashioned by Peter Hall and John Barton, cast its huge shadow over the RSC's work for nearly a decade and has acted as a reference point for most stage productions of the histories in Britain ever since. It certainly occupies a prominent position in the official narratives of the RSC, of twentieth-century Shakespearean production and of the post-war British theatre; it was also the key to the establishment of the RSC's serious reputation within the Shakespearean critical community.[4] With the production history of Shakespeare's plays becoming ever more comprehensively documented, the cycle repeatedly returns to haunt critical writing; and as theatre history becomes an increasingly significant presence within textual history, this authoritative theatrical inscription of the *Henry VI* plays has entered into the crucial area of the critical apparatus which sustains and mediates the playtexts themselves.[5] The obdurate legacy of *The Wars of the Roses* seems to offer a refutation of the idea that theatre art is ephemeral and transient: perpetuated in the proliferating discourses of theatre history, the cycle has acquired the enduring status of myth.

Even in 1963, the engineers of the event seemed to suspect – and indeed ensured – that it was theatre history in the making. The fact that the cycle was mounted at all was itself a vindication of Hall's policies as artistic director of the RSC since its inception in 1961. The company faced the imminent quadricentenary of Shakespeare's birth at the end of three years of financial near-crisis, bitter rivalry with the National Theatre and struggles with the Arts Council over its level of subsidy. This cycle, the RSC's first such large-scale enterprise, was a determined articulation of the company's claims upon substantial public funding: the construction of England's own Oresteian myth was to be viewed as a matter of self-evident theatrical, critical and cultural importance. The scale of the project demanded a coherence and a continuity in the structure of the RSC, in the deployment of its personnel and in its repertory policy, that had only become possible as a result of Hall's reorganisation of the Stratford Festival enterprise along the lines of a permanent ensemble company. Only in such propitious circumstances of consistent and generous state support, it appeared, could Shakespearean production move beyond the intermittent successes of the star-centred one-off performance (the pattern for the pre-RSC Stratford era) that appertained in the commercial theatre; only within the ethos of subsidy could the history plays be produced systematically and intelligently (that is, cyclically) at all. The achievement of the cycle was the first example of the RSC's public service pro-vision. Assembling plays that had been variously treated as minor-league lyric tragedy, melodrama, shapeless chronicle, patriotic and sentimental pageant, or not staged at all, *The Wars of the Roses* standardised their heterogeneity in order to validate histories as a dramatic genre within a serious, scholarly and cosmopolitan theatre practice.

The landmark status of *The Wars of the Roses* derived partly from its reclamation of theatrically and critically neglected plays (which was effected, as I shall discuss below, through some deft editorial manipulation), and partly from its definitive exposition of the house style which the RSC had been building under Hall's direction from 1960 onwards. Together with fellow directors John Barton and Clifford Williams, Hall introduced a new regime of systematic actor-training at Strat-ford, with sonnet classes, fencing classes, democratic under-studying and the cultivation of a university-style atmosphere of seriousness and dedication. He also instigated what many saw as a revolution in Shakespearean production, chiefly in verbal delivery and stage design. In both aspects, the RSC strove to eradicate the fuzzy romanticism permeating Shakespeare at Stratford in the 1950s. As far as verse-speaking was concerned, the objectives were verbal clarity, precision and accuracy, in place of the booming oratory and dandified lyricism of the heroic tradition on the one hand and the prosaic mumblings of sub-Method acting on the other: a new middle way of acting that combined the favoured features of both traditions. In design terms, the tendency was towards bold, schematic, anti-illusionist statements in place of the comfortably nostalgic, decorative elaboration of pictorial design. On the first count, the histories provided ideal material for the practice of a dry, ironic and intellectual verbal style. As a halfway house within Shakespeare's oeuvre between the tragic sublime and comic whimsy, they relieved the pressure upon actors to affect pathos on the one hand, and to be charming and amusing on the other. Rhetoric could be scaled down, scepticism given a free rein, and the plays naturalised, psychologised and ironised. This approach appeared to reap handsome dividends in the more 'mature' plays of the Second Tetralogy. Thus *Richard II* in 1964 was a production which contravened the lyrical tradition of Benson and Gielgud. As the reviewer from *The Times* noted, there were 'no "arias" . . . even Gaunt's apostrophe to England is a political speech in which a line such as "I die pronouncing it" is delivered as an argumentative debating point'.[6] In *Henry IV*, the emblematic aspects of the texts were translated into the language of realism; thus the allegorical figure of Rumour appeared as 'a ragged, one-legged soldier with a bandage round his head, carrying contradictory reports from the field of Shrewsbury'.[7] Ian Holm's Henry V embodied the sceptical spirit of a decidedly anti-heroic production:

> no heraldic Henry, moving in spotless armour across a blood-soaked battlefield, but a man discovering his kingship within himself and through his comradeship with other men. It was an essentially democratic Henry, almost as tattered and mud-spattered as the 'Old Contemptibles' with whom he marched . . . a thoughtful, anxious Henry.[8]

The emphasis reflected what could be seen as a defiantly

modern perspective, 'democratic twentieth-century heroism',[9] to be contrasted with the effeteness, and the evasiveness of theatrical tradition. Villainy was also scaled down: the climax of the cycle was a production of *Richard III* whose titular hero, played in Pinteresque style by Ian Holm, was criminal rather than demonic, where 'verse was no longer an isolated consideration':

> A humpbacked man with a club-foot was talking to us in a voice that riveted our attention, and Shakespeare was suddenly being acted in the accent of twentieth-century thought . . . a schizoid Richard whose royal ambitions are fed on infantile fantasies.[10]

This was a performance without 'Satanic magnitude': 'instead of the boar, the bottle spider or the hunchbacked toad, Mr. Holm remains a high-spirited minor.'[11] By placing a premium upon spontaneity and directness, the RSC reformed bombast into self-expression and self-articulation: here was the immediate focus of the contemporary relevance sought from Shakespeare, a resurrected interiority that emerged as the transcendent agent and victim of history. As Ronald Bryden pointed out, this approach rescued the histories from obscurity: 'it rationalizes and humanizes those miles of blank verse, explaining, motivating, lending historical and psychological solidity . . . It makes the kind of sense a novel or film does.'[12] Parallels also suggested themselves with the contemporary political scene, with contemporary politicians – as Hall noted thirty years later: 'the Macmillan crisis and Quintin Hogg throwing his hat into the ring, the Profumo affair'.[13] Between the fifteenth and twentieth centuries, political motives were assumed to remain constant, even instinctual, and the aggressive modernity of the RSC's new style brought this point to life.

The humanisation of Shakespeare effected in the early productions of the RSC was frequently described as a mode of realism. Theatre history teaches that this is a slippery and relative concept at the best of times; in the context of the Shakespearean traditions against which the RSC's innovations were evaluated, and in the broader context of the British theatre of the early 1960s, it designates a complex and contradictory stylistic and generic field. Realism denoted not only a set of theatrical styles (ranging from Osborne–Wesker kitchen sink to Brecht) but the cultural, philosophical and political milieu within which they operated; it was an attitude as much as a dramatic mode. In this respect, its most important aspect (and the most frequently misinterpreted) is the so-called 'Brechtian' dimension to the RSC's work. In 1964 Hall declared that the RSC had 'moved into this almost neo-Brechtian approach to the plays' – a circumspect revision of Brecht which entailed asking the simple question: 'what do they mean?'[14] Such theatrical rigour seems to echo the account of the Epic Theatre given by Kenneth Tynan eight years before, in his review of the Berliner Ensemble's 1956 visit to London. Tynan saw Brecht as a puritanical realist and humanist, his stagecraft as artisan-like and functional: 'Reality is preferred, reality of a memorable and sculptural ruggedness . . . we see nothing but solid, selected objects.' In place of the vacuousness and decorative frivolity of the boulevard theatre, Brechtian realism signified sobriety and common sense: 'the beauty of Brechtian settings is not of the dazzling kind that begs for applause. It is the more durable beauty of *use*.'[15] Here indeed was a lesson for Hall and a model for Shakespearean production: a theatrical vocabulary deprived of political force in the passage from Brecht to Brechtian, while retaining the distinction of being apparently anti-Establishment, anti-heroic, pragmatic and socially aware.[16]

The basic theatrical vocabulary of *The Wars of the Roses* reflected a ruefully pragmatic, even nihilistic stance. The staging and design offered a potent combination of significant detail and large-scale scenic abstraction. It was the scenic dimension of *The Wars of the Roses* that created its initial impact and accounted for its subsequent memorability, not the intelligent, quietly emphatic performances of its cast. This displacement of foreground by background was part of the cycle's grand theatrical and political statement. However individualised, the actors in the drama were still the little people, who either suffered themselves to be crushed in the machinery of history (David Warner's Richard II was thus 'a royal butterfly broken on the wheel'[17]), or became armoured and indistinguishable from their environment, in an image of

indestructible masculinity: 'the warring factions of York and
Lancaster moved about the stage, in and out of each other's
trust and party like the pieces of some effortless, shining
machine.'[18] Accounts of the production have centred on this
aspect, documenting the swinging and rotating three-sided
towers or *periaktoi*, the huge emblematic maps and grilles that
moved the action from England to France and back, the council
table marking the fluctuations of power, the leather and metal
costumes, the awesome, baroquely detailed weaponry, and the
steel plate covering the walls and floor, enclosing history within
the 'great steel cage of war'.[19] Creating an extraordinarily
flexible and mobile stage environment, and a sense of rapid,
vertiginous historical movement, this design also spoke of
innovation, of modernity and of power. Solid realism and
impressive stage technology punched a hole in the flimsy canvas
of the 1950s tradition, installing a reassuring architectural
density, grandeur and authority: 'a comparison with 1951 is
suggestive . . . walls of an unbelievable solidity go round and
round, and presumably up and up. In comparison, Miss
Moisewitch's [sic] timbers were stoically static.'[20]

For all its aggressive modernity this Shakespearean style
wasn't all that Brechtian, even in the limited sense adumbrated
by Tynan, and even though there might be references to
Brecht's drama in the incidental detail (battle scenes choreographed to evoke Breughel, Mother Courage's canteen wagon
appearing in *Henry IV*), the apparently radical edge to the
production derived rather from its effect of immediacy and
harshness, its stern and unyielding *realpolitik*.

The scaling down of the human participants and scaling up of
the blankly unforgiving background presented Shakespeare's
vision of history – as Hall saw it. There was the Elizabethan
World Picture:

> Shakespeare believed that there was a natural order in
> nature, starting with the lowest forms of life and moving up
> through the beasts to man and to God. All Shakespeare's
> thinking, whether religious, political or moral, is based on a
> complete acceptance of this concept of order. There is a just
> proportion in all things: man is above beast, king is above
> man, and God above king. Revolution, whether in the

individual's temperament, in the family, or in the state or in the heavens, destroys the order and leads to destructive anarchy.[21]

However, this idealistic belief in order and hierarchy was tempered by a more cynical, 'realistic' perspective:

> Shakespeare knew that man in action is basically an animal. Before man developed religion or philosophy, he had an instinctive will to dominate. This lust may be excused as self-defence, or the need to obtain food – but it is as basic to an animal as the desire to eat, to sleep or to procreate. Man must hunt in order to get food, just as his women must bear his children and protect them as part of an instinctive pattern.[22]

From the conflict between what Shakespeare 'believed' and what he 'knew' emerged the powerful Social Darwinist politics of the cycle. The crushing and imprisoning walls of the set presented political and human motives and aspirations, writ large: a relentless, vicious, amoral struggle for power. It has been pointed out more than once that both the specific imagery and the general reading derive from Jan Kott's *Shakespeare Our Contemporary*, with its Grand Mechanism or implacable roller of history realised on stage.[23] It has also been observed that this interpretation, while ostensibly radical in its intentions, simply inverts the terms of Tillyard's Elizabethan world order to equally conservative effect.[24] In bold, schematic terms the history enacted in *The Wars of the Roses* was that of a secularised mystery cycle, a universal drama of fall, decay and corruption with no hope of redemption in this world or the next.

The full picture emerged in 1964, when the cycle ran in its complete form, *Henry VI* following on from the Second Tetralogy. Between the deposition of Richard II and the death of Richard III stretched not only a century of feudal conflict but the whole of English, and ultimately human, history. *Richard II* was staged in an English Garden of Eden that became a Gethsemane haunted by Warner's 'white-robed Christ figure'[25] of a king; *Richard III* took place among the Nazi or nuclear bunkers of the twentieth century, where Richard's 'storm troopers' stomped through a 'slaughterhouse at Pontefract as something out of a nightmare concentration camp'.[26] For all its relevance, there was a deeper, more mythological pattern of history to be traced here. The cycle drew heavily upon the perennial ideologies of pastoral: here the passage from the Golden Age into the terrors of modernity is reflected in the enclosure of the protagonist's world in alienating and de-humanising metal. As Ronald Bryden observed, the story began in 'a remote, forested England' which 'underwent a technological revolution' as 'the wooden rusticity of Richard's kingdom was replaced by steel and armour: an iron age of war and political despotism was dawning'.[27] This was not really about the Middle Ages, but more recent history: this treatment articulated more immediate anxieties. Out of the cycle's historical eclecticism there emerged a modern tale of mechanisation, an upgrading of the medieval Wheel of Fortune to the wheels of industry, a spectacle regarded by Hall with horrified fascination. The pattern of debilitating nostalgia, pastoral and counter-pastoral derives partly from Tillyard, whose image of a stable, ordered Elizabethan society acts as a counter to the chaos and horror of the twentieth century; but it may be more closely linked to the other mode of literary historicism informing Hall's position, that of the *Scrutiny* school as articulated in general terms by F. R. Leavis and with particular reference to Elizabethan drama and society by L. C. Knights.[28] *The Wars of the Roses* followed the pattern of Leavisite cultural analysis, evoking the destruction of the pre-capitalist organic society and of a unified national culture, and the brutalisation of sensibility, by the forces of industrialisation. Nazi imagery aside, there were even more local and contemporary resonances, beyond the traumatic immediate past. For the 1964 audience, assailed on one side by Harold Wilson's rhetoric of the 'white heat of technology' as the motor of social and economic transformation, and on the other by Doomsday scenarios of nuclear annihilation, the cycle might also have presented a disquieting vision of a closely threatened future.

The design of the cycle enacted an armour-plating of both self and society that in turn suggested that history could be seen as a process of dispossession and alienation of man from his true identity. For Hall and Barton, this corruption of selfhood was one of the tragic aspects of history, and was perhaps most vividly staged in the personal fates of Richard II and Henry VI. David Warner played both roles in the same mould, as awkward, injured martyrs, embodying an anachronistic, impotent moral sensibility at odds with a world of violent intrigue: his 'sophistication and gentleness obviously doomed him to incompetence as ruler of such a historical milieu'.[29] In Harold Hobson's review of the production, Warner's Henry VI emerged from his background as 'one of Shakespeare's greatest parts':

> Henry is never active, and he would – with some reason, seeing what action was in the fifteenth century – that no-one else were active either. He suffers only, and endures, never resisting, never striking back . . . Yet his sad, distressed face beneath his fair hair, meeting each new misfortune with an absolute absence of protest or indignation spreads over the darkest waters of the play a quiet and persistent golden glory.[30]

A very mid-twentieth century anti-hero, indeed: in his passivity and eloquent silences, this Henry was an absurd, tragicomic figure from the world of Beckett, Ionesco and Pinter, miscast in history. His victimisation at the hands of an unfeeling environment emphasised the extent to which the cycle's design and setting materialised a universal will to power. The bloodied 'great steel cage of war' provided the arena for 'man in action' by articulating his deepest aggressive and destructive drives. Throughout the cycle the spectacle of conflict predominated. The walls of the torture-chamber set complemented the fearsome, intricate weaponry wielded throughout the cycle, the massive broadswords, chains, maces and spikes; a harsh man's world in which the armour and weapons 'clanked, and . . . suggested the smithies of their forging'.[31] With ghoulish enthusiasm, the directors also took every opportunity ingeniously to elaborate incidences of violence in (or implied by) the texts: these included ending *Henry IV, Part 1* with 'Vernon in death agonies, swinging in a noose; he was then cut down and Worcester climbed in to take his place';[32] staging the drowning

of Clarence in an onstage Malmsey butt; tethering Richard II
with a massive, heavy chain during his prison scene, and so on.
Decapitation featured as a recurrent motif which had a cumulative effect: *Richard III* was overlooked by a gallery of the
impaled heads of all those executed throughout the cycle. The
new technological era was also one of tribalism.

This clear emphasis seemed to reflect the responsibilities of
'realism': Shakespearean history depicted not in the traditional
stage language of pageantry and romantic heraldry but as a
nightmare of predatory violence. Although it might be billed as
a reclamation of the authentic Shakespeare, Hall's Social
Darwinist reading of history and politics went hand in glove
with the RSC's other experiments in what was broadly (and
inaccurately) termed the Theatre of Cruelty in the early 1960s:
Peter Brook's 1962 *King Lear,* the 1963 LAMDA season, the
Marat/Sade in 1964, *US* in 1966.[33] Without provoking the
controversy courted by these confrontations with the RSC's
patrons, its audiences and the Lord Chamberlain's office, the
horrors of *The Wars of the Roses* nonetheless aimed to unsettle
its audience in a manner which suggests a deeper sense of
unease, even desperation. In this connection, the RSC's adoption of Jan Kott is highly revealing. Reviewing *Shakespeare
Our Contemporary* in 1965, Ronald Bryden noted its remarkable appeal to Western liberal readers, and attributed this to a
curious 'nostalgia for violent action' affected by male middle-
class intellectuals.[34] This paradoxical emotion, which Bryden
sees as symptomatic of fears of personal and cultural impotence
and irrelevance, can be mapped on *The Wars of the Roses*, and
offers a partial explanation of its theatrical appeal. I have
already suggested that the cycle demonstrates quite clearly the
influence of Kott, Tillyard and Leavis; Christopher McCullough and Alan Sinfield have argued from different angles that
the RSC's cultural profile can be read as an articulation of
specific class aspirations, that is, the colonisation of the cultural
high ground by members of a newly educated bourgeoisie.[35]
The involvement of Kott might be read along the same lines:
the appropriation of an Eastern European literary critic
steeped in the literature and philosophy of the Absurd, in order
to reread Shakespeare, is a means of reimagining the English
reader's own position within contemporary political culture.

For the reader in the early 1960s, Kott offered the opportunity of an existential identification with dissident avant-garde intellects behind the Iron Curtain; this was one way of escaping the sense of decline and malaise, the homogenising tedium and lassitude of post-Imperial Britain, and the encroaching horrors of mass culture, television and paperbacks. Reading Kott delivers the vicarious experience of violent oppression – captured in Peter Brook's anecdote of intrigue and arrest that prefaces the English translation of the book. Kott reconstructs the post-war Polish police state in the image of Shakespeare's England by drawing upon the vocabulary of the European Theatres of Absurdity and Cruelty; Hall and Barton followed suit in *The Wars of the Roses*, dovetailing past and present in a grotesquely tragic fantasy of history. Having seized the apparatus of Shakespearean production and turned it against the traditionalists in the uncompromising, taboo-shattering Kottian terms of relevance and modernity, the alienated intellectuals of the middle class could claim a degree of cultural (if not political) power – even if this power manifested itself in the form of anti-politics. Read in this light, the carnage and mayhem of *The Wars of the Roses* become understandable: in a meaningless, tedious universe the sadistic or murderous act comes to figure as existentialist self-affirmation, not least (and maybe at most) as a demonstration of mastery over the theatre audience.

The biographies of the RSC's key players are relevant here, given the extent to which Hall in particular succeeded in imprinting his own aspirations upon the company. Hall's story is a familiar one: he reached the commanding heights of the Shakespearean theatre via the meritocratic route of grammar school, scholarship and Cambridge University, followed by a spectacularly successful career as a West End theatrical impresario. An icon for the iconoclastic, youthful, educated audience that the RSC aimed to cultivate, such a figure might well be expected to produce as dynamic and forward-thinking a production as *The Wars of the Roses* – but (naturally) the success story was not without its tensions. The cycle was a vindication of three years of personal struggle for Hall as well as collective endeavour by the company, and it is tempting to read the incessant civil warfare of the cycle as a representation

of more immediate domestic and personal battles for survival
and sovereignty. If *The Wars of the Roses* were ostensibly about
the making of England, they were also very much about the
making of the RSC itself. Hence the tussles between individual
wills and the collective decision-making of the king's council reproduced tensions within the RSC between actors and directors, and between the traditional star-centred hierarchy and
Hall's efforts to create an ensemble; the heated debates around
John Bury's celebrated council table mirrored Hall's protracted
wranglings in the meeting-rooms of the Arts Council over the
company's levels of subsidy; and the conflict between York and
Lancaster replayed the feud between the Houses of Stratford
and London's South Bank for the sovereign status of the
national theatre. Such a local reading might also be placed in
broader social and personal contexts: in particular, the cycle
played out in luridly violent terms the traumas of class conflict
and social mobility. In this sense the violence depicted in the
cycle was as much mental as it was physical. Although we can
only speculate about the extent to which Hall's own personal
trajectory was embodied in the production, it is clear that *The
Wars of the Roses* reflected a characteristically *petit bourgeois*
perspective in its simultaneous scorn (shot through with fear)
for the brutal and decadent aristocracy and contempt for the
working class, represented in the Cade rebellion as (supposedly
comic) uppity trade-unionists. Alternatively, we might follow
and extrapolate the RSC's Cambridge connection for the
cycle's guiding rationale: where could we find a better model
for the world of *The Wars of the Roses* than in the rigid
hierarchies, arcane rituals and systematic brutalities of the
English public school and Cambridge college system?

Peter Hall's contribution to *The Wars of the Roses* was, of
course, only partially what ensured its critical and commercial
success. Its other ground-breaking element was due to the work
of another key RSC player, John Barton. He was responsible
for reviving the craft of wholesale Shakespearean stage adaptation and affording it a previously unheard-of legitimacy, by
reconstituting the neglected *Henry VI* plays as two parts out of
three. Since the details of the adaptation have been extensively
discussed in accounts of the production, it is necessary only to
offer a brief summary here.[36] Hall and Barton claimed that the

originals were not viable as they stood: in the words of the former, 'a mess of angry and undifferentiated barons, thrashing about in a mass of diffuse narrative';[37] in those of the latter, 'immensely diffuse and uneven in quality'.[38] In other words (and here Hall and Barton were only reiterating the received theatrical and critical wisdom), the plays lacked the focus provided either by recognisably 'real' characters or by 'great' poetry. There were ways around some of these difficulties. Presenting the plays as a cycle meant that they could gain in cumulative grandeur and expansiveness what they lacked in intensity; as for the language, what was disparagingly regarded as clumsy, feeble and repetitive Elizabethan stage rhetoric could be cleverly reread as satirical in intent, deliberately hollow and fraudulent, 'an ironic revelation of the time-honoured practices of politicians'.[39] The lack of in-depth, individualised characters was, for an RSC in pursuit of its own mode of Brechtian realism, more troublesome: Barton felt that one of the 'basic weaknesses' of *Henry VI, Part 1*, for instance, was that 'the characters are one-note parts with no complexity or development'.[40] So, in order to bring the texts into line with what was expected of a more 'mature' Shakespearean style, the requisite qualities had to be manufactured.

This was initially achieved by rearranging the parts of the trilogy around strong central characters: Henry in the first part, Edward in the second, Richard in the third. Great interest was generated by the rewriting of Henry as a complex tragic protagonist, which stemmed from the intensified focus upon the relationship between Henry and the Duke of Gloucester in the first part of the trilogy, *Henry VI*. However, the extensive surgery practised upon the texts also necessitated an element of prosthesis, in that Barton not only cut and rearranged the text, but added material written by himself, in the form of pastiche Elizabethan blank verse. The climactic point in the first part was the Bishop of Winchester's death-bed admission to Gloucester's murder (interpolated by Barton) in the final scene:

[WARWICK] *Dost thou confess thy part in Gloucester's death?*
[CARDINAL] *Thou might'st have sav'd him: but in holy*
cowardice

>   *Thou durst not do it –*
> [KING]   *I thought all for the best.*[41]

This established 'one of the main moral points in the trilogy':

> that self-seeking and wickedness breed guilt in the doer and
> rejection by other people. More important, it should beget
> an enormous guilt in Henry, and the play should end with his
> appalled acceptance of the fact that his weakness has been
> responsible for the death of Gloucester.[42]

Thus, with a little editorial intervention, the text could be
realigned with a traditional character-centred realist dramaturgy, and the newly self-reflective, conflict-ridden, haunted
Henry became a prototype Plantagenet Hamlet (and a rehearsal for Warner's own portrayal of the Prince in 1965).

This was a representative instance of how Barton's editorial
practice worked within a legitimating framework of assumptions derived from a humanist understanding of Shakespeare:
the early history plays, with their vocabulary of emblems and
icons rather than character psychology, might well be at odds
with this. However, since the realist perspective constitutes the
dominant ideology, it made such interventions seem natural
and pragmatic decisions. Critical discussion of the ethics of the
adaptation has frequently operated within established textual
parameters, manoeuvring between traditional Shakespearean
authority, the suspected presence of collaborators, the 'appren-
tice' status of the texts, the vagaries of Elizabethan theatre
practice and publishing, and the imperatives of the contemporary theatre. At the centre of the debate are the twinned
problems of authorship and authority: who wrote (or was
entitled to write) what, and when. Since full authority could be
withheld from the texts as they stood, Barton was entitled to
cross the threshold of conventional Shakespearean scripting
into more active and creative participation, 'not as an improvement of absolute Shakespeare but as a further revision of only
partly revised originals'.[43] A generous gesture, perhaps; but, as
the above example suggests, Barton's scriptwriting can be seen
to possess a theatrical and ideological orientation that goes
further than mere services to Shakespeare and to the expec-

tations of contemporary audiences. Many of Barton's blank verse passages, apparently designed (like dialogic footnotes) to elucidate the transhistorical 'political and human meaning' of the fuddled originals, resound with more immediate contemporary concerns. At an early point in *Henry VI*, Barton supplied Talbot and the Duke of Bedford with an expository dialogue about the conflict between national and self-interest:

> [TALBOT]   *What, can they jar at such a time as this?*
> [BEDFORD]   *Ah, Talbot, thou and I are simple men:*
>   *All our ambition is for England's good.*
>   *But for the rest, albeit their words are ours,*
>   *Of England and of true inheritance,*
>   *They do but sanctify their inward malice,*
>   *Which is a vile abuse of those true sanctions*
>   *That, under God, do tend on government.*[44]

'Sanctions' was one of Hall's political and moral keywords: 'those justifications which politicians use in the Press or on television to mask the dictates of their party politics or their personal ambitions'.[45] In an age of mass media electoral politics, the disparity between political ethics and political language, and between private motives and public performance, was becoming ever more troubling: it was already an issue in 1963. Translating this sentiment into the reassuring sonorities of mock-Elizabethan blank verse is one way of elevating the resulting sense of impotence and disenfranchisement to the status of transhistorical truth. The nostalgic archaism of Barton's pastiche was thus part of its ideological instrumentality; in this, it fulfilled the traditional institutional function of Shakespearean stage production. Unlike other twentieth-century adaptors of Shakespeare (such as Brecht, Charles Marowitz and Edward Bond), Barton sought relevance not through contradiction and juxtaposition but by forging a seamless unity of style, tone and imagery, speaking in an Elizabethan rather than a contemporary idiom.

This aspect of the adaptation is, for me, one of its most curious features. Reviewers were more or less unanimous in their admiration for Barton's ability to mimic the early Shakespeare. Frank Cox offered an assessment in *Plays and Players*, describing the adaptation as 'a triumph of scholarship and theatrical awareness':

> John Barton's achievement in extracting from the sprawling immaturities of the three parts of *Henry VI* their workable elements cannot be too highly rated . . . by inspired weeding, contraction and even in places by brazen invention he has virtually created from a seldom revived mess of swordrattling chronicles a positive addition to the canon of popular works.[46]

Barton even earned the rare praise of a leading article in *The Times*, which judiciously declared that his 'cuts, transliterations, and extensive flights of pastiche blank verse in no way do violence to the spirit of the original text', and used the occasion to interpolate its own casually racist version of relevance:

> what emerges is a view of history that restores the connexion between political tactics and the basic human passions.
>   For modern audiences the bloodstained chronicle of York and Lancaster may be splendid costume drama, but it offers little insight into the current mechanics of western diplomacy. Where it may have such an application, however, is in some parts of Asian and African politics.[47]

The link between primitivism and violence is one 'connexion' which *The Wars of the Roses* assiduously promoted: as usual, the ideological ends legitimated the theatrical means. On reflection, though, praise for this uncanny knack of producing plodding pentameters whose very *raison d'être* is to merge with their background seems an ambiguous form of compliment – but this ambiguity turns out to be entirely apposite to Barton's role in the production, and to his distinctive contribution to the development of the RSC.

Barton's personal history may be as relevant here as Hall's: if the *petit bourgeois* dimension of *The Wars of the Roses* was motivated by the latter, other aspects of the production might be traced to the former. In contrast to his co-director, Barton's origins were privileged; a pupil of Eton, he went on to become a Fellow of King's College, Cambridge before receiving an invitation from Hall to join the RSC. Whereas Leavisite critical, cultural and class aspirations underpinned Hall's position, Barton's connections were with theatrical academic George Rylands, and with Cambridge's Marlowe Society. Barton's career nonetheless traces a similar pattern of displacement and alienation to that of Hall. Michael Greenwald begins his biography of the director by recording how, at Eton, Barton sought refuge from the ritualised violence of school sport (to which he was physically unsuited) in amateur productions of Shakespeare's history plays; his subsequent academic career was dominated by theatre directing at the expense of scholarly obligations.[48] When he joined the RSC, however, Barton was haunted by the scholarly and academic associations – pejoratively regarded by theatre professionals as antithetical to creativity (or even competence). His 1960 RSC production of *The Taming of the Shrew* had been an unhappy, near-disastrous experience; according to the cast, because of his over-intellectualised approach. Curiously, Barton's real aspiration throughout was to become a dramatist in his own right – two of his verse dramas (in the style of T. S. Eliot and Christopher Fry) were directed by Hall at Cambridge. If Hall's prolific directorial output at this time were symptomatic of compulsive over-achievement, Barton may have also had something to prove; scholarship and directing would nonetheless still seem like second-hand artistry, and Barton's successes would be persistently dogged by the spectre of failure.

Writing pastiche Shakespearean verse for *The Wars of the Roses* could well have offered a partial, if unsatisfactory, resolution to the conflict between the roles of writer, academic and director. Barton did not share Hall's enthusiasm for contemporary playwriting, and his orientation as a writer, as demonstrated in the Cambridge verse plays, was clearly antithetical to the major developments in the drama of the 1950s and 1960s. Rewriting Shakespeare provided an outlet for Barton's revivalist style, anachronistically more akin to the dramaturgy of Fry and Eliot than to the contemporary theatre. This aristocratic authorial role had its compensations, not the least being that Barton has entered theatrical history as one of Shakespeare's more renowned collaborators. In this respect, he may turn out to have the last laugh on those practising dramatists with whom he was competing. Acting as a medium for the spirit of early Elizabethan drama, Barton in 1963 anticipated postmodernism by humourlessly executing its characteristic artistic stratagem of blank parody; merging his own script with Shakespeare's, and cultivating each to speak in the accents of the other, he succeeded in pulling off a fetishistic near-identification with the revered master-author. Theatre reviewers, when debating the merits and weaknesses of the script, frequently mistook Barton's lines for Shakespeare's, and vice versa. What more could an aspiring neo-Elizabethan dramatist ask for?

The Wars of the Roses firmly established the RSC's proprietorial rights over Shakespeare, for the next decade and beyond. Its major consequences were to confirm the credentials of the company as a large-scale publicly subsidised arts corporation, and to establish an enduring critical, theatrical and political agenda for the RSC and for Shakespearean production in Britain. *The Wars of the Roses* demonstrated that it was in the staging of such cycles that the RSC's unique and important cultural contribution lay; it also proved how the skilful reconstitution of the margins of the Shakespearean canon could provide a grounding for the effective colonisation of its centre. Moreover, despite the nihilistic historiography promoted by the cycle, it embodied a certain cultural optimism. As it reached its climax in 1964, the Conservative party were finally voted out of office after thirteen years, and Britain seemed poised on the threshold of significant social change: perhaps most important for the RSC, one of the promises of the incoming Labour government was a renewed commitment to culture and the arts. If *The Wars of the Roses* seemed to regard social mobility and the promised technological revolution with some degree of trepidation, Labour's corporatist approach at least held out the hope that the future of such epics was not in doubt. History, however, was to take a rather different turn.

Chapter Five

Anarchy in the UK: Henry IV (1975) and Henry VI (1977)

The distance between the monumental *Wars of the Roses* cycle and the much smaller-scale cycle of history plays mounted by the RSC under the direction of Terry Hands in 1975 marks eleven years of increasingly turbulent political as well as theatrical history. Britain's long-term industrial and economic decline, which had begun to become painfully apparent in 1964, had by 1975 accelerated to the point of imminent crisis. As in every other state-sponsored industry, the theatre faced a rapidly worsening situation with dwindling sources of subsidy becoming ever more in demand. For the RSC, 1975 was another anniversary year (the centenary of the foundation of the Shakespeare Memorial Theatre), and therefore an appropriate occasion for another staging of the Second Tetralogy. This time, however, the comprehensive historiography of the 1964 cycle was succeeded by an altogether less panoramic, and rather more shambolic, vista of English history. The scaling down of aspirations mirrored the political movements in the country at large, as the grand corporatist industrial and economic policies pursued by a succession of Labour and Conservative governments fell apart, giving way to crisis management and survival tactics. The parallels with the RSC's critical years of the early 1960s were glaringly apparent, but by this time the situation seemed to verge on the desperate. The erosion of subsidy provided a constant reminder of the extent to which Shakespearean production was at the mercy of the political and social circumstances outside of the theatre: the oil crisis; Britain's battles with the EEC; a succession of inconclusive general elections; a revival of nationalist politics, particularly in Northern Ireland; the resurgence of the extreme Right; and an escalation of industrial struggle, leading to a State of

Emergency, power cuts and the three-day week. Not a propitious set of circumstances in which to attempt to recreate the success of *The Wars of the Roses*; and to cap it all, there was the fact that the 1974 Stratford season, veering from the eccentric to the plain dull, had proved to be a near-disastrous financial and critical low point for the company.

Once again, the histories provided a focus for the hoped-for renewal and regeneration. Whereas the identity of the RSC in the 1960s had been fashioned on the template of *The Wars of the Roses*, it now fell to Hands to reconstruct that identity for the next decade, and the new circumstances within which the company found itself. To the surprise of many observers, however, Terry Hands approached this task by apparently disregarding many of the systematic principles upon which cycles had traditionally been based. Possibly because John Barton had directed what seemed to be a definitive production of the play only two years previously, Hands chose not to start with *Richard II*. This might have seemed logical had the two *Henry IV* plays been presented in tandem (as in the inaugural Shakespeare Memorial Theatre production in 1932, and the 1982 Barbican production), but onto these was battened *Henry V*. The eccentricity of this makeshift trilogy was further compounded by Hands's decision to ignore chronology and to open the season with *Henry V*; the final curiosity was that the cycle was rounded off with a revival of Hands's 1968 production of *The Merry Wives of Windsor*.

It was all rather odd. Stratford audiences were presented with a history cycle that seemed asymmetrical, even arbitrary, in construction: it appeared to be simultaneously three-quarters of a recognised tetralogy, a trilogy of plays about Prince Hal, and three plays (one fairly tenuously related to the others) about Falstaff. The patterns didn't quite fit, particularly if the *Merry Wives* was brought into play: a strange contrast to the commanding long-range planning and execution of *The Wars of the Roses*. But, in a way, this was the point, even if it was not consciously intended as such, and it signalled a change of ideological and theatrical direction for the RSC tantamount to a reinvention of its institutional identity. The ramshackle, improvised quality of the 1975 season revealed the implicitly tendentious basis of cycle manufacture: throwing together four plays and allowing audiences to make what unifying sense of them they could, without editing, interpolation or rewriting, indicated the extent to which Hall and Barton had tailored the histories to suit the purposes of a monolithically deterministic historiography.

Hands's *laissez-faire* approach to the material in textual and cyclical terms was indicative of a difference of ideology as well as of style and strategy. Although Hands did not join Trevor Nunn as Joint Artistic Director until 1978, it was already clear by the mid-1970s that he had become a dominant force in the company. Both Hall and Nunn had emphasised their socialist convictions, and even though the former's dream of an ensemble company and a popular theatre had proved to be short-lived, the latter still declared in 1974 that he wanted the RSC to be 'a socially concerned theatre. A politically aware theatre. In reality not in name.'[49] Hands has always been more circumspect about declaring either his political beliefs or any defined cultural agenda. It was clear, however, that he was determined to steer the RSC away from the Brechtian realism enshrined in the previous cycle, and simultaneously away from the concern with public politics and Kott/Hall-style relevance, towards what he called 'a freer world, a more theatrical world'.[50] In an interview given in 1980, he signalled his distaste for Hall's approach:

> *The Wars of the Roses* was a study in power politics: its central image was the conference table, and Warwick, the scheming king-maker, was the central figure. But that's not Shakespeare. Shakespeare goes far beyond politics. Politics is a very shallow science.[51]

The repudiation of politics, for Hands, meant concentrating upon the private self rather than the public role. In this light, the Henry trilogy made sense as an exploration of family (father and son) relationships, of conflicts within the individual, of personal development. This change of emphasis was characteristic of the cultural and intellectual movement of the early 1970s towards introspection, and in this sense the 1975 Henriad was to reflect the temper of the times. But, as it turned out, it also paralleled the ideological manoeuvrings on the political right which would eventually create the basis of its hegemony over the next decade, in its reconstruction of the traditional nuclear family as the locus of political and moral values. Appealing to the siege mentality fostered among the bourgeoisie in the terminal stages of the Heath government, this return to family values was to prove a potent ideological force.

Issues of personal freedom and integrity were at the centre of the cycle, its main purpose being 'to investigate the crab-like growth of Prince Hal', in the words of *The Times* reviewer, which encouraged the spectator 'to concentrate on the old values of individual character rather than on any panorama of English society'.[52] In the *Henry IV* plays the focus of interest was provided by Alan Howard's Prince Hal and his relationships with his Good and Bad Fathers, Emrys James's Bolingbroke and Brewster Mason's Falstaff:

> The Stratford productions of *Henry IV, Parts One and Two*, directed by Terry Hands, reveal with exceptional clarity the Oedipal nature of Prince Hal's struggle. Alan Howard's Hal is a young prince, growing up. His mind is being formed by two mutually opposing fathers. His natural father, the King, is tortured by guilt and obsessed by ideals of kingship. His debased 'father', Falstaff, is impervious to guilt, scornful of honour and duty, but relishes the simple pleasures of life, sack, sex and getting away with things.[53]

The attraction of this patriarchal narrative, presumably, is that it excludes women as well as history from the Oedipal triangle in yet another RSC man's world. Howard's nervy, scrupulous, neurotic prince, who seemed to anticipate the mood of the decade to come by appearing 'like that graduate who fritters away his time at university, and then resolves to be a millionaire by 30',[54] had as his antagonist James's vicious and grasping Henry IV, 'a snarling, sardonic, guilt-laden autocrat'.[55] Mason's genial Falstaff, meanwhile, was 'not a gigantic comic performance, rather a precise character creation that snugs in with the production'[56] who offered the prince the warmth and affection he desperately sought.

The emphasis upon private personalities and the interpersonal dimension displaced the power and public politics of the *Henry IV* plays so that they became largely symptomatic of the personality disorders of the central characters. In a later interview, Hands made it clear that this was indeed his view: 'Politics, like the swelling associated with dropsy, is a fat and watery exterior to the real problem, which is a disease of the heart. Shakespeare and the theatre in general should be concerned with the real sickness.'[57] This perspective allowed for a less deterministic historiography than that of *The Wars of the Roses*, which was perhaps part of the cycle's attraction. Hands's efforts to structure the cycle along the lines of a *Bildungsroman* enabled Hal to achieve moral and spiritual awareness, and personal integration, by resolving his troubled relationship with his father and by exorcising the demons within and outside himself. The political reverberations of this personal odyssey were again symptomatic, with Henry becoming an effective ruler and achieving a unity of self and nation in the heroic self-assertion of *Henry V*.

The narrative follows a familiar humanist pattern and, like many treatments of the histories that dwell upon the universals of human nature and of character psychology, it was pursued in the productions at the expense of historical and social specificity and detail. In this respect, the enforced scenic minimalism of the cycle's staging operated in the service of its central ideological project. For the 1975 season, which derived its impetus from the anti-illusionist *Henry V*, the scenic resources of the Stratford theatre had been cut down to a minimum, and the action swept across the bare boards of the steeply raked stage, with only emblematic indications of location such as curtains for the Eastcheap scenes (a sharp contrast to the great, weathered oak beams of the 1964 production), a tangle of branches suspended overhead for most of *Henry IV, Part 2*, a few sticks of furniture which doubled for tavern and palace, and selected props. Nonetheless, the economics of necessity produced what was for many a more essentially Shakespearean theatrical experience: from this stark setting the text, and the psychologised, universal individual, emerged more strongly and clearly than ever before. If the imposing machinery of *The Wars of the Roses* had spoken of the imponderable history and ambiguously celebrated technology, the half-empty space of the 1975 staging simply foregrounded humanity and the individual spirit, preaching theatrical self-reliance and the triumph of initiative over adversity.

Within Shakespearean theatre history, the rhetoric of the unworthy scaffold, whether in the Elizabethan or the modern theatre, has always been extremely potent, and it has become part of RSC mythology that theatrical riches are most frequently produced from scenic rags. The idea that theatrical capital might be accumulated from the basis of 'starting from scratch',[58] which Hands defined as the guiding principle and imperative of the season, has contradictory ideological implications, some potentially radical, others less so. Here, it would seem that this particular brand of poor Shakespeare was not unrelated to one of the enabling fictions of what was emerging in 1975 as the distinctive ideology of Thatcherism: the story of the self-made man, working his way to the top of the ladder through enterprise, entrepreneurial zeal, ingenuity and lots of hard work.

It was not only in terms of theatrical style that the RSC could be seen to be following the lead of the Conservative party and its apologists: this emergent heroism was set against a jaundiced depiction of the condition of England. The world of this Henriad, while ostensibly outside of real history and politics, was still very much an image of contemporary Britain, as obliquely relevant to its time as its previous RSC incarnation. The wintry branches adorning *Henry IV, Part 2*, the dead leaves and disused cannons, the expanses of bare boards and the white stage walls created an almost Beckettian void, a world simultaneously sterile and in a state of decay and decline, a site for historical endgames. Yet this was not the mythically pure and timeless empty space framed by Peter Brook's celebrated pristine white box for his 1970 *A Midsummer Night's Dream*. There seemed rather to be a deliberate flaunting of the threadbare, tawdry qualities of this theatrical world (and it was in this sense that the imagery of sickness took hold): a very poor Shakespeare, indeed. Here was an apt image of the shabbiness and squalor of 1970s England, and while the 'British disease' was debated in the country at large, it stalked the stage of the Royal Shakespeare Theatre in the persons of a sore-encrusted Bolingbroke and a syphilitically crumbling Bardolph.

Given this emphasis, the inclusion of the *Merry Wives* becomes readily comprehensible. Although theatrically reasonably popular, the play has been critically undervalued, dismissed as a hastily written, poorly constructed hack work, its relationship with the histories as arbitrary and tenuous. Here, though, this very second-rate quality made the play an appropriate coda to this history cycle. This run-down England was ripe for the reappearance of an enfeebled Falstaff as a clumsy, lecherous drunk, surrounded by the pathetic remnants of the Eastcheap gang and a cast of stereotypical foreigners. Falstaff's humiliation at the hands of a pair of independent-minded women offered a grim comic satisfaction which had prescient echoes in the political world; and by firmly banishing the male public world of the histories, the *Merry Wives* could also be interpreted as a celebration of the virtues of bourgeois family life.

The two parts of *Henry IV* and the *Merry Wives* were well received and moderately successful, but the big commercial and critical success of the season (and another landmark production in the RSC's history) was *Henry V*, which remained in the repertoire for four years. More by accident than design, this production also provided a makeshift bridge between the 1975 season and the cycle of three *Henry VI* plays directed by Hands in 1977. If the former had gone some way towards dislodging the definitive status of *The Wars of the Roses*, the latter represented an even more strenuous attempt to banish the ghosts of the RSC's past. Two years on from 1975, the social and political mood in Britain seemed attuned to the extremities of the *Henry VI* plays, as the prevailing sense of malaise had darkened into apocalyptic visions of a country in crisis. With the Labour government attempting to rectify the deep contradictions within the capitalist economy by imposing, with mounting desperation, increasingly right-wing economic policies; with the issues of European Community membership and Scottish and Welsh devolution threatening the disintegration of the United Kingdom and a consequent fragmentation of national identity; with the trade union movement in a position of unprecedented strength, the voice of the authoritarian Right was becoming ever more strident and insistent. The

Henry VI plays, which could be readily interpreted as a
nightmare vision of anarchy and insurrection unleashed by the
failure of governmental authority, seemed apt texts for the
times.

The 1975 cycle – *Henry V* in particular – had been theatrically successful because of a combination of textual and
pictorial *laissez-faire* and powerful fantasies of charismatic
authoritarian rule forged amid adversity. The new-found sense
of confidence generated by this work underpinned the decision
to present the *Henry VI* plays in their unadapted entirety, for
the first time in the British theatre since the Birmingham
Repertory Theatre productions (directed by Douglas Seale) of
1952–3. Whereas Hall and Barton's interventionist treatment
had been motivated by anxieties about the quality and commercial viability of the texts as they stood, Hands declared that the
RSC was now mature enough to take the plunge and 'trust
Shakespeare'.[59] This he saw as a matter of duty: 'it was our
responsibility to do the plays without cutting or reshaping . . .
just to put it all very crudely, very naively down on the stage –
everything that was there, warts and all.'[60] Being prepared to
trust Shakespeare and to stage his imperfections seems like a
high-risk strategy, but underpinning it was a faith in his and the
RSC's improvisational capacity to conjure theatrical magic out
of unpromising material. In any case, those warts, seen in a
different light, would 'turn out to be beauty spots':[61] the texts
would work in performance, often in unexpected and startling
ways. For Hands and his actors, Shakespeare was a more
reliable authority than he had been for Hall and Barton.

The 1977 *Henry VI* cycle, stylistically speaking, represented
the culmination of a long movement away from the subfusc
rationality and realism of the 1960s, towards a more flamboy-
ant, sometimes operatic, and unashamedly star-centred, mode
of acting. As G. K. Hunter noted:

The actors . . . act their hearts out in giving Stanislavski-
esque 'depth' to the characters: Joan La Pucelle swaggers
and giggles as one supposes a maidenly soldier would have
to, in real life; Elinor Cobham preens and sighs; Edmund
Mortimer acts his age as well as expressing it. Emrys James,
on the other hand, camps up the Duke of York with fluting

exaggerations and Anton Lesser outacts Olivier acting
Richard III. Between these separate effects the plays fall to
the ground.[62]

Although Hunter detects the presence of Stanislavsky, this
sounds more like the deadly cocktail of sub-Method naturalism, competitive virtuosity and self-admiring heroics that Hall
fought to eradicate a decade before – except that here the dregs
of the RSC's own traditions have been added. The charismatic
centre of the production was Alan Howard as Henry VI, who
had also dominated the 1975 RSC season, and who appeared to
come straight from the ranks of an old-fashioned natural
theatrical aristocracy:

> Alan Howard comes to the part at the peak of his great
> powers, with a stunning Henry V and an overwhelming
> Coriolanus in the same repertory. He brings to the trilogy
> the experience of playing this Henry's father and as Prince
> before that. He brings, too, high intelligence and great
> personal power – not qualities usually associated with Henry
> VI. His speaking is superb, his playing uniformly interesting
> and unexpected. This is a Henry who has the capacity to be
> as revolutionary as Joan or Cade. Far from being a pale
> weakling, he can see too much, and call on powers far
> beyond the rest.[63]

The repudiation of one kind of realism alleviated the pressure to edit out the inconsistencies and fill in the gaps in the
texts. Hands was prepared to accept their episodic construction, their contradictoriness, and their diversity. Even so, he
still regarded the three plays as a unified cycle. He read *Henry
VI, Part 1* as 'a series of tableaux vivants, of emblems', *Part 2*
for 'the full richness of the chess game played in the English
Court' and *Part 3* as 'rather like German Expressionism . . .
monstrous horror and then this sort of ribald black comedy
which is actually slightly grotesque'.[64] This pattern of progression (from formalised medieval to avant-garde modernity) is
similar to the narrative development of *The Wars of the Roses*;
here, however, it is read as a pre-eminently stylistic rather than

historical movement. Yet this potentially unsettling discursive plurality was ultimately not as radically opposed to the dictates of realism as it might initially appear, since the drama of individual subjectivity offered a reliable developmental focus to the trilogy. Its deep structural cohesion was for Hands provided by a series of interlocking personal histories: 'There are three "inner plays", one in each part (Talbot, Jack Cade, and the three York brothers) and a "superplay" of all three parts and four main characters (Henry, Warwick and York) that is fed by such others as Suffolk, Gloucester, and Winchester.'[65] The application of a standard character-centred dramaturgy thus provided a comprehensive hierarchy of discourses, within which the conflicting narratives of the three plays could be systematised, and stylistic contradictions effortlessly resolved. In *Part 1*, 'people tend to be emblematic at first, slowly deepening into humanity as the play proceeds', and in *Part 2*, the 'characters are really established';[66] but it was only in *Part 3* that 'Shakespeare has prised open the public figures and revealed their secret selves',[67] in other words, that 'the dramatic imagination catches fire and the historical puppets start speaking like human beings'.[68]

As in Hands's *Henry IV* cycle, the *Henry VI* plays narrated a myth of rediscovery, personal development and emergence, articulated through the increasingly realist expressivity of the plays' language and the intensified naturalism of some of the performances. This centred on the growth of moral and spiritual awareness in Alan Howard's Henry VI, who embodied most clearly the movement towards personal, national and authorial integration and maturity. Henry's achievement of self-awareness and existential autonomy thus appeared to parallel Shakespeare's gradual discovery of psychology:

it's Alan Howard's Henry who does the most to bind the trilogy together: his, if anyone's, are the moral binoculars with which we peer at the black events unfolding below . . . It's a fine performance, and one that tends to prove, by the substance and resonance it slowly and inconspicuously achieves, that the probationer who patched together both part and play was, after all, our Shakespeare.[69]

There is a neat irony in 'moral binoculars', given Howard's personal short-sightedness, which in itself may partly explain why cast and action had to arrange themselves around him, and why he was able to deliver such a powerfully self-contained performance. In the event, Howard's portrayal of Henry provided a suitable mould for 'the making of both England and Shakespeare'.[70] It seems likely that this mythical convergence of the authorial, national and psychological had more to do with the combination of an inevitable re-emergence of the naturalised practices of quasi-Stanislavskian acting, routine bardolatry and the excitement generated by the event, than with the unsolicited revelation of the texts' true identity; but this would seriously contradict the avowed policy of textual *laissez-faire*. Then again, Hands and the RSC would hardly have trusted Shakespeare had they not firmly expected this ideological confirmation.

Like *Henry IV*, the 1977 *Henry VI* cycle had resonances for the present. The action took place on a stage even emptier than that of the 1975 Henriad, in order to 'present the actor as cleanly and as clearly as possible' and to 'help the audience's imagination – but not impose upon it'.[71] *Part 1* was presented on a cavernous black raked stage, decorated with a few cannons and barbed wire; *Part 2* on a carpet of improbably green artificial grass, the emblem of English pastoral; *Part 3* against a background of camouflage netting which also suggested 'a kind of Arthurian forest'.[72] The result was that 'scene melts into scene, each one contrived with a masterly simplicity that announces its content at once, so that there is as much continuous action as a football match'.[73] With the historical setting this vague and indicative, the weight of personal responsibility devolved all the more clearly to the individual, and politics became a matter of individual actions and decisions – as long as these were confined to the aristocracy. The commons, particularly as they emerged in the Cade rebellion, were treated with thinly disguised fear and contempt: 'All of the Cade scenes had been backed by a sort of mindless banner, the vacant grin of a silly turnip-lantern face with blood running down it.'[74] The moral that emerged, and its relevance to the contemporary political scene, was unequivocal. According to an enthusiastic Bernard Levin, the cycle followed 'Shake-speare's own clear view':

> that the worst horror that can be visited upon mankind is anarchy . . . so Cade's rebellion, for instance, is seen through the author's eyes rather than those of, say, the Baader-Meinhof gang, and becomes both a profoundly disturbing glimpse of the dog beneath the skin and an accusing finger pointed at the warring nobility, robbed of their moral authority over the mob by their own treachery, greed, and ambition.[75]

Interweaving the corruption of government, terrorism and mass insurrection, Levin's demonology crystallises Conservative fears of Britain's imminent descent into violent anarchy. Not all reviewers of the production saw it this way: Colin Chambers wrote in the *Morning Star* that 'there is a portrayal of the Cade uprising which, even allowing for Shakespeare's lack of sympathy, is so grotesque as to spur you on to armed revolution.'[76] On the whole, though, the right-wing view prevailed. For the audiences of 1977 and 1978, with the mass media making the most of IRA terrorism, of picket-line violence in industrial disputes, and of confrontation between neo-Nazis and the anti-racist movement, and with a mood of nihilism and anger spreading among the country's youth, the prospect of anarchy and social collapse was an alarming one; and *Henry VI* exploited and extrapolated these fears as lurid fantasy. In a year which saw the Sex Pistols' riotous 'Anarchy in the UK' as one of the top-selling British singles, Hands's *Henry VI* was high culture's warts-and-all version of punk, offering a violently nihilistic vision of a Britain with No Future: 'Apocalypse was in the air and the rhetoric of punk was drenched in apocalypse: in the stock imagery of crisis and sudden change.'[77] In a further repudiation of Hall and Barton, Hands left *Richard III* out of the sequence, withholding the tentative closure that is effected by the accession of Richmond at the end of that play; with the collapse of the post-war political consensus at the end of the 1970s, the union of the red rose and the white was, even for the RSC, too far out of line with reality. Ironically, the absence of that play from the RSC's repertoire at this time did not prevent its opening line from entering into the political lexicon and into political history: thanks to the popularising efforts of the *Sun* newspaper, the escalation of industrial militancy that coincided with the demise of 1970s labourism and the final performances of *Henry VI* would be ever after commemorated as the Winter of Discontent.

Chapter Six

Victorian values: Henry IV (1982) and The Plantagenets (1988)

Trevor Nunn's inaugural Barbican production of the two parts of *Henry IV* in June 1982 began a new chapter in the RSC's history. Opening in the final week of the Falklands War, these histories once again provided a bridge between the RSC's political and theatrical past and its anticipated future during the years of seemingly unassailable Thatcherite ascendancy. The long-delayed move of the company's London base from the Aldwych Theatre to the Barbican Centre (which was eventually funded by the City of London) launched the RSC into a brave new 1980s world of consumerist culture. The Conservative government's aggressive pursuit of monetarist fiscal policies, its assaults upon the surviving institutions of corporatism and the welfare state, and particularly its savaging of subsidies for the arts, meant that the RSC was to be placed at the mercy of the market-place as never before. Equally threatening to the traditional identity of the RSC was the populist Right's ideological onslaught against the values and culture of the left-liberal bourgeoisie, those middle-class radicals and liberals who had previously formed one of the company's key audience constituencies. The nineteenth-century liberalism espoused by the Conservatives had a strongly utilitarian strain which, in a society newly fashioned in terms of the revived ethics of obsessive work, compulsive achievement and wealth accumulation, was deeply antagonistic to the culturist aspirations embedded in the RSC. During the 1980s, theatre workers were expected to feel the cold winds of competition, show initiative and offer value for money, like everyone else.

The RSC's tactical response during the decade was to play the Thatcherite game, diversifying its activities in the theatrical market-place and accepting large-scale corporate sponsorship, relying on an internal mechanism of subsidy through lucrative West End transfers (starting with the musical *Les Miserables*, directed by Trevor Nunn, which transferred from the Barbican to the Palace Theatre in 1983). Liberal or progressive cultural politics were definitely off the agenda: in 1988, Terry Hands (who took over as sole Artistic Director in 1987) denied that the RSC had ever had any radical aspirations and likened the company to 'a merchant bank or an underwriting firm . . . maverick, buccaneer, private. We are not the National Theatre and never will be.'[78] This last assertion seems ironic, given that the RSC's early successes had effectively constituted it as a national theatre in all but name; but Hands's determination to steer the RSC away from the pejorative associations of state support seemed to pay off. The RSC managed to weather the climate of the 1980s when many of the regional repertory theatres and small-scale touring companies did not – at what was, by comparison with its rivals, still a disproportionately high level of subsidy.

Nonetheless, by the end of the decade a number of commentators felt that the RSC's survival tactics had led to a neglect of its traditional role as the custodian of a vital part of the national heritage; according to the *Guardian* theatre critic Michael Billington, it had 'sold its soul' (Shakespeare) in a Faustian pact with the market-place that threatened to undermine its identity, making many 'question its very *raison d'être*'.[79] Hands was later to distance himself from his former enthusiasm for theatrical venture capitalism, stating in 1992 that 'not only did the Thatcher years bring the regional theatres, our breeding ground, to catastrophe, they damn well nearly destroyed the RSC itself.'[80] But by then the damage had been done. Meanwhile, the RSC continued to present theatre as a consumer product, acting at the Barbican as cultural caterers to the City and beyond, serving up a theatrical fare not dissimilar to the mass-produced, overpriced, shrink-wrapped sandwiches on offer in the theatre foyer: bland, homogenised and ultimately unsatisfying.

In 1982, *Henry IV* had one eye on this grim future and the other on the traditions of the 1970s. This dual perspective was embodied in the set design, which was as simultaneously assimilatory and agenda-setting as was the selection of the plays themselves. The production – and thus the Barbican stage – introduced itself with a mesmerising, totally wordless *coup de théâtre*:

> At the beginning of Trevor Nunn's production of the first part of *Henry IV* at the new Barbican Theatre, the stage lights go down at the same time as the house lights and in darkness we hear the opening notes of Guy Wolfendon's solemn, haunting music as a scattered host of twinkling candles advances slowly from every nook and on every level of the black recesses and cells of the honeycomb set. It is a breathtaking moment, and, when I first saw it, was greeted by a stunned silence followed by excited cheering.[81]

This is the sort of once in a lifetime theatrical experience that Shakespeare's history plays might well be seen to exist for, an epiphany brought on by a near-perfect convergence of sound, vision, event and environment. And this was all before a line of the text has been spoken; indeed, it might well have been superfluous, for the mass of candles was a stage effect offered not to illuminate the word but to supplant or replace it – a more or less complete inversion of everything the RSC had stood for in the previous decade. The rest of the production did not disappoint. After the austerity of the last history cycle, the RSC was back in the business of opulent spectacle, densely textured *mise-en-scène* and labyrinthine over-abundance. History was back, in the guise it was increasingly to adopt in the culture of Britain in the 1980s, as heritage: here was richness and magic, bold pictorial statement, the operative mode of RSC designer Shakespeare.

John Napier's set for the *Henry IV* plays offered a surfeit of detail, combining 'a magnificent folly of balconies, gangways, rotting beams and rusting armour',[82] 'a series of black-timbered, interlocking trucks laced with crossbows, quivers and other implements of war . . . like some vast Satanic ship of state',[83] 'beams and spars, crossbows and spears, even a crucifix, all forming cells and spaces, recesses and rooms, ropeways and platforms'.[84] Napier and Nunn had recycled their design for *Nicholas Nickleby*, which had been the RSC's last major success at the Aldwych Theatre; conjuring the ghosts of the theatre recently vacated, suggesting the continuity between the RSC's past and its future, the medieval, Victorian and modern within the enveloping security of heritage. Perhaps the RSC was conscious that the chrome and concrete expanses of the Barbican complex formed a potentially alienating and intimidating site for Shakespeare, and hoped that christening the space with the bric-à-brac associated with Dickensian (and Hogarthian) richness would be a way to infuse it with some warmth and humanity. But whereas the success of *Nickleby* had been actor-centred, arising from ensemble narrative and improvisation, and anti-illusionist scenic minimalism within the relatively intimate confines of the Aldwych, *Henry IV* celebrated the technological resources of the huge new stage, rather as *The Wars of the Roses* had in the Royal Shakespeare Theatre nearly twenty years before. In *Nickleby*, the whole company had remained on stage throughout the performance in a collective act of storytelling; for *Henry IV*, the supporting cast remained as mute witnesses, decoratively perched over the action on walkways and gantries, observing but not participating in the historical and theatrical events unfolding below. In *The Wars of the Roses*, John Bury's schematic sets had presented a modernist vision of history; Napier's baroque inventiveness signalled the onset of postmodernism.

Against this picture of history as *bricolage* was placed the moral ambiguity and psychological complexity of the central characters, once again arranged as an all-male Oedipal triangle, a struggle between Prince Hal and two father-figures, Bolingbroke and Falstaff. Michael Billington observed that Nunn 'treats the plays as if they were a long novel called Fathers and Sons'.[85] The cycle, accordingly, centred on conflicts of loyalty and feeling. Patrick Stewart played Bolingbroke with acute attention to naturalistic detail, as 'a man in whom almost everything is clamped down under control and neutralised . . . obsessively working himself to death with papers and state-business, knowing that everything he did was pointless'.[86] Joss Ackland offered a surprisingly peevish Falstaff, 'a richly provoking performance as an oddly melancholy Lord of Misrule', whose 'troubled humanism remained, indomitably, the focus of the plays'.[87] At the centre of the cycle was Gerald Murphy's adolescently rebellious Hal:

who, judging by his hair and manner, might today be found tooling off on his motorbike to a pop-festival, a snort of cocaine in his pocket . . . comfortable only with his substitute father, the one who cradles him and offers him love, Falstaff. No wonder the old man is tempted to exploit him. No wonder the Lord Chief Justice and the rest of the ruling class are so nervous about the end-effects of that exploitation.[88]

However, the subversive possibilities aroused by this Hal's flirtation with the Eastcheap counter-culture were finally closed off in an emotional death-bed reconciliation between natural father and son:

Here, he finally accepts that his father is his father, that he loves him, and that he must succeed him; but not without a great deal of snarling and writhing and distraught emotional somersaulting. The battle is over, painfully won for the British establishment.[89]

The battle appeared to be over for the RSC, too: perhaps in Hal's capitulation to the ruling class we can detect echoes of the company's leave-taking of its former radical loyalties, surrendering relevance for a more traditionally institutional role.

Manufactured nostalgia about a vanished past has always had an ideological role to play within English culture; but in the 1980s, the appropriation and manipulation of images of the past was to become a semiotic battleground, not only in the political use of idealised histories to ratify social, economic and military policy, but in the growth of the museum and heritage industries within the culture as a whole.[90] For all its potential for sentimentalisation, *Nicholas Nickleby* had deployed images of history in an oppositional, subversive fashion, satirising 'Victorian values' by echoing Dickens's outrage at the social consequences of nineteenth-century liberalism. Its final image was of the titular hero breaking out of the comfortable family tableau to gather up in his arms one of the nameless, starving waifs who remained as a silent, accusing chorus out in the cold: a moment which demonstrated both the strength of feeling contained within the charitable gesture and the limitations of such individual action. In the move to the Barbican, this moral and political impetus seems to have been sidetracked: at best, *Henry IV* offered, in the very density of its visual texture, to wrap protective layers around Shakespeare's vulnerable humanism.

Retaining the proscenium-arch, end-on configuration for the Barbican Theatre meant that the RSC perpetuated the pictorial and scenic mode of production as its dominant main-house, large-scale style. In the same season that *Henry IV* set the agenda at the Barbican, the Royal Shakespeare Theatre at Stratford saw the spectacular debut of Adrian Noble and Bob Crowley, the director–designer team who went on to establish the definitive house style for the remainder of the decade. Alongside *Henry IV* and Nunn's Edwardian *All's Well that Ends Well*, their *King Lear* inaugurated a new era of pictorial production. Yet while the splendours of showcase productions formed the economic core of the RSC's activities, they seemed increasingly to compensate for a sense of dissipation and beleaguerment. With a succession of Conservative governments eagerly breaking up and selling off the old state monopolies, the culture industry came to face similar prospects of privatisation, and the RSC faced the prospect of serious competition. Its new rivals succeeded in establishing their stake in the Shakespearean market-place through the exercise of appropriately Thatcherite individualism and entrepreneurial initiative. In 1981 Declan Donnellan founded Cheek by Jowl, which toured small- to medium-scale venues nationally with acclaimed, apolitical productions of Shakespeare.[91] In 1986 director Michael Bogdanov and actor Michael Pennington secured sponsorship from the Allied Irish Bank for their English Shakespeare Company: their first major project was their own version of the history cycles (entitled, apparently without irony, *The Wars of the Roses*), staged in Bogdanov's trademark modern dress.[92] A year later RSC renegade Kenneth Branagh revived the traditions of the actor-manager and the unashamedly star-centred Shakespearean production by forming the Renaissance Theatre Company; one of his major initial successes was to borrow some of the ideas from the 1984 RSC production of *Henry V* (in which he starred) in his own film version of the play. In such a diverse market-place, the

RSC's traditional Shakespearean hegemony looked rather precarious, and these external pressures were augmented by internal ones. The single most important theatrical event within the RSC during this period was the opening in 1986 of the Swan Theatre, an imitation Jacobean playhouse constructed within the shell of the old Shakespeare Memorial Theatre; almost immediately the quality of its productions cast the main-house work in a deeply unfavourable light. Not only did the radical theatrical impact of its thrust stage effectively undermine whatever lingering credibility the picture-frame still possessed in the eyes of many observers, but its repertoire of the neglected and undervalued plays of Shakespeare's contemporaries threatened to dislodge the house dramatist from his traditional position of privileged pre-eminence. By 1988, the conditions were ripe for another history cycle rescue operation.

When Adrian Noble turned to the *Henry VI* plays for the 1988 season, it would appear that he intended them to perform the consolidatory and definitive role that they had in previous RSC cycles. The great adventure of a *Henry VI* cycle for the 1980s would be an invocation of former glories, a harbinger of the future, a training ground for a new company, and a reminder of what the RSC could do with, and to, Shakespeare. And the company made sure that the production would be commemorated. For all its theatrical importance, it had taken seven years for the script of *The Wars of the Roses* to enter into print; Noble showed rather less tardiness, and the script of the cycle was published to coincide with its transfer to the Barbican in 1989.[93] Following Hall and Barton, Noble set out in it the rationale for the treatment of the text. He did not start out with Hands's declared confidence in the plays as they stood:

> I found sections of the *Henry VI* plays not only clumsy, but fairly tedious. I felt that *Henry VI Part I* had great theatrical possibilities, but contained many *longueurs* and seemed repetitive. *Part II* seemed the best of the three, a major play. *Part III* seemed to wither alarmingly in the last two acts.[94]

Hence it was 'an easy and pragmatic choice'[95] to condense the three plays into two, retitled *Henry VI* and *The Rise of Edward IV*, and to finish off the trilogy, called *The Plantagenets*, with the rechristened *Richard III, His Death* (a curious archaism which made it sound like a rediscovered Elizabethan play). By the late 1980s the RSC was far less concerned to demonstrate its 'scholarly' identity than it had been in the 1960s; in an interview in *Plays and Players*, Noble posited the question of authorship but left it almost as an aside: 'I'm not of the opinion that all of the Henry VI plays are great writing. I don't even think that the majority of *Henry VI Part One* was written by Shakespeare.' Moreover, Noble's understanding of 'great writing' seemed to differ from Hall and Barton's, at least insofar as considerations of stylistic cohesion, realism, linearity and organic unity went. He felt that his predecessors had 'cut out vast amounts of the contradictory qualities within those plays',[96] and was determined to preserve the 'relish of the contradictions and paradoxes in the world of the Plantagenets'.[97] This was also a political approach, which involved a shift from Hall and Barton's teleological and homogenising ordering of their cycle. Noble did not want to endorse the Tudor Myth, but neither did he intend to subvert or question it; his solution was to play upon the texts' fictional–factual ambiguity, emphasising the ideological complexities of their dramatic historiography. Whereas Hall and Barton, and subsequently Hands, were eager to close the gap between themselves and Shakespeare, and consequently afforded the *Henry VI* plays the transcendent status of myth, Noble attempted to distance himself from Tudor propaganda by locating them within the equivocating discourse of drama documentary. With debates about the fictioning of history for ideological ends very much an issue (particularly in television drama) during the 1980s, this afforded the cycle some neat up to the minute relevance.

Noble could nonetheless ascribe to Shakespeare a clear authorial standpoint which was not political but moral: 'the plays revolve around a private and individual choice coming into harsh conflict with a complicated and violent political scenario.'[98] This emphasis was embodied in the cycle's composite title: *The Plantagenets* advertised a dynastic saga catering for what one of Noble's interviewers described as the current 'taste for serials, soaps and history cycles'.[99] Here was a decidedly more market-led rationale for adaptation than

Tillyardian scholarship: upwardly mobile culturist aspirations seemed now to have been superseded by downwardly mobile populist ones. The distance between 1963 and 1988 was also marked by the difference in the nature and extent of editorial intervention by the director. *The Wars of the Roses* had taken shape according to the dual vision of Hall and Barton as authors and scholarly directors; Noble followed the now more common RSC practice of employing a reputable professional dramatist to rework the material. He began work on the trilogy with Charles Wood, the author of a number of celebrated and controversial plays on the subject of warfare (including one of the most notorious television drama-documentaries, screened in 1988, *Tumbledown*[100]), a writer whose work had repeatedly subverted militaristic and historical myth, and, according to Noble, 'the greatest living writer on war and soldiers'.[101] Work on the adaptation proceeded as far as the first draft, which then went into rehearsal: initially, according to Noble, rehearsals 'centred around passionate debate about the script and extensive improvisations of battles and acts of violence'.[102] The participatory model of collective editorship and authorship (a veritable share-owning democracy) recalled *Nicholas Nickleby* and Hall's ensemble ideals, and Noble felt that the creation of an ensemble at Stratford was one of the cycle's major achievements. The aim was to create a feeling of epic history, narrative economy and speed were prioritised over character development; a shift which was supposed to democratise the production. Noble claimed that the cycle effected a healthy shift away from the predominant egocentricity of the theatre of the 1980s:

> the greatest tribute I can pay to the acting company is that they rapidly learned to balance the need to project and develop their own character with the needs of the work as a whole. We all had to learn to value narrative over 'character moments' and to value storytelling over psychology. One of the most ego-less and purposeful companies imaginable emerged surely and deftly in Stratford.[103]

In the event, the narrative that emerged was in some respects not all that different from that of *The Wars of the Roses*. There were obvious structural similarities between the two cycles.

The first half of Noble's *Henry VI*, like Hall and Barton's, compressed most of *Henry VI, Part 1*, mainly by eliding battle scenes; the second half presented the highlights of *Henry VI, Part 2*, up to the deaths of the Duke of Gloucester, the Bishop of Winchester and the Duke of Suffolk, and concluded with the tableau of Margaret clutching Suffolk's severed head. *The Rise of Edward IV* covered the edited remainder of *Henry VI, Part 2* and *Henry VI, Part 3*, notably transposing the first and second scenes of Act Three of the latter, so that Richard of Glouces-ter's first major soliloquy closed the first scene of the second half, providing the link with *Richard III, His Death*. As *The Rise of Edward IV* ended, Richard stepped forward with the first lines of *Richard III* (echoing the 1953 Birmingham Reper-tory production). The conclusion and climax to the trilogy was a shortened but 'fairly straightforward reading'[104] of *Richard III*, now integrated into 'a landscape of death, of mourning, of grieving, that is the true counterpoint to Richard's inventive genius and so becomes the seed-bed for his downfall'.[105] Although the details might vary, the general scheme and pattern were the same as *The Wars of the Roses*: English history seen as a rolling epic of crime and punishment, guilt and expiation.

The Plantagenets did depart from *The Wars of the Roses* in its gender politics. While there was common ground between the two cycles in terms of their emphasis upon individual moral choice and responsibility, Hall and Barton seemed more interested in developing this theme through the male protag-onists than the female. As Hugh Richmond has pointed out, the stage history of these plays tends to demonstrate that 'male directors looking for cuts still find the women's roles the most tempting',[106] and female parts which are already prone to marginalisation and stereotyping are often simplified still further. Most of Barton's textual interpolations had been consistently supplied to the male characters; more recently, actresses in the 1984 RSC production of *Richard III* had found themselves struggling with the director to preserve their lines. Nonetheless, the 1980s saw increasing numbers of female performers of Shakespeare (both within the RSC and beyond) rejecting the traditional role of decorative or demonised dispensability, and attempting to overcome textual, theatrical

and institutional subordination by insisting upon the integrity
of their characters' experience. In this instance, with the texts
of the *Henry VI* plays and *Richard III* to some extent up for
grabs, there might be expected to be more potential than usual
for such liberal feminist foregrounding of Shakespeare's
women. Responsive to this new mood, Noble records that he
was 'fascinated by the roles of women in the play and Shakespeare's ambivalent attitude towards them'.[107]

The texts represented woman as object, in the figure of Joan
of Arc (which I shall discuss below), but more interestingly for
naturalistically inclined performers, woman as subject in
Margaret of Anjou, played by Penny Downie. According to
Noble, the part was 'A King Lear for women'[108] thus she was:

> Shakespeare's first great female characterization, whom in
> many ways embodies the journey of our Plantagenets – from
> innocent formality in her early scenes with Suffolk, through
> the terrible transformation brought about in her by civil war,
> to the refugee in *Richard III* who hands on, quite crucially,
> the gift of cursing to the grieving Queen Elizabeth, whose
> encounter with Richard changes the course of the play.[109]

The adaptation developed and strengthened Margaret's role,
creating a more purposeful, consistent and intelligent character
than the original texts might suggest. Her decisive moment
came at the end of *Henry VI*, when she violently interrupted
Henry's conventionally pious comments over the death-bed of
Winchester:

KING HENRY: Forbear to judge, for we are sinners all.
                (*Enter* QUEEN MARGARET *with* SUFFOLK'S
                head.)
QUEEN MARGARET: Ah! barbarous villains! Hath this lovely
                face
                Rul'd like a wandering planet over me,
                And could it not enforce them to relent,
                That were unworthy to behold the same?
                Oft have I heard that grief softens the
                mind,

> And makes it fearful and degenerate;
> Think therefore on revenge, and cease to
> weep.[110]

Combining lines from Act Four, Scene Three and Act Three, Scene Two of *Henry VI, Part 2*, this climactic sequence offers a sharp juxtaposition of vengeful conviction and impotent religiosity, impassioned femininity and feeble, inept masculinity. As one reviewer pointed out, it was a 'turning point in Margaret's mental history', powerfully conveyed by Penny Downie: 'She lets you see that this same atrocity will at once turn her into a monster and preserve, at some deep core, a capacity for intense human feeling.'[111] This complex, universalised interiority goes some way beyond the narrow compass of experience usually allotted to Shakespeare's women: so much so, in fact, that Downie's authoritative performance became 'the axis of the production'.[112] Celebrated by another male reviewer as 'aggressive, sarcastic, sensual and brave, her mind eventually cracked by years of unsupported conflict, loneliness and loss',[113] this female Lear-surrogate compelled attention, not least because she presented a mesmeric image of female violence.[114]

But if Margaret's tormented inner life provided one powerful focus of interest throughout *The Plantagenets*, the cycle also provided some more literal images of female suffering, particularly in *Henry VI*, with the development of the material dealing with Joan La Pucelle. Noble found that *Henry VI, Part 1* offered contradictory perspectives upon the role:

> Joan, to the English, is a witch who uses demonic powers to defeat the otherwise invincible Talbot; however, to the French she is a great heroine . . . we have two distinct and opposing views of the same phenomenon – both totally credible and accurately portrayed. A modern audience is faced with a simple question: who are right, the French or the English?[115]

Audiences were thus presented with a dialectical representation that was also the site of male (mis)readings of female sexuality: 'Is she a witch, or isn't she?'[116] In this production,

she evidently wasn't, since neither Joan's spirits nor those of
Margery Jourdain appeared on stage; the demonisation was
actually ideological, indicating the military imperative 'to shape
the enemy into something worthy of slaughter'.[117] This
provided the impetus for one of the production's more memorable tableaux, Joan's burning at the stake, which came towards
the end of the first half of *Henry VI*. Hoisted on a ladder over a
mound of corpses high upstage (where she was to remain like a
grotesque parody of the crucifixion until the end of the act,
through two scenes of diplomatic manoeuvring), bathed in red
light, she became the addressee of one of the adaptation's few
textual interpolations:

YORK: Break thou in pieces and consume to ashes,
           Thou foul accursed minister of hell!
           Joan grilled!
           Sceaboles! Arbaron! Elohi!
           Elmigith! Herenobulcule!
           Methe! Baluth!
           Ferete!
           Bacuhaba! Guvarin!
           By the empire which ye exert over us,
           Fulfil this work that I may pass invisible
           To whom I wish!
WATKINS: Fear him who was immolated in Isaac
           Sold in Joseph
           Slain in the lamb, fear him,
           Fear him who was crucified in man!
           (*He thrusts the cross at her.*)
           Fear him who was triumphant over hell.[118]

The victimised, objectified Joan provided the antithesis to the
predatory Margaret, shortly to appear on stage below; the
image of her burning implicitly condemned state-sanctioned
male violence. But the very power of the image (an aestheti-
cisation of torture) itself poses uncomfortable questions, not
the least being that by transforming a person into a symbol
the *mise-en-scène* has begun to operate in the manner of the
ideology it purports to criticise. Who was being objectified,
and by whom: Joan, or the actress playing her, Julia Ford?

Fifteenth-century misogynists, or Adrian Noble, Bob Crowley and the RSC?

As an example of how the politics of the stage image might under closer inspection prove problematic, this moment encapsulated the dubious ideological orientation of the production – and of the whole scenic mode of Shakespearean production that it exemplifies. In terms of staging, *The Plantagenets* was the triumphant culmination of several years of increasingly elaborate, picture-book history, as witnessed in the gothic cathedral setting for the 1984 *Richard III* and the animated clockwork Book of Hours illustration that formed the background for the 1986 *Richard II*. The success of *The Plantagenets* stemmed less from its expert abridgement of the text than from its visual splendours. Noble claimed that the look of the production arose out of the rehearsal blocking and improvisation but, given that most reviews were given over to rapturous descriptions of the scenery, this does not seem to have been the effect achieved in performance. As Michael Ratcliffe put it in the *Observer*, 'rich heraldry returns to the Histories':

> Huge bannered walls at the start of *The Plantagenets* blaze with lilies, lozenges and lions in blue, red, black and gold, but the punctured floor steams like the sidewalks of Manhattan, as though history – fifteenth-century English history at least – were one long dash across the crust of hell . . . Three glittering French horsemen rear out of the darkness like jewels on black velvet. Battle standards of fluttering silk are raced across the bare stage as the war abroad slides sickeningly into the war at home. Ladders rise out of the earth to scale battlements of gleaming brass; the glorious sun of York becomes an ominous disc of bristling steel as Richard's fortunes wane. Richard (Anton Lesser) dies with his hump pierced by a black flag, the nation's sickness cured.[119]

Ratcliffe's conclusion was that the concern of this cycle was 'not political but aesthetic', thus distinguishing it in intentions and effect from Hall and Barton's (and Bogdanov's) *The Wars of the Roses*, and incidentally rendering the RSC safe for Thatcherite Britain. No doubt this was a welcome accolade but, in truth, the production was deeply political. To begin with,

Noble's 'moral' reading of the cycle interpreted its close in a manner which would have received the endorsement of Tillyard, let alone that of Hall and Barton:

> this bleak, divided, brutalized world is healed by the Tudor Richmond, who 'unites the white rose and the red'. This sense of healing, of renewal, is perhaps my lasting memory of *The Plantagenets*, and perhaps the strongest 'message' of the tetralogy – an anguished cry for peace.[120]

Maybe this articulated a liberal message for Noble: a vaguely ecological, feminised pacificism rather than feudal despotism, but to many reviewers it was the latter viewpoint which irresistibly suggested itself. The *Daily Telegraph* reviewer, as a representative of the right-wing press, noted with approval that the cycle endorsed 'Shakespeare's concern for social order based on submission to a just, or even an unjust, authority'.[121] Battered and overwhelmed by a relentless succession of images of devastation alternating with gorgeous pageantry, the spectator was in precisely this position of submission, to the autocracy of director and designer, and reactionary politics emerged on a large scale almost by default. In the midst of otherwise adulatory reviews, one solitary voice of criticism addressed this issue. Writing in *City Limits*, Lyn Gardner observed that the cumulative historiographical effect of the cycle was of 'a constant sea of chaos':

> And if chaos *is* a constant (rather than the result of actions) then change (and potential revolution) is impossible. Only totalitarianism can triumph. No wonder, then, that after 9 hours, the audience gave Henry VII such a welcome – you could tell by his haircut that this was the sort of chap to make the trains run on time . . . At the end, as Henry VII gets down to business, the music (composer: Edward Gregson) swelled, sounding suspiciously like the score for 'Star Wars' crossed with 'Chariots of Fire'. The audience cheered. Now *that's* a lesson for our time.[122]

This lesson was implicated in the very style of the production. With Simon Dormandy striding onstage as a Richmond presented in the slicked-back mould of those heroes of 1980s Britain, the estate agents and stockbrokers, and generating the braying triumphalism of the Conservative party conference, we might well ponder how far the RSC had moved from its original radical aspirations. The surrender to charisma and dema-goguery, and the willingness to suspend disbelief in the care-fully stage-managed image, are symptomatic of the wider political culture of the Britain of the time: a society obsessively preoccupied with politics at the level of signification. The self-referential Noble–Crowley style, combining anachronism with pageantry, simultaneously startlingly inventive and totally derivative, pointed to the postmodernist future of RSC Shake-spearean production by recycling its own past. Stepping for-ward to proclaim the end of warfare at the end of the grand narrative of *The Plantagenets*, Richmond also heralded the end of opposition, the end of intervention and perhaps the end of history itself.

Part III

Heroes and Villains

Chapter Seven

Shakespeare through the looking-glass: Richard II (1973)

John Barton's 1973 production of *Richard II* is one of the best-documented Shakespeare productions of the post-war period; it is also often cited as the most influential, if not the definitive, modern production of the play.[1] Such is the almost mythic status of the production that it is worth beginning with a reminder of how novel it seemed to its first audiences. It opened amid high expectations. Apart from a poorly received *Richard III*, directed by Terry Hands in 1970, *Richard II* was the first major production of a mainstream history play since *The Wars of the Roses*; it was directed by John Barton, who had established a reputation for daring and innovation; and, most intriguingly of all, the roles of Richard and Bolingbroke were to be alternated in successive performances between two of the RSC's well-established stars, Ian Richardson and Richard Pasco. Right from the start of production, audiences were in for a few surprises. The first was the set. Given the established practice of the RSC since the early 1960s, it is unlikely that anyone would have still been expecting Victorian-style pictorial design; but – for a play which has long been draped in pageantry and period charm – the spectator was presented with an unnervingly sombre, austere and abstract stage setting. No sea-walled gardens or ivy-covered castles here; instead a stark, spare framework, as described in detail by one of its designers, Timothy O'Brien:

> Picture two walls, set at right angles to the front of the stage, parallel to one another 8 m apart, 8 m long, 8 m high at the upstage ends and zero centimeters high at the downstage ends which were 3 meters from the first row of the audience. These triangular walls were 80 cm thick and had a staircase

built into their steep incline with a closed string on either
side of the steps, much like the walls of the great sun clocks
in Jai Singh's observatory in Jaipur. Next a bridge was
designed to span from one wall to the other and fitted with
wheels to run in grooves cut in on the on-stage closed string
of the pair of walls. The bridge had a level floor 2 m deep
from front to back . . . To symbolize the business of the
play, a portable pyramid of golden steps was set downstage
before the audience arrived and on it stood the robe and
crown of the king.[2]

Even in the tone and style of this account we can catch a hint of
the spirit of the production: here is a model of hierarchical
ordering and clockwork precision, a set designed for neither
representation nor evocation, but for exposition. This was a
structure which from the outset laid open the ceremonial and
symbolic machinery of the play; it also announced the production's self-reflexive, overtly theatrical style. To the alert spectator, musing on Barton's reputation as a scholar and intellectual heavyweight, the strongly schematic quality of this
picture would perhaps have signalled that this was to be no
straightforward staging of *Richard II*.

This impression would have been confirmed by a glance at
the programme, which furnished clues to the production's
intentions, particularly in an essay by Anne Barton, the director's
spouse, on 'The king's two bodies'. Combining the Barton's
own concern with Shakespearean metadrama with the analysis
of medieval political theology offered by Ernst Kantorowicz,[3]
this essay fleshed out the bones of what was on stage, supplying
a historical and textual rationale for the production, and clearly
indicating its interpretive line. For Anne Barton, the doctrine
of the two bodies, which held that the king simultaneously
occupied a 'body natural' and a 'body political', was a way of
resolving the contradiction between the monarchical role and
the human being occupying it: 'One of these bodies is flawless,
abstract and immortal. The other is fallible, individual and
subject to death and time.'[4] Barton saw this doctrine as a
source of tragedy, since it inevitably involved conflict between
the private and the political self. If this seemed rather arcane
and antiquarian, its immediate relevance lay in its connection

with Shakespeare's (and the production's) other area of concern: 'the latent parallel between the King and that other twin-
natured being, the Actor'.[5] In this production, the idea of
the two bodies would be explored through Richard's political
tragedy, but also through the rising and falling fortunes of
Richard and Bolingbroke, and through their self-dramatisations.
This placed the production in the vanguard of contemporary
Shakespeare criticism; the idea of Richard as actor had long
featured in the play's critical history, and had been thoroughly
explored in Anne Bartons's *Shakespeare and the Idea of the
Play*, published a decade earlier,[6] but metadrama was very
much in vogue in the early 1970s.[7] The inclusion in the
programme of rehearsal photographs of Pasco and Richardson
underlined the connection between this reading and the production's double casting. Together with the set, the programme
provided clear pointers as to how, and with what level of
seriousness, the production was to be read.

There was much to ponder here, and more surprises were to
follow. The performance began not with Richard's time-
honoured 'Old John of Gaunt' but with an elaborate and
entirely interpolated induction: a production which was dominated by ritual opened with a curious little ceremony. As the
lights dimmed for the start, there entered a balding man
dressed in doublet and hose, masked to resemble the
Droeshout portrait of Shakespeare, and carrying a large book.
This figure mounted the pyramid of steps centre stage and
stood alongside the stand on which were hung the king's robe
and crown. With a hand gesture he cued music and the entry
of the entire cast, uniformly dressed in brown tunics and
breeches, who formed lines on either side of the stage. Pasco
and Richardson, until now indistinguishable from the rest of
the cast, stepped forward to take the book from the actor
representing Shakespeare. While they leafed through the book,
Shakespeare took the crown from the stand and held it out
between them; the actors seized the crown on either side. A
brief tableau, and then a nod from Shakespeare to Pasco or
Richardson nominated the actor who was to play Richard for
this performance. Shakespeare then disappeared into the background and the action moved into a coronation ritual, with
Richard (as well as Pasco or Richardson) assuming the mantle

of kingship as an actor costuming himself for his part. Robed, crowned and masked, Richard ascended to the top of the central steps and sat down. Removing the mask, he checked the book for a final time and then, with his first words, Shakespeare's *Richard II* began.

Robert Speaight noted that this sequence ensured that 'the play was stated before it was performed'.[8] Establishing the key concerns of the production as well as its distinctive style, it created a metadramatic frame for the action of the play, making explicit links between the double casting of the production, the idea of performance and monarchical ceremony – and, at a deeper level, between role-playing and the concept of identity itself. During the induction, key props and items of costume were introduced which were to reappear as recurrent motifs throughout: the robe, the crown, the mirror. The heavy emphasis on ritual and artifice also prepared the ground for the staging techniques of the production as a whole. Since many of these have been extensively documented and discussed elsewhere, I shall offer only the briefest of outlines here. For the most part, the spectator was denied the seductions of illusion, as both *mise-en-scène* and much of the acting embraced the stylised, the emblematic and the ritualised. Movement, grouping and gesture were highly choreographed, formalised and symmetrical, with many speeches directed straight out to the audience, and others divided and distributed among the cast in choric fashion. Barons appeared on wooden horses or on stilts, the Queen and her attendants in half-masks. A pot of earth placed in a downstage corner provided a touchstone for the repeated references to England and England's ground. The Duchess of Gloucester emerged as a ghost from a floor-trap, her voice melodramatically overlaid with echo effects. For the Flint Castle scene, Richard appeared on the bridge high above the stage, wearing a huge, circular golden cloak which transformed king and actor into 'glistering Phaethon' – an image of the sun-king which 'set' as the bridge descended to the floor. The lighting was uniformly bright, sometimes harsh; when not part of the action, actors sat on benches running across the back of the stage, stiffly observing it.

It was the expository, ritualistic and emphatically symbolic style of the production, more than anything else, that rendered

it so startling and, in places, controversial. Some reviewers
welcomed Barton's formalisms, and his trick of visualising the
play's imagery, as lucid, inventive and intellectually as well as
emotionally satisfying; others condemned it as pedantic, heavy-
handed and redundantly literal-minded. John Elsom of the
Listener, for example, praised an interpretation which he
regarded as 'splendidly coherent and close to the Shakespearean text', and cited a typical example: 'the discontented nobles
rise in stature, on stilts covered by black cloaks, perfectly
illustrating the metaphor that the country's flowers are being
choked by envious weeds.'[9] Conversely, Benedict Nightingale
of the *New Statesman* found the whole tone of the production
'pompous', and the illustrative technique presumptive and
patronising, and charged Barton with 'ossifying the abundance
of *Richard* . . . using shrieking capitals to accentuate his
interpretation.'[10]

In many reviews of the production (as in many subsequent
accounts), the evaluation of style is inextricable from discussion
of the merits of the expository method and, crucially, the
nature of the directorial role – and of Barton's use (or abuse) of
the Shakespearean text. These were vexed issues within
performance-centred Shakespeare studies in the early 1970s.
Thus when Stanley Wells initiated his account of the production by noting that it was 'the most strongly interpretative
production of a Shakespeare play that I have ever seen. It was
also exceptionally stylized',[11] his association of directorial
licence with stylistic innovation was representative of the
overall critical response. The implication seems to be that a
more natural, straightforward and less overtly directorial mode
of production would have been a more illusionistic one: an
assumption which is as much ideological as it is aesthetic. Peter
Hall had identified one aspect of the problem back in the early
1960s when he wrote that common-sense assumptions about
what Shakespeare 'really meant' often went along with a
yearning 'for more pictorial Shakespeare, a taste which is more
Edwardian than Elizabethan'.[12] The RSC's task, as Hall saw it,
was to confront these assumptions in the business of producing
a 'contemporary Shakespeare'; a programme which licensed a
degree of stylistic and formal adventurousness that was
inextricably linked to the interpretative role of the director.

However radical this appeared, it stopped short of undermining the ideological foundations of the tradition it opposed: neither Shakespeare's universality nor an essentially humanist understanding of character was ever seriously in doubt. This was very much the case with Barton's *Richard II*: it was disconcerting, up to a point, because its stylistic rigour refused the usual conciliatory gestures towards pictorial illusion; it challenged by historicising, rather than modernising, the text. Yet because this unsettled what might be aptly termed liberal theatrical expectations, it seemed an avant-garde strategy: hence the paradox whereby an ultra-conservative theatrical vocabulary ('Graeco-Elizabethan' was the term used by the director and designer[13]) was described by some reviewers as 'Brechtian'.[14] Indeed, it is possible to parallel Barton's theatrical historicism with the critical methodology of Tillyard: in both cases, an insistence upon the historical otherness of Shakespeare's drama conflicted with liberal humanism – but from a deeply conservative rather than a radical position.

It is in this light that we can read the political subtext of the arguments about the proper limits of the director's power which were focused by this production: they are a way of debating the principles of liberalism. Viewed negatively, director's Shakespeare is a form of extremism, to be differentiated from the centrist eclecticism of directorial practices which aim for critical consensus – usually constructed on the basis of a shared understanding of the text. This was a perennial problem for the RSC, in its attempts to reconcile the traditional authority of Shakespeare with the creative interventionism of relevance, but Barton's repudiation of realism in *Richard II*, because it was perceived in terms of the imposition of a distinctly auteurist signature upon the work, presented the problem in a particularly acute form. Thus the production inevitably raised issues of appropriation and legitimacy, with Shakespeare (as ever) the ground of contention, between directorial licence and autonomy on the one hand, and literary and cultural authority on the other. Assessing Barton's method in his review of the 1973 Stratford season for *Shakespeare Survey*, Peter Thomson examined this opposition in terms of its hidden agenda, pointing out that critical and academic claims that director's Shakespeare was gimmick-ridden and dogmatic often seemed to conceal the demand for the theatre to concede authority to the literary academic, resulting in ' "Shakespeare as I'd make the actors do him" ', or even 'a stronger demand for no productions at all'.[15]

Rather strikingly, the production seemed to incorporate an at least incidental awareness of these issues of authority and appropriation in its own metadramatic form. The question of its legitimacy as an interpretation was, I would suggest, intriguingly addressed (although not resolved) in the induction. In this respect, I would draw attention to a highly diverting detail: the presence of the figure of Shakespeare as the inaugurator of the action. This device has received little attention: many reviews do not mention it, while those that do pass over it as a rather jokey wheeze. Peter Ansorge refers to the appearance of 'an apologetic looking Shakespeare',[16] but elsewhere his identity seems to be in doubt: Miriam Gilbert records 'a figure, vaguely like Shakespeare',[17] while Liisa Hakola is sufficiently cautious as to suspend 'Shakespeare' in quotation marks throughout her account of the production.[18] In view of the concerns outlined above, however, this superficially incidental, apologetic and ambiguous appearance seems to me crucially symptomatic of Barton's directorial project. In his eyewitness record of the rehearsal process, James Stredder notes that the inclusion of Shakespeare came about as a response to the problem of finding a rationale for the centrepiece of the induction, the coronation ritual:

> There was a mechanical problem setting up the mime: some figure was needed to introduce it. Barton thought of having an Elizabethan prompter, the Lord Chamberlain, even himself (as the play's director), but finally he decided on the the figure of Shakespeare contemplating the idea of kingship.[19]

If introducing the performance is, at least implicitly, a way of authorising it, then this is a revealing series of substitutions: responsibility for the production was being deferred back to the mythical source that has supposedly prompted it: Shakespeare's imagination. Thus Barton seemingly anticipated and forestalled criticism by conjuring forth Shakespeare from the

pages of the Folio/promptbook that he carried, installing him as
the origin and guarantee of theatrical meaning. Shakespeare's
bald head, ambiguous smile and heavy tome were the signifiers
of literary and critical legitimacy: rest assured, he seemed to
say to the audience, here is an interpretation which – however
outlandish it might seem – was firmly rooted in the text, and
which had received the blessing of the author.

Barton's Shakespeare might well be regarded as a half-
serious theatrical figure of speech, but by providing the production with a source and a centre he nonetheless fulfilled what
Barthes has defined as the author's primary function: 'to
impose a limit on that text, to furnish it with a final signified.'[20]
In the circumstances, Barton's use of the device was a prudent
manoeuvre, not only in relation to the issue of authority, but
also because the notion of metadrama, once introduced, may
be more disruptive than a conservative reading such as Barton's
might wish. Read deconstructively, Shakespearean metadrama
interrogates the play itself, introduces a radical indeterminacy
of meaning and undermines the representational status and
authority of both text and performance. The presence of
Shakespeare was a way of keeping the 'idea of the play' safely
within an authoritative framework.

It is here that we may turn to the other distinctive feature of
the production, the double casting of Pasco and Richardson in
the parts of Richard and Bolingbroke. This related very clearly
to the staging and overall style: with two distinct, finely
nuanced characterisations of both central characters in play, it
seemed to offer a suggestively open, pluralist approach to the
playtext, drawing attention to the coexistence of different
interpretative possibilities, haunting one actor's performance
with echoes of the other. There was a textual rationale
underpinning the doubling, in that Barton saw Richard and
Bolingbroke as mirror images, a pairing which fitted into the
overall conception of doubling, twin-natured beings, and kings
and actors. As Anne Barton explained:

> Like the two buckets filling one another that Richard
> imagines in the deposition scene, buckets which take a
> contrary course within the deep well of the crown, Richard's
> journey from king to man is balanced by Bolingbroke's

progress from a single to a twin-natured being. Both movements involve a gain and a loss. Each, in its own way, is
tragic.[21]

Barton's idea of the fatal reciprocity of the characters (which
was further strengthened by the interpolation of passages from
Henry IV, Part 2 to beef up the part of Bolingbroke) was less
remarked upon than the fact that their doubling 'provided a
fascinating exercise in comparative histrionics'.[22] Since this has
been discussed in detail elsewhere, I shall cite only the key
points. The major variations between Pasco's and Richardson's
portrayals of Richard were temperamental, marking the difference, as Benedict Nightingale noted, between the former's
'extrovert, amply justifying the comparisons with the sun
applied to him' and the latter's 'introvert, understandably
mistrusted by his barons'.[23] Particular details in each performance highlighted this: 'Pasco throws a near epileptic fit when
confronted with Gaunt's accusations of inadequacy; Richardson merely turns away in disgust, obviously appalled by the
stench which can come from a dying noble';[24] in the deposition
scene both remained 'unusually dignified . . . Pasco proudly
proclaiming "no" when Henry asks if he's content to abdicate,
Richardson sighing out the word with half-humorous regret'.[25]
As well as offering two distinct characterisations, Pasco and
Richardson appeared to represent two acting traditions, with
the former in the lavish, romantic Gielgud mould and the latter
in the ironic and intellectual 1960s RSC style. But diversity
remained within carefully defined limits: for the most part,
Richardson and Pasco followed the directorial conception by
emphasising the similarities between the characters rather than
their differences. To this end, the two actors were made up
with wigs and beards to resemble each other as closely as
possible, becoming virtual mirror images in the final scenes.

   This was vital; for it was in the relationship between Richard
and Bolingbroke that the production was able to contain its
own metadrama, as well as the more challenging implications
of its style. If the one aspect threatened to destabilise the act of
representation, and the other seemed alien and bizarre, the
acting placed the production in more familiar psychological
territory. Whatever anti-illusionist implications there might

have been in the staging, the comments of both Richardson and Pasco concerning the process of rehearsal and performance suggest that theirs was still a traditionally Stanislavskian approach: as Richardson put it, 'Dickie calls upon the experiences of his life, and I call upon those in my life to fill out the emotional motif of what I want to play.'[26] Far from inducing a critical disparity between actor and part, the idea of role-playing was, for both Richards, incorporated into a naturalistic character. Richardson again:

> For my Richard, his very marriage is an acted scene, all his life has been a performance. And suddenly when he's lost it all, he thinks 'my God what am I?' And he has to come to terms with a capital N – Nothing. Dickie plays the prison scene beautifully as a wounded martyr. I play it as a liberated human being who has at last discovered what it is to be real.[27]

Inner space and identity, being and nothingness: these were the real existential concerns of the production. Echoing a recurrent theme of post-war Shakespearean criticism, the production negotiated between personal, social and theatrical role-playing in quest of the authentic, interiorised self. If this seemed difficult to reconcile with the patently non-naturalistic rhetoric and artifice of the text, metadrama again provided an answer, as Barton later proposed: 'the characters in the play are consciously using rhetoric as characters';[28] ultimately, the real presence of the recognisable true self (the corollary of the Shakespeare-author figure) remains accessible to the actor, still in control.

The chief effect of the double casting, framing these twinned characterisations, was to create a hauntingly resonant subtext. It reached its uncanny apotheosis in the penultimate scene, in the most blatantly manipulative, ingenious and controversial of Barton's directorial interpolations: the substitution of the disguised Bolingbroke for Richard's Groom. The scene was played with the pair facing each other, and as Richard completed his diatribe against 'jaunting Bolingbroke' (v, v, 94), his companion lowered his hood to reveal the face of his antagonist and *doppelgänger*; holding between them the empty mirror frame that Richard had retained from the deposition scene, they gazed at each other in solemn understanding. It was a moment which was both portentous and ambiguous, and reviewers (while not disputing its surprise value) were divided as to whether it was a justified interpolation, and uncertain as to whether it should be read literally. Benedict Nightingale found it 'tendentious', as 'The two men touch, smile and stare sympathetically at each other, showing us (presumably) the hollowness of the crown;'[29] Peter Thomson conceded its 'meretricious effectiveness' but considered that 'there is nothing else to say in defence of this invention'.[30] Peter Ansorge's more sympathetic view, however, was that it reflected 'the mutual understanding and, even, love between the great rivals of this *Richard II*;'[31] while Miriam Gilbert offered the most positive exposition of what was for her 'in theatrical terms, the obligatory scene':

> This substitution . . . is aimed at increasing our sense that Bolingbroke is painfully aware of his own guilt . . . The scene as played asks us to imagine a Bolingbroke who, while acknowledging his tongue-tied state, can still confess his sense of emotional involvement to the man he has trapped in a literal prison.[32]

As these accounts suggest, there is also the strong hint of a homoerotic subtext to the relationship between the two kings, so that Bolingbroke's inarticulacy professes the love that dare not speak its name: a dangerous area of indeterminacy that even the rigid frame of Barton's production might not be able to contain.[33] There was a range of fairly naturalistic interpretations of this scene, but it was possible to read it in expressionist terms. According to Stanley Wells, Barton intended it as 'a subliminal moment', so that Richard (and the audience) 'cannot actually tell whether it was dream or reality'.[34] Richard David was also uncertain as to 'whether we were to suppose that Bolingbroke indeed came disguised as a groom, or that Richard's imagination had stamped Bolingbroke's features on the visitor'.[35] Whatever its status as fiction, the import of the image was clear: common humanity and fellow-feeling transcended politics. I would also suggest that the ambiguity of the meeting needs to be read *mythically*, in that its subtextual depth and suggestiveness was its primary ideological function. By engineering this confrontation between not only Richard and Bolingbroke but also the fictional world of the play and its metatheatrical frame, Barton created a magic moment which, however textually, historically and politically nonsensical it was, still contained its own transcendent truth. It was a powerfully sentimental gesture, and a profoundly anti-historical one, a transitory vision of wholeness and reciprocity, designed to arrest the movement of history itself by denying historical difference and change.

In this final meeting, the thematic climax of the whole production, self-reflexive circularity and symmetry encapsulated Barton's view of history and politics. Framed in the metadramatic terms of a secularised *Theatrum Mundi*, this *Richard II* saw the interplay between actor, role and king in terms of the conflict between personal integrity and the pressures of history, and the rituals of power as scripted and choreographed in a tragic, endlessly repetitive pattern. The image of the player-king was also a poignant metaphor for transience and mortality: for Barton, politics was ultimately a meaningless charade in the face of death. The production concluded, accordingly, with another coronation sequence to mirror its opening – except that here the crowned figure was that of a Morality Death, standing centre stage, flanked by Richard and Bolingbroke. Here was a *Richard II* without a possibility of a sequel, with no way forward but a reversion to its own beginning, and to a repetition of the whole doomed ritual all over again.

The question that remains is that of the relevance of all this to the cultural and political circumstances of 1973. Clearly the production struck a chord with audiences: a critical and commercial success, it played to capacity houses in both Stratford and London, was taken to New York, and was successfully revived for the 1974 season. However, unlike previous RSC hits – such as Peter Hall's 1965 *Hamlet* and Peter Brook's 1970 *Dream* – its success stemmed not from its apparent modernity but from its conservatism; from the fact that it seemed to eschew 1960s-style 'relevance' altogether. As dramatic historiography, it was the antithesis of *The Wars of the*

1. *The War of the Roses* (1963): Richard III (Ian Holm)
   confronts Richmond (Derek Waring).

2. *Henry VI* (1977): Anton Lesser as Richard, Alfred Lynch as Edward, Jack Klaff as George and Anthony Naylor as Clifford.

3. *The Plantagenets* (1988): Joan of Arc (Julia Ford) is burnt at the stake.

4. *Richard II* (1973): The coronation sequence,
with Ian Richardson as King Richard.

5. *Henry V* (1975): Alan Howard as King Henry, Philip Brack as Exeter, Derek Smith as the Archbishop of Canterbury, Oliver Ford-Davies as the Ambassador, Anthony Naylor as Clarence.

6. *Richard III* (1984): Antony Sher as Richard.

7. *King John* (1974): Emrys James as King John, Jeffrey Dench as Pandulph.

8. *King John* (1988): Robert Demeger as Hubert, Nicholas Woodeson as King John.

Roses; by reconstituting *Richard II* almost as a cycle in itself, Barton seemed to have established a new synchronic mode of Shakespearean history. In 1963, the histories had been directly connected with post-war European history, with reference points in the Cold War, the corridors of power and parliamentary and party politics; ten years later, Barton seemed to go out of his way to avoid references to the contemporary political scene.

Yet it is in its very determination to avoid contemporary significance that the production's cultural politics are most evident. It opened against a background of mounting political and economic crisis in Britain, during a period which saw an upsurge in industrial conflict, rising inflation, and the beginnings of a right-wing backlash against the liberal social legislation of the 'permissive' 1960s. In the course of the production's two-year life, the Conservative government led by Edward Heath switched from a conciliatory to a confrontational industrial policy – resulting in the three-day week, and the miners' strike which installed Harold Wilson's Labour government in 1974. It was the period which marked the sudden and catastrophic disintegration of the post-war consensus, the key moment when, as Alan Sinfield has described it, 'the compromise of welfare-capitalism became a contradiction'.[36] A few reviewers found parallels with the contemporary political scene, like the *Listener*'s John Elsom, who admired Barton's 'ability to convey the relevance of the play to modern audiences': 'Aren't prime ministers equally actors? Barton's main *coup de théâtre* lay in asking Richardson and Pasco to swop roles, "Wilson" and "Heath" . . . .'[37] Perhaps it is possible to detect such prescient echoes in the casting and performances of Pasco and Richardson, the one evoking Heath's patrician lugubriousness, the other Wilson's machiavellian wit and showmanship; but on the whole reviewers preferred to avoid such explicit parallels. With so much history happening outside the theatre, Barton's *Richard II* offered an escape from contemporaneity into an endlessly fascinating hall of psychic mirrors. Moreover, if the events of 1973 made one thing clear, it was that 'politics' was not simply confined to the manoeuvrings of politicians nor to the vicissitudes of the electoral system: the increasing strength of the trade union

movement signalled the possibility of a substantial shift in the
balance of power away from the institutions of capital and the
state. Amid such turbulence and uncertainty, *Richard II*, for all
its elements of surprise, quietly affirmed an alternative England, offering the prospect of a simpler, more predictable and
more ordered world: a world where revolutions ran along
quaintly choreographed lines before freezing into stasis; where
stars are stars and everyone else knew their place; a world
where even Kott's Grand Mechanism of history appeared to
have jammed. Barton's historicist vision of order was as much a
reaction to the contemporary political scene as Tillyard's had
been, thirty years before; and, for all its metadramatic complexities, *Richard II* offered a theatrical equivalent of Tillyard's
vision and critical method. It is small wonder, then, that this
production has attained the enduring status of a theatrical
myth.

Chapter Eight

Playing soldiers:
Henry V (1975 and 1984)

I have aready briefly considered the 1975 production of *Henry
V*, directed by Terry Hands and starring Alan Howard, in the
context of that year's cycle of history plays. There it was
discussed as the culmination of a rather muted national epic, a
Bildungsroman structured around a three-cornered Oedipal
contest between Prince Hal, Bolingbroke and Falstaff, and set
against the backdrop of an England in a state of terminal
decline. The novelty of this season was that it did not quite fit
together as a cycle in the recognised sense, not least because
the Henry plays were presented out of chronological sequence,
with *Henry V* opening in March, *Henry IV Part 1* in April, and
Part 2 in June. The linear development and pacing of *The Wars
of the Roses* in 1963–4 had helped to ensure that the cycle was
received and evaluated as a totality, thus contributing to the
sense of an ensemble epic: the heroics of individual performances were ultimately subsumed into a larger picture of history.
This season, however, opted for the logic of the box office by
centring the season on the play that could be most counted
upon to be a sure-fire success. Hands and Howard's *Henry V*
belonged to an older tradition of star-centred Shakespearean
production; as the most popular and critically acclaimed production of the 1975 season, it succeeded in transcending the
confines of the cycle itself. *Henry V* remained in the RSC's
repertoire until 1978, established Alan Howard as the RSC's
definitive Shakespearean hero and monarch for the second half
of the 1970s (he went on to play Henry VI, Richard II, Richard
III and Coriolanus), and consolidated Hands's position as the
RSC's leading director; it also created a potent company myth,
which was to underpin the RSC's work for nearly half a decade.
In this chapter, then, I shall examine some of the theatrical and

contextual factors that led to the formation of this myth, as well as some of its ideological implications.

The story has several times been told of how *Henry V* reversed a near-catastrophic decline in the financial and artistic fortunes of the RSC in the mid-1970s.[38] Inevitably, parallels between the form and subject matter of the play and the process of the play's production suggest themselves: true to the traditionally inspirational spirit of the play, it is a story of gutsy determination, hair-raising risks and inspired improvisation in the face of overwhelming odds. The closing months of 1974 saw the RSC starved of both cash and sympathy: it had been a critically and commercially disastrous season; the Aldwych theatre was under threat; the antiquated heating and air-conditioning system of the Royal Shakespeare Theatre was in a state of illegal inefficiency; the company was a quarter of a million pounds in deficit; and, in the context of national economic crisis, a rapidly diminishing level of state subsidy threatened its very existence. But if the RSC perceived itself as economically beleaguered, it was also under attack for its alleged profligacy and for its (still) massively disproportionate claim upon Arts Council funding. In such circumstances, the choice of *Henry V* to lead the 1975 season was almost mandatory; it was to act as a call to arms not only for the RSC but (in an ideologically deft conflation of company and national self-interest) for the country as a whole; it would beat the RSC into shape, silence the dissenters and trigger all the right patriotic and nostalgic emotions.

This was a very different mobilisation of the play to that of the 1964 Stratford production, and an index of how far the RSC had travelled from its original liberal aspirations. In the context of *The Wars of the Roses* (and against the background of the war in Vietnam), *Henry V* had been downbeat, anti-heroic and anti-war. Ian Holm's Henry was 'a grimy and exhausted little general who is trying to piece together his scattered feelings for continuing the struggle';[39] the French campaign was 'bloody, clobbering and unpleasant';[40] this was a production in which 'mud draggles tattered surcoats, blood deluges face, smoke hangs somberly over dark, fevered billets'.[41] It was a pacifist reading against the grain of the play's post-war theatrical history, and appeared sufficiently radical for John Arden to claim in a letter to the *New Statesman* that it had discovered the 'secret play inside the official one',[42] revealing the reality behind bogus nationalist rhetoric and pageantry. Eleven years later, with the war in Vietnam drawing to its ignominious conclusion and with the British state now bloodily embroiled in an escalating colonial war of its own in Northern Ireland, the RSC seemed to have reverted to a more conservative reading. In 1976 the RSC produced a volume commemorating the production which included the text of the production, photographs, interviews, extracts from reviews, and essays by members of the company and others; judging by the overall tone, the RSC was keen to promote a celebratory view of both play and production. For once, the RSC flourished its 'royal' connections, with a foreword by Prince Philip which endorsed 'the marvellous spirit of the play', which was an 'appropriate choice' for the company and the nation as a whole. Meanwhile Trevor Nunn evoked the play's 'special message of courage to the English in times of gathering darkness, fear, and falling empires'.[43] As for the production itself, the reviewers in the right-wing press were not disappointed: Charles Lewsen of *The Times* exulted in the spectacle of Henry's 'attempt to forge himself in the painful fires of authority and battle';[44] Harold Hobson wrote in the *Sunday Times* of 'the theatrical, visual, and above all the spiritual splendour';[45] while the *Daily Express* reviewer described the production as 'rousing stuff, a reminder of national greatness . . . a gutsy, reviving production at a time of national adversity'.[46] Yet the production also pleased reviewers of the centre and the Left, who praised its even-handedness, its avoidance of conventional heroics and militar-istic chauvinism. This was 'no call to arms, no aggressive fantasy, rather the invocation of a passing dream', according to W. Stephen Gilbert in *Plays and Players*;[47] one which left the audience 'free to conclude' with Benedict Nightingale 'that [Henry's] adventure was a moral outrage'.[48]

That the production was able to provoke such contradictory responses is a measure of Hands's skill in steering the produc-tion between the 'extremes' of rampant patriotism and paci-fism, thus alienating neither ideological wing of the RSC's audience constituency. My interest here is in how this was effected through the production's formal and stylistic strategies, which were crucial to its ideology. In her history of the company, Sally Beaumann characterises the right-wing critical appropriation of the production as instances of misreading shaped by an 'accumulated heritage of prejudice', so that it was 'frequently to be praised for the wrong reasons'.[49] Compare this judgement with that of Ronald Bryden, who pointed out that most critics also missed the point of the production's stylistic vocabulary: 'praise of the production seemed to focus on its elements of spectacle . . . illusion, after all, seemed to be what the determined reviewers insisted on deriving and taking away from their evening.'[50] In the case of *Henry V*, at least, spectacle and illusion are associated with nationalistic delusion, stylisation and the aesthetics of the empty space with sceptical interrogation, even pacifism: a major element in the production's success was its adept theatrical negotiation of these stylistic and political oppositions.

As in Peter Brook's *Dream* and John Barton's *Richard II*, metadrama was again the central strategy. The cue was provided, of course, by the self-reflexive and interrogative structure of the play itself; in particular in the first Chorus which, as 'the dictionary of this new method', urged the RSC to 'start from scratch'.[51] In what was to form the framework for the whole season, Hands and his designer, Farrah, divested the Stratford stage of much of its traditional apparatus of illusion and spectacle, presenting a stripped-down space which exhibited the stage as a piece of theatrical machinery. The brickwork of the proscenium and the side and back walls of the theatre was exposed and painted off-white, and the bare boards of the stage floor were tilted to form a steep rake. According to Farrah:

> I felt that what we wanted to create was not a box of illusions, but something that freed the audience's imaginations and made them conjure their own illusions. And, because we were beginning the play as if the actors were rehearsing, we wanted an area that was clearly defined, but which could also be seen to be an organic part of the building that everyone – actors and the audience – were part of.[52]

As Peter Brook had stated in *The Empty Space*: 'we must open our empty hands and show that there is nothing up our sleeves. Only then can we begin.'[53] By allowing the spectator visual access to normally hidden areas of the stage, Hands and Farrah seemed to commit themselves and the company to a new theatrical economy of democratic openness, neutrality and inclusiveness – although such candour did not go so far as to preserve the rusting gas pipes and electrical fittings that were found covering the back wall. But even this avowedly anti-illusionist stage was not as neutral as Farrah claimed; this empty platform was also a semi-representational space, bristling with ballistic connotations: 'It was a stage designed to launch the actors into the audience . . . like the great deck of an aircraft carrier.'[54] In design terms, it was both statement and anti-statement, a double effect which was characteristic of the production's overall metadramatic style.

Scenic illusion was banished in favour of a spectacularly emblematic style. Props were kept to a minimum, costumes appeared only gradually. Nonetheless the production still afforded the visual pleasures traditionally appropriate to the play, such as when the aircraft-carrier stage floor suddenly reared up to form the Breach at Harfleur, then sank detumescently at the end of the scene to reveal Ludmila Mikael as Princess Katherine, 'rising like Venus from the sea'.[55] The major items of scenery were two large canopies, ingeniously used throughout to powerfully suggestive effect. The first scenes rattled around the bare frame of the stage, with the first canopy rolled up and suspended on wire hausers overhead. At the end of the first act, a hand signal from the Chorus (Emrys James, who played Bolingbroke in the *Henry IV* plays) cued it to unfold, forming 'a beautiful, heraldic, glorious roof over the heads of the actors'.[56] At the end of the second scene in the French court (III, v), which in this production marked the point when the heroic rhetoric of conquest gave way to the muddy realities of a war of attrition, this heraldic vision descended to the floor, revealing its reverse side of grey tarpaulin. During the interval, which followed Henry's meeting with Montjoy and the order for the execution of Bardolph (III, vii), a second canopy was added to cover the remainder of the stage and the back wall. While there was no attempt to persuade the spectator that the canopies were anything other than what they

were, the effect proved more atmospheric, more potently
suggestive of the battlefield than conventional pictorial scenery
would have been. Following the victory of Agincourt both
canopies were raised overhead to reveal their undersides: red
and blue complemented by textured gold, a pleasing combination which 'seemed just right for the reconciliation in the
French court'.[57]

This synthesis of the emblematic and the semi-representational
was not only ingeniously economical in itself, but also part of
the production's metadramatic form. The bold simplicity of the
design was as much a comment upon traditional scenography
and spectacle as it was an indulgence in them, part of the
production's central preoccupation with theatre and theatricality.
In the bridge scene (III, vii), the contrast between the two sides
of the canopy juxtaposed the 'dream' and the 'nightmare reality
of war'; more complexly, the positioning of the tarpaulin on
stage was itself used to thematise the relationship between
Henry and his army:

> the scenery is 'on' the stage. It does not cover the whole
> stage-floor area, and it is far removed from the audience . . .
> Henry (and the actor playing Henry) has the choice during
> the scene of joining the army on the canopy, or remaining
> isolated off it, downstage . . . Shakespeare has never left
> his twin themes of theatre and reality, of real and acted
> kingship. Neither have we.[58]

Such devices created a rich interaction between the varie-
gated styles of the production, and between its numerous levels
of role-play, emblem and illusion. But they also struck the right
note of ideological balance and complexity, since the perpetual
ambiguity made it possible to sustain heroic and anti-heroic,
pro-war and anti-war, uncritical and ironic readings all at once.
Here were the secret play and the official play simultaneously
visible as never before, as opposing, yet interdependent, sides
of the same fabric. Just as in Hands's terms the play had
'enough in it to satisfy every pacifist, warrior, poet, peasant,
scientist and sectarian ever invented', so 'Nothing is what it
seems. Ever.'[59] With reality and theatricality so entangled, this
Henry V at once offered both celebratory spectacle and

sceptical interrogation, both involvement and detachment: on the face of it, a perfect liberal reading.

But if the overall scenic inventiveness of the production was much admired, other elements of the self-consciously theatrical and minimalist-spectacular approach were more controversial. The piecemeal introduction of costumes as the play progressed was a particularly divisive issue. There are echoes of Barton's technique in *Richard II* of gradually inducting the spectator into the fictional frame of the play. Here, however, the formalities of ritual were supplanted by a more loose-limbed theatricality that created rather more unsettling interpretative possibilities than the architectonic ironies of Barton's production. In a device which matched the opening up of the stage space, the production began by prefacing the play with a display of the mechanisms of its rehearsal. As the audience took their seats, they were faced with the spectacle of the cast, dressed in tracksuits, jeans and T-shirts, lounging, strolling about, exercising on the stage, and even chatting to members of the front row. Eventually Emrys James as Chorus came forward 'looking like an Italian film director on location'[60] in his trendy black open-necked shirt, to introduce the play in an equally casual and chatty fashion. The Archbishops of Ely and Canterbury then appeared, the latter in a lightweight business suit, then Alan Howard's Henry, kitted out in a blue tracksuit, shades and black leather gloves. But for any spectator disconcerted by this image of half-dressed modern-dress Shakespeare, the arrival of the French Ambassador struck a more reassuring note, as well as hinting at the visual splendours to come: characterised as a Bishop, resplendent in brightly coloured robes, his was the first period costume to appear. With him came the first prop, the casket of tennis balls; at the end of the act a huge black cannon was wheeled on. The argument between Nym, Pistol and Bardolph (ii, i) was played on the forestage while Henry and his army armoured and costumed themselves behind them. In the following scene Henry reemerged, now dressed entirely in biker-style black leather (and, for me, eerily reminiscent of 1970s pop icon Alvin Stardust), among the 'opulent fashions of the royal courts of England and France – and the shining armour of conflict'.[61] From then on there was no looking back, as the production

relaxed into a more reassuringly pictorial, semi-illusionist
costume style, a seductive eclecticism which combined the
unspecific modernity of 1960s RSC Brechtianism with traditional pageantry.

The stylistic progression in both costuming and staging fitted
the theme of victory achieved through improvisation in the
teeth of overwhelming odds. In this sense, the play and its
mode of production were offered as a metaphor for the
situation of the RSC. The early scenes – rather than celebrating
the unworthy scaffold – had both cast and audience struggling
within and against its limitations: the reward for imaginative
efforts was the alchemical transformation of rehearsal into
opulent spectacle. Many reviewers did not appreciate the
point. The denial of costume, in particular, was widely condemned as a perverse and tedious gimmick: a 'stylistic
oddity',[62] or 'some sort of alienation effect . . . a device carried
to inordinate lengths'.[63] Quite simply, the opening of the
production looked too much like one of the RSC's own 'fringe'
productions: the jeans, tracksuits and sneakers of the staged
'rehearsal situation' were very much in the casual, uncostumed
style of the Theatregoround touring productions of the late
1960s and early 1970s. What was acceptable for audiences of
schoolchildren became outrageous when transferred to the
main Stratford stage. Revealing the sweaty, scruffy and subversive body of the actor beneath the costumed Shakespearean
persona was disrespectful enough (for many reviewers, the cast
uncomfortably reminded them of base football players); even
more troubling was the possibility that this might destabilise the
play itself. Hence the reversion to a more reassuringly semi-
illusionist and spectacular mode of staging as the production
progressed. In the most judicious and generous assessment,
Benedict Nightingale of the *New Statesman* brought out the
ideological implications that were implicit in other reviews:

> Alienation, that fashionable commodity, is afoot. But, just
> as we're resigning ourselves to a severe Brechtian sermon
> about the evils of imperialism, the production relents . . .
> Why, then, the rehearsal-room opening? Presumably Mr
> Hands fears we'll be ravished and lulled by too much
> spectacle too soon. He wants us to enter the play in a

detached, critical frame of mind, because of the nature of the production he's about to offer us. He is not going to heroise Hal and glamorise conquest, nor does he want to slant things the other way, satirising and condemning a bloodthirsty crusade.[64]

In this fashion, Hands and his cast were able to cover all possibilities, in both theatrical and ideological terms.

The various modalities of costume were used strategically and self-consciously, emphasising the element of role-playing but also creating a hierarchy of 'authenticity' which set the French army against the English in theatrical as well as military terms. The former, stylised and statically presented so as to resemble figures within a tapestry (as in Olivier's film of *Henry V*[65]), first appeared in 'black and blue brocades as linear and iridescent as in a stained-glass window . . . persons from a fairy tale or a *chanson de geste*',[66] and for the battle scenes in imprisoning golden armour. As beautiful yet unreal, inhuman figures, the French (conveniently for a queasily partisan English audience) belonged in the world of the 'official' play, in the language of conservative theatrical tradition; in complete contrast to the English, who in grey and brown capes and helmets were more of the twentieth century than the fifteenth, evoking the First World War as much as Agincourt. Their world was the timeless one of the 'secret' play, the reality of mud, misery and attrition, dogged determination and desperate improvisation; yet this ultimately sustained a more solid, more affecting heroism than the narcissistic hubris affected by the French. Yet again, the production's political manoeuvrability lay in its juxtaposition of the two modes of heroism within opposing theatrical vocabularies.

The formal sophistication of this production afforded it a degree of openness and plurality that, as we have seen, invited diverse ideological appropriations: its intense and complex theatrical self-consciousness allowed scope for both empathy and detachment, and for both celebration and condemnation of nationalist myth and military adventurism. Ultimately, however, the production was authoritarian in its implications; partly because the movement towards the closure of conventional pictorial representation erased many of the contradictions generated in the opening scenes, but also because the production retained a fundamentally (if complexly) heroic view of its central character. Alan Howard as the king had many of the physical characteristics appropriate to a traditional reading of the role, with 'a voice like gunfire, a combination of sacramental authority and the common touch, and a capacity for creating the big moments while also choosing unexpected moments for their arrival';[67] thus his Henry 'acquits himself like a pride of lions', uttering 'some of the most ringing and thrilling calls to valour ever heard in a theatre'.[68] But, true to the equivocal spirit of the production, Howard's Henry was no one-dimensional hero. Hands began by emphasising the 'doubts and uncertainties inherent in the role';[69] while Howard felt that 'Henry's situation was very much what Hamlet's might have been, if he had lived.'[70] Consequently a considerable (and to some reviewers, inordinate) emphasis was placed upon Henry's self-questioning and introspection, the disparity between the public figure and the conscience-stricken private man, and his pained ambivalence towards his own position and towards the conduct of the war itself: he was 'all imagination and self-awareness',[71] a troubled leader who, while attempting to inspire his troops, was 'sorely in need of comfort himself, and knowing that he will have to do his best in a terrible situation without it'.[72] This interpretation provided a compelling focus for empathy, to the extent that Henry's personality and behaviour became an emotional filter for the moral and political concerns generated by the play. Indeed, in the context of the director's view that 'the play is not really about war',[73] the chief concern was Henry's personal journey of self-discovery. This shift of emphasis was one way of obscuring the more disturbing implications of the play and its subject matter; by attributing to Henry a highly developed sense of guilt and responsibility, the production also powerfully limited the spectator's capacity to respond *against* Henry, the war or the play. One of Howard's repeated manoeuvres was to pre-empt the spectator's response by juxtaposing Henry's actual or verbal brutalities with his appalled personal response – notably following the sentencing of the Cambridge conspirators (ii, ii), when 'he holds his head and staggers in sudden nausea, as if he could see their chopped necks';[74] and on the surrender of Harfleur

(III, iii), where 'he practically vomits after hurling the barbarous threats',[75] and 'the relief of his tension is such that he very nearly breaks down. He is like a man saved at the eleventh hour from hell'.[76] Such touches enabled Howard's Henry to keep candour with the audience, but they also offered the spectator the opportunity for catharsis: as moments of intense empathy, they provided a safe outlet for the shock, revulsion and outrage that might otherwise have rebounded upon Henry himself. In this way the king became the thing wherein was caught the conscience of the play.

By presenting an appealing image of complex, self-reflective heroism, Howard's finely nuanced and sensitive portrayal of the king offered *Henry V* an ideological centre – one that was perhaps all the more authoritative because it recognised and incorporated doubt, contradiction and uncertainty. Again, a metadramatic preoccupation with role-playing was central to the interpretation, so that the play followed Henry through a series of rehearsals of more or less authentic and sustainable identities. And just as the staging moved gradually into illusion, the progression was towards realist characterisation, from externals to interiority. The whole complex structure of self-reflexive theatricality was centred upon this: Henry's self constituted the point at which the production's various languages and styles converged. Thus the reconstituted heroics of Howard's developing and deepening characterisation were the true force of unity and coherence in the production. Henry's self-fashioning as a unified person had political implications, and herein lay the conservative appeal of this *Henry V*: for all its complexities and equivocations, it finally endorsed the necessity for strong, charismatic leadership, as an emblem of national unity. The political order expounded in the production was a curious combination of the authoritarian and the apparently egalitarian. As Hands saw it, the production's vision of unity was based on 'individuals aware of their responsibilities, both to themselves and each other, voluntarily accepting some abdication of that responsibility in a final non-hierarchic interdependence – a real brotherhood'.[77] The contemporary relevance of this was as much economic as it was military, of course. As Ralph Berry has remarked, it was 'oddly reminiscent of an argument in favour of an incomes policy or a voluntary pay code':[78] in other words, a call for the working class to collude in the management of the contradictions of welfare capitalism. More ominously, the production's potent combination of strong leadership, initiative, self-reliance and an illusory egalitarianism renders it a proto-Thatcherite parable, and a timely one at that. Theatrically, metadramatically and thematically, Hands's *Henry V* effected an alliance between authority and individualist 'freedom' that was also to act as Thatcherism's central dynamic. Although the production might have begun in doubt and uncertainty, it ended in resoluteness and conviction – the most compelling of all success stories.

The RSC next tackled *Henry V* in 1984, in a production directed by Adrian Noble and with Kenneth Branagh in the title role. A year after Margaret Thatcher's Conservative government had been re-elected by a landslide, and two years after the Falklands War, which had been a decisive factor in that election victory, it opened against the immediate background of a miners' strike that was proving to be one of the bitterest and most protracted disputes in British industrial history. Whereas in 1975 Terry Hands could almost plausibly claim that *Henry V* was not really about war, in 1984, recent memories of military conflict inevitably meant that the play was very much about it. The 1975 production had largely avoided any connection with contemporary military conflicts, preferring to hark back nostalgically to the First and Second World Wars, but in 1984 the presence of contemporary history was more keenly felt; and, moreover, while the mythology of Dunkirk and D-Day might serve as a force for ideological cohesion, the cultural reverberations of the Falklands War were potentially far more divisive. While many had fantasised the campaign as a rediscovery of Imperial identity and national destiny, others had seen it as a combination of violent desperation, adventurism and political opportunism, spawned by national delusions of grandeur: that it was a cynically perpetrated and unnecessary conflict rather than an inevitable and righteous crusade.

In such circumstances, *Henry V* was a hot potato; particularly for a company which was finding itself increasingly vulnerable to political scrutiny from its corporate and state sponsors. Tact and circumspection were clearly essential: using the play to present any real criticism of the conduct of the Falklands War would have been, at the very least, inopportune, and at worst dangerously provocative. Once again, the play offered to test the RSC's political credentials; as in 1975, the production seemed to succeed in striking the right compromise between the official and the secret versions. By definition, this was a 'post-Falklands' production, and was billed as such; but in this case, the foregrounding of relevance did not necessarily imply a critical or oppositional stance. As Graham Holderness points out, ' "post" (as in "post-modernism") does not always translate easily as "anti" or "counter" ':[79] here it signalled a contemporary interest that seemed liberal or radical enough in itself without giving voice to a more challenging critique.

The link with postmodernism is an apt one, since the production's visual style matched its political ambivalence and inclusiveness. In terms of their eclecticism, self-referentiality and intertextuality, the design and staging were recognisably postmodern in orientation, inventively mixing and mismatching diverse theatrical styles, historical periods and cultural referents. At the beginning of the production a token of Brecht's Epic Theatre appeared in a white half-curtain strung across the proscenium, which was opened to disclose a Victorian-style splendour of rain, smoke and flashing lights. A female cellist sat on the forestage to provide an ironic counterpart to the rhetorical posturings of the early scenes, to be sent off at the end of the first act as Ian McDiarmid's sardonic and sceptical Chorus ushered in the spectacle of war. Gorgeous period costumes, armour and pageantry jostled khaki and combat fatigues which looked, as one reviewer noted, 'as if they had come from the fashionable end of South Molton Street';[80] swords were used alongside electric torches. At the end of the play, the diplomatic manoeuvrings in the French court were played out under harsh white light on the forestage; behind them partially obscured by a gauze curtain, scavengers armed with prams moved among the candlelit corpses left on the battlefield. Some aspects of the staging recalled the 1975 production: the bare bricks of the proscenium walls, the golden armour sported by the French, and the threadbare tarpaulin (a grim parody of Farrah's magnificent canopies) which sheltered

the sodden English army during Henry's meeting with Montjoy
(iii, vi). Amid this hallucinatory *bricolage*, images of the
Falklands War flashed like dream fragments: the sheet metal
wall equipped with aluminium ladders to represent the ram-
parts of Harfleur, the SAS-style camouflage paint smeared on
the faces of the English army, the heap of swords that recalled
newspaper pictures of piles of surrendered rifles at the end of
the campaign.

This was a production with something for everyone. Balanc-
ing pain with pageantry, patriotism with pathos, the production
offered the pleasures of spectacle in conjunction with a liberal
humanitarianism which was unexceptionable precisely because
it did not ask the really awkward and divisive questions. Herein
lay its consensual and conciliatory appeal. By offering a kind of
postmodern anti-heroic hyper-realism, the production enabled
the sensitive spectator to differentiate between superficiality
and profundity, between gung-ho militarism and the harsh but
nonetheless necessary and inevitable realities of war; and so it
was possible to be critically 'post' (but not anti) Falklands. As
Holderness has argued, the production provided the occasion
for a necessary distinction to be made between the xenophobic
excesses and populist bloodlust of nationalism and the plangent
melancholy of the patriotic emotion: 'patriotism is associated
with "poetry", with emotion, with the heart, with tears,
"nationalism" with "mindless" aggression, with "tub-thump-
ing" jingoistic assertiveness.'[81] Such was the broad appeal of
this bitter-sweet patriotism that the production was able to
unite critics of the right, centre and left in praise for its even-
handedness, maturity and honesty. Thus it was a production of
'intractable moral ambivalence',[82] it was 'stirring, thoughtful,
unjingoistic',[83] 'not a *Henry V* of easy patriotism',[84] and
'painfully honest'.[85]

Kenneth Branagh's portrayal of the king provided the moral
core of the production. At 23 years of age, he was the youngest-
ever actor to take on the part at Stratford, and the acclaim he
gathered for his performance launched him into his highly
successful career as an actor, director, writer and producer. His
was a heroic narrative in itself: as a number of commentators
have pointed out, Branagh's subsequent film version of *Henry
V* (1989) offered some suggestive parallels between the play,

the making of the film and Branagh's own career.[86] While the film, with its interweaving of the languages of commercial and military adventurism, was plausibly read by many as a rousing semi-autobiographical parable of Thatcherite initiative and self-reliance, the stage production (from which it drew a number of its key images and some of its cast) presented the spectacle of a star being born. Like Alan Howard before him, and to much the same ideological effect, Branagh was keen to engage with what he saw as the emotional complexities of the role. In one published account of the rehearsal process, he reveals that he was drawn to Henry's compassion, piety and genuine humanity; while in his autobiography he records how the process of preparation for the role involved a consultation with Prince Charles, as an appropriately postmodern repre- sentative of monarchy, in order to gain access to the 'real' experience of kingship.[87] In Noble's production Branagh aimed for a detailed, balanced and non-judgemental portrayal that would displace the focus of interest from the political to the personal:

> I know many people who questioned the wisdom of putting the play on so soon after the Falklands conflict. And so on Day One we determined to throw aside the shackles of limiting preconceptions, remembering always to ask why those particular words are necessary to this king . . .[88]

For Branagh, Henry was driven and shaped by 'tremendous repression', in that he was 'unable to release huge amounts of humour and indeed of violence';[89] but it seems to me that what is most repressed in this account is the force of contemporary history itself. The post-Falklands dimension was simply too dangerous to be allowed into play; as was perhaps also that of the continuing war in Northern Ireland, which Branagh, as an Anglicised working-class Protestant from Belfast, might have been particularly well placed to explore.

Branagh's emphasis upon Henry's humanity steered the play away from such controversies, and reviewers accordingly praised the range and the sensitivity of his performance, which 'highlights . . . the painful cost of war to the individual',[90] and which 'impresses with his stern youth, his ferocity in anger, his

quiet regrets when giving harsh commands and, finally . . .
rough country boy charm'.[91] Henry's impulsiveness, his
emotional spontaneity and his painful progress towards the
acquisition of maturity were his main humanising qualities: he
physically assaulted both Scroop and Montjoy, displayed a cute
gaucheness in the final scene with Princess Katherine, and
occasionally gave way to tears. In one particularly painful
interpolation, the execution of Bardolph (III, vi) was carried
out onstage, in front of Henry: as one reviewer noted, 'the
effect is to increase the king's humanity, not to lessen it.'[92] As
in the 1975 production, Henry's complex humanity was ideologically instrumental: once again, the conscience-stricken hero
internalised the conflict between the secret and the official play.
In all this, a key determinant of the audience response was the
charismatic presence of the rising star Branagh himself. In
many critical accounts Branagh emerges as the fetishised object
of semi-(homo)erotic fascination, variously described as
'blond, stocky, boyishly well-graced . . . an embryonic matinee
idol if ever I saw one';[93] 'stocky, fair and unassuming';[94] 'a raw,
stocky warrior',[95] an 'excellent troubled boy-hero';[96] and having 'the aspect of a cubist cherub'.[97] Such comments are
evidently intended to celebrate a charismatic physicality that
might easily lend itself to a conventionally heroic portrayal of
the king, a good-looking muscularity that might well suit 'a
manly, no-nonsense show of valour and sensitivity'.[98] Yet there
is also, I would argue, a curious sexual and gender ambiguity in
these apparently straightforward descriptions of Branagh/
Henry; a physicalised ambivalence which reveals a different,
more problematic and unstable strain of post-Falklands topicality. Admiring Branagh's muscles is one way of aligning
military prowess and strong leadership with the traditional cult
of manliness, but the recurrent preoccupation with Branagh's
boyishness and sensitivity positions him rather less certainly on
the terrain of heroic masculinity in these critical accounts. I
interpret boyishness here as a sign of androgyny, indicating not
only youthful exuberance, naivety and immaturity, but also a
degree of conventionalised femininity, manifested in Branagh's
Henry's sensitivity, his waywardness and impulsiveness, his
tearfulness. This androgyny and gender ambiguity, as well as
being an intrinsic part of Branagh's star appeal, can also be

seen to have an important ideological role in the production, for it provided a space for the negotiation of the conflict between pro- and anti- views of Henry and his campaign. Branagh's Henry combined broad shoulders with a big heart, masculine resolution with feminine intuition, the potential for violence with a caring disposition.

Here, I would suggest, was the most intriguingly topical aspect of the production. If Branagh's Henry had a political role model, it was not the Prince of Wales but the Prime Minister, Margaret Thatcher. As Beatrix Campbell has argued, part of the ideological potency of the Thatcherite movement stemmed from its regendering of patriarchal conservatism, redefining it on the terms of a leader who simultaneously exploited and denied conventional femininity: 'she is just *like* a man. Yet she is unmistakably a woman. Uniquely among politicians, in the public mind she belongs to one sex but could be either.'[99] Provoking both loathing and abject subservience, Thatcher's paradoxical double identity as a paradigm of radical conservatism was a source of strength rather than weakness. It proved particularly effective during the Falklands War itself, when her self-representation as a combination of Winston Churchill and Boadicea manifested the self-conviction, the determination and the violent nationalism that pushed the image of masculinised military leadership almost to the point of grotesque self-parody. In the aftermath of war, this militantly heroic political and personal style, with its disturbingly andro-gynous confusion of the 'natural' zones of male and female power, behaviour and personality, could be as much a source of embarrassment and (largely suppressed) disquiet as of emula-tion. It was this combination of sexual ambivalence and fascination that permeated the critical response to Branagh's boyish Henry, as his manly charm made brief sense of the cultural and political contradictions generated by the war itself. In this sense was this Henry, as he shed tears on the battlefield among the victims of his own resolute approach, a thoroughly postmodern military hero – and this *Henry V* a comprehen-sively post-Falklands one.

Chapter Nine

Murder in the cathedral:
Richard III (1984)

While Noble and Branagh's *Henry V* addressed the nation by
juggling images of immediate and not-so-immediate military
conflicts, the same season included another history play that
seemed to have fixed its sights more firmly upon the past:
Richard III, which was directed by Bill Alexander, designed by
William Dudley and which starred Antony Sher in the title
role. In visual terms, this production set itself against the Jan
Kott-inspired postwar theatrical tradition (spearheaded by the
RSC itself) of modernist 'relevance'. As we have seen, Hall and
Barton's 1963 *Richard III*, with its steel walls and floors and
fearsome military technology, had resonated with echoes not
only of Hitler's bunker and the gas chambers, but also of a
totalitarian near-future; this imagery had persisted in subsequent productions of the play right through the 1960s and
1970s. By 1984, however, Bill Alexander and William Dudley
clearly felt that this style of brutal immediacy had become a bit
passé: as Dudley put it in an interview, it was 'the worst
possible idea to set it in Orwell's Britain . . . That neo-fascist
thing is such a cliché.'[100] What was offered instead was a more
opulent and romantic vision of a bygone medieval world, in a
baroque and breathtaking return to the splendours of
Victorian-style spectacular theatre. The setting for the play was
a huge and elaborate cathedral chancel in limestone and red
brick, complete with stained-glass windows, carved wood
screens, plaster arches and the huge tombs of the Plantagenet
kings stretching upstage. Modelled partly on Worcester
Cathedral, this set equally evoked the crushing weight of
history via other landmarks of English heritage, from West-
minster Abbey, St Paul's and York Minster to the Holy Trinity

Church, Stratford and (most apt for the RSC) King's College, Cambridge.

Offering itself to be read as partly emblematic, partly realistic, the set provided a clear diagram of the play's moral (or Morality) structure. Scenic illusion was achieved by atmospheric lighting, which created 'a realistic setting for almost every scene';[101] more importantly, the ecclesiastical setting underlined moral and political polarities in a highly traditional reading of the play. Whereas the open spaces and blank metal walls of previous productions had suggested an amoral and godless universe, this 'pageant-like' version was also 'religious and morally straightforward . . . typified by the way it puts Richard, at the last, in black armour on a black horse and Richmond in gold plate on a gold palfrey'.[102] There was not a hint of Kott's scepticism here: to all appearances, this was a world of clear-cut heroism and villainy, good and evil, blacks and whites. Like *Henry V*, this was a production which could be characterised as postmodernist; except that here, as a theatrical product of what Robert Hewison has termed the 1980s 'heritage industry',[103] the appeal to nostalgia was much more overt. The repudiation of modernist minimalism and the empty space in favour of the scenic spectacle, historical authenticity and moral certainties of the Victorian theatre appealed to the simpler tastes of Stratford audiences, but in an appropriately postmodern fashion it also hinted at a more sophisticated spirit of knowing self-consciousness and quotation: in particular, the faking of Victorian Gothic replicated an architectural style which was already itself based upon simulation and nostalgic pastiche. At least to look at, this production offered the reassurance of solidity, hierarchy and tradition: history set in stone, or in the simulacrum of stone.

The central component of the appeal of this *Richard III*, however, was Antony Sher's now-legendary portrayal of the title role; even the monumental design statement of the set was subordinate to its star actor. Sher's Richard has been well documented, not least by the actor himself: throughout the year-long period of preparation and rehearsal for the part, he kept a diary, which was subsequently published.[104] Sher's autobiography may well be the production's most enduring legacy, not least for the detail with which it documents an actor's appropriation of Shakespeare in the contemporary theatre. In the first instance at least, and unlike the RSC stars of the 1970s, Sher does not seem so concerned with penetrating the heart and soul of Richard as a character; indeed, Sher's account mirrored the design aesthetic in one respect, in that it could be said to show a postmodern preoccupation with surface rather than depth, with representation rather than with essence. Sher's first flash of inspiration is to play Richard as 'Laughton in *The Hunchback of Notre Dame*';[105] in the pages that follow, Sher muses upon a series of prototypes, exploiting and reacting against more or less appropriate models for Richard drawn from other performances and myths and echoes of other performances, including those of Ian Holm, Jonathan Pryce, Chkhivadze and Olivier. Initially intent upon constructing a Richard that is unique, Sher runs up against a relentless and disconcerting intertextuality that is endemic to the postmodern condition, discovering that his own characterisation is irrevocably inflected with the traces of others. Determined to claim the words of the text as his own, he finds that they are quotation rather than utterance: 'It seems terribly unfair of Shakespeare to begin his play with such a famous speech. You don't like to put your mouth to it, so many other mouths have been there.'[106] Crushed speechless by the weight of cultural tradition, the actor is alienated from the text, a rupture which, as Sher half-recognises, mirrors the postmodern division between self and speech ('It's as hard as saying "I love you" as if you had just coined the phrase for the first time'[107]); disconcertingly, originality and authenticity are no longer possible as everything seems recycled, borrowed or second-hand.

Moreover, as Sher notes, the particular problem for any postwar performer is that those words have been authoritatively stamped by Olivier's definitive version: 'His poised, staccato delivery is imprinted on those words like teeth marks.'[108] Throughout the rehearsal period, the more Sher strives to repress echoes of Olivier's mannerisms, the more his mentor–antagonist returns to haunt him, to the point of invading his dreams and his own self-portraits ('the lips I have drawn are not my own, but Olivier's'[109]). In his attempts to fashion a self-contained characterisation in an overcrowded field presided over by Olivier, Sher engages in an omnivorous inventiveness, assimilating a wide range of cultural referents and figures from popular mythology. In a process of character-building that follows Strindberg as much as Stanislavsky, Sher trawls widely through popular culture, drawing particularly upon the iconography of horror and gangster movies: models include Marlon Brando in *The Godfather*, Quasimodo, Frankenstein and the Elephant Man; other influences include *Alien* and *Jaws*. His Olivier-style preoccupation with the character's physique eventually lead him to settle upon the condition of kyphosis, not only as a model for Richard's physical form but also as a framework and rationale for his motivation and behaviour: 'I had set out to look for a physical shape . . . what I found is something about being *disabled*.'[110] That something, quite simply, is that disablement produces frustration and anger; underpinned by 'an absence of love. Caused by a hating mother',[111] this became the driving force behind Sher's Richard III. Here, then, was the Stanislavskian superobjective to match the physical characterisation, both, it seemed, rooted in medical and psychological fact.

That this psychological insight was not picked up by the production's reviewers is hardly the point: what mattered was that it afforded Sher a direction and a purpose for the physical energy that was expended in the production. Equipped with a large, authentically kyphotic hump and a pair of steel crutches, Sher offered an interpretation of Richard which was both dazzlingly athletic and startlingly inventive. The crutches, which transformed Sher's Richard into a quadruped, were a prominent feature: as well as using them to propel himself 'at great and alarming speed across the stage',[112] they also proved surprisingly versatile:

> they become a staff to beat Lady Anne's attendants, a phallic symbol to probe under her skirt, incisors to grip Hastings's head, a sword to frighten recalcitrant children with, and a cross to betoken Richard's seeming saintliness.[113]

The crutches were also powerfully redolent of the animal imagery of the play, with reviewers variously describing Sher as a spider, lizard, crab, bluebottle, ape, blowfly, bat, praying mantis, toad, hedgehog, rat and waterboatman. The very diversity of the epithets testifies to the agility and manic inventiveness of the performance but also to the way in which its relentless physicality appealed to the unconscious; like a nightmarishly mobile Rorschach inkblot, Sher's Richard called forth a wide range of phobic associations (and some odd attitudes towards disablement).

Intriguingly, as S. P. Cerasano points out, this indicates a striking difference between intention, means and effect. In Cerasano's account of the critical reception of the production, this characteristic of the response is seen as a gross dereliction of duty on the part of the reviewers themselves, indicative of a disparity between the complex terms in which Sher conceived and executed the character and the simplistic terms in which it was received:

> Embarrassingly few probed the ways in which Sher's concept of Richard brought (or didn't bring) the production together in the exciting and unusual way suggested by the actor's own remarks. A reader stranded on a desert island, with only the reviews of Sher's *Richard III* in hand, would conclude that this production was really a gymnastics exhibition pretending to be Shakespeare.[114]

According to Cerasano, Sher's psychological complexity and thematic richness was received in terms of slogans and clichés; evidence that the reviewers had, not to mince words, 'failed most abysmally'[115] to provide a fair, accurate and useful record of the performance. Read symptomatically, however, the reviews of the production reveal something more interesting than a failure to do justice to a monumental performance. Like the physical rhetoric of the performance, the rhetorics of stardom and physicality have ideological dimensions. At the most obvious level, the shameless celebration of Sher's one-man show could be seen as the strongest reflection yet of the individualism and self-sufficiency of the Thatcher epoch, a triumph of histrionic demagoguery over the more democratic and collectivist spirit of ensemble playing. As Jack Tinker put it in his *Daily Mail* review:

There is little enough justice in the world and even less in the theatre.

So I shall not waste time begging pardon of everyone from the humblest spear carrier to the haughtiest noble, for riding rough-shod over their individual excellence in this extraordinary, exciting and tumultuously successful production.

It must be enough for them to know that they trod the same stage with an actor whose performance has scorched its mark in the annals of Stratford like a thunderbolt . . . From his first appearance, he establishes himself as master of the role, the stage, the production and, if I am any judge, an era.[116]

The opening aphorism indicates that the thespian hierarchy reinstated by Sher's performance is a 'natural' one which offers a model for society as a whole: lesser members of the cast have to accept (even be grateful for) their subordinate status. Other reviewers followed suit in focusing upon Sher at the expense of the other performers, as well as confirming that Sher's dominance of the role and his 'supporting' cast was matched by his hypnotic mastery of the theatre audience. For Eric Shorter, 'His showy style and nervous energy and unrelenting "attack" hook us for whatever he does';[117] while Michael Billington summarised it as 'a performance filled with that most exciting of all theatrical qualities: danger'.[118] Thus is rampant egotism both hypnotic and terrifying, the subject of extravagant praise and wild applause.[119]

On the surface, the Sher *Richard III* had all the elements that might already account for its populist appeal: a star performance, the delights of spectacle and an old-fashioned struggle between good and evil. There was, however, a further dimension to Sher's performance, which, set in its immediate historical context, constituted a more chilling aspect of the production's crowd-pleasing appeal. As with the ambivalently gendered heroics of Branagh's *Henry V*, but in different terms, Sher's villainy had a sexual dimension. Reviewers noted particular moments such as his prying with the crutches under Lady Anne's skirts, the 'disgusting phallic business with his scepter'[120] and the 'sheer orgasmic bad taste'[121] of the interpolated bare-backed coronation sequence at the end of the first half. Many also (implicitly or explicitly) eroticised Sher's power and physicality: it was a performance of 'much sexual power',[122] 'the very embodiment of vaulting ambition and none the less seductive for that',[123] 'a gross and indecently energetic display',[124] an 'evening of considerable theatrical thrust',[125] and so on. Michael Ratcliffe summarised:

> It is a performance inspired by the sheer joy of acting: unpredictable, dangerous but wholly under control . . . It is a very sexy performance, making as clear as I have ever seen it the nature of Richard's power over wretched women . . .[126]

Faced with such a seductive display of physical virtuosity, it takes only a slight twist for Richard to become attractive, for his villainy to become a transgressive, secretly enviable display of masculine prowess. Here the term 'performance' conflates histrionic and sexual achievement and conquest: occupying an illicit and ambiguous zone between eroticism and obscenity, Sher staged an image of violent, powerful and dominant masculinity that was simultaneously terrifying, excessive to the point of parody, and a source of admiration, emulation and pride. The excited ambivalence it provoked may well attest to the general sexiness of theatrical villainy, and of the Shakespearean variety in particular; stepping outside from the production, however, it is also characteristic of a patriarchal culture's response to the more violent and murderous aspects of male sexuality. In their study of the discourses of sexual murder, *The Lust to Kill*, Deborah Cameron and Elizabeth Frazer point out that, within a dominant culture where gender is an ideological blindspot, the male sexual killer is a necessarily contradictory figure, sandwiched between 'two kinds of discourse': the ' "cultural" discourse in which he is a hero, at the centre of literary and philosophical celebration; and . . . a "scientific" discourse in which he is a deviant'.[127] Out of the contradictions and ambiguities generated by the clash between these conflicting systems of representation, patriarchal culture has woven a mystique around the phenomenon of the sexual murderer. There is always a question mark attached to his motivation and behaviour, whether these are viewed as the product of madness, monstrosity or just pure evil; the result is that the killer remains a fascinating, unfathomable and thus (for men) potentially attractive figure.

In the context of Britain in the early 1980s, these considerations had a particular force and cogency. *Richard III* was staged in the shadow of the trials of Dennis Nilsen, who murdered sixteen men in his London house between 1978 and 1983; and of the so-called Yorkshire Ripper, Peter Sutcliffe, who had killed at least thirteen women between 1975 and 1981.[128] In *Year of the King*, Sher records how he was drawn to consideration of these figures, especially the latter, as models for Richard: reading Gordon Burn's biography of Sutcliffe,[129] he finds himself 'quoting the book constantly in rehearsals' – and then wondering at the 'disgust and anger'[130] that this aroused in some of the female members of the cast. Sher professes bafflement, even irritation at this response, attributing it to censorship, to a wilful desire 'not to know, not to understand':[131] the implication is that his own project is precisely the opposite. Although Richard is by no stretch of the imagination a sexual murderer, he, and the play, might nonetheless offer access to the psyche of the killer, providing the opportunity to re-examine the questions of psychology and motive posed by cases such as those of Nilsen and Sutcliffe. Indeed, it could be that these figures were not just incidental to the production but central to it. As Nicole Ward Jouve has shown, the crimes committed by a Sutcliffe or a Nilsen, and the range of conflicting meanings attached to them, had the capacity to provoke a crisis in subjectivity itself, revealing the complicity between masculine identity, everyday misogyny and murderous deviance, and blurring the boundaries between sanity and madness: 'hearing the voice of God, Sutcliffe had heard the secret voice of Society . . . For Society supported him: it did not stop him.'[132] Sher's *Richard III* responded to the demands of a culture deeply in need of reassurance, reinstating the hierarchies of star casting alongside the pleasures of transgression, restoring history in solid lumps of stonework and reconfirming the polarity of good and evil.

In its final results, neither knowledge nor understanding were particularly evident, whether in Sher's portrayal or, as we have seen, in the critical reaction to it. By subordinating everything to Sher's ostentatious and charismatic display of masculinity and physical virtuosity, the production exploited the ambiguities of the murderer as cultural hero to mystify rather than to explain. A really radical questioning of the motives of a Peter Sutcliffe would have also meant an interrogation of the 'normal' masculinity and misogyny within which his crimes are implicated; an interrogation, that is, of what Cameron and Frazer identify as the masculine 'quest for transcendence', whereby 'murder has been used as an act of self-affirmation'.[133] Caught up in its own quest for histrionic transcendence in the context of a Victorian Gothic never-never land, the haunt of a medieval Jack the Ripper, Sher's performance was singularly ill-equipped to pursue this line of investigation. Indeed, *Year of the King* reveals that Sher (assisted by 'Monty' the psychotherapist) endorsed the widespread misogynist rationale for the male killer's crimes, actually attributing blame and responsibility to the female, in the shape of the 'hating mother':[134] in this respect Sher's Richard was no different from the Sutcliffe constructed within popular mythology. Ultimately, this is what made this Richard tragic; and, for all its capacity to terrify and repel, it was Sher's athleticism that transformed the villain into a hero. This, then, was the nature of Sher's achievement in *Richard III*: to confirm the sexiness of murder.

Part IV

Shakespeare Bastardised

Chapter Ten

Barton's Bard: the 1974 King John

In previous parts, I have been mainly concerned with plays and productions which have been central both to the corpus of the RSC, and to the established canon of Shakespearean histories. In this part, I wish to take a detour into the periphery of the RSC's involvement with the histories, by focusing upon the two plays which have, for the most part, remained on the margins of criticism and theatre history: *King John* and *Henry VIII*. The productions discussed here are atypical, and less representative of the RSC's dominant style: in its own way, each stands as a significant exception to the company rule. While operating on the boundaries of canonical and theatrical acceptability may lead (and has led) to marginalisation and critical condemnation. It may also offer a considerable degree of licence, and scope for a more radical intervention in Shakespearean history than is usually the case. As we shall see, the uncertain status and reputation of these plays has in part contributed to some intriguingly eccentric (and, in places, potentially radical) appropriations, even within the institutional context of the RSC. In this sense, the margins of the canon may ultimately prove more significant than its apparent centre.

When John Barton came to direct *King John* for the 1974 Stratford season, he was faced with a play which presents problems to a critical and theatrical industry geared towards the production of cycles and sequences. Like *Henry VIII*, it is isolated from any Grand Scheme of history; and the play itself seems to be devoid of moral, political and generic reference points, offering neither tragic catharsis nor comic resolution. While the task of making sense of a neglected and, to many, unpalatably cynical and baffling play might well have seemed a daunting one, it also offered Barton a freer hand than usual. Like the rarely performed *Henry VI* plays, although on a smaller scale, the attraction of this play was that it provided the opportunity for textual reconstitution and 'improvement'. Buzz Goodbody had directed a raucously satirical, cartoon-style touring production for the RSC's Theatregoround in 1970, but it had not been afforded a main-house production at Stratford since 1957.[1] Goodbody's production, which owed as much to Lewis Carroll and A. A. Milne as to Shakespeare, had taken an irreverent approach to the play and to the conventions of the RSC house style, presenting nursery history agitprop, with costumes in the shape of playing cards, toy props and cardboard scenery, programme references to Nixon and Heath, and a sustained reliance on slapstick and sight gags. Described by Colin Chambers as a 'blistering attack on politicians, as if it had been written in 1970 by a Howard Brenton or a Howard Barker',[2] this production received only a limited airing, was not widely reviewed, and was certainly not much liked: for Peter Thomson, writing in *Shakespeare Survey*, 'its flippancy was ill-judged and often puerile'.[3] This treatment had not helped the play's reputation; four years on, the circumstances for Barton's production were not auspicious. As I have noted in previous chapters, 1974 was financially a near-disastrous year for the RSC, and Barton's production formed part of a Stratford season which, after the grand planning of the 1960s, seemed unified only by Barton's directorial dominance. As well as *King John*, the season featured the equally unpopular *Cymbeline*, directed by John Barton and Barry Kyle; Barton's *Twelfth Night*; a revival of Barton's *Richard II* from the previous year; and, what proved to be a highly controversial production, Keith Hack's Edward Bond influenced *Measure for Measure*.

Nevertheless, the critical and theatrical neglect of *King John* afforded Barton, at the outset, one major advantage: its unfamiliarity suggested that hardly anyone in the audience would know (or care) enough about the play to be able authoritatively to evaluate his intervention and adaptation. The play's supposed defects have been repeatedly identified: lacking a clear governing idea, identifiable hero or central character it has no focus and unity; its plotting is arbitrary and disconnected, episodic in the manner of a chronicle history (in

Brechtian terms, 'Epic' rather than 'Dramatic'[4]); the psychology and motivation of the central characters is ambiguous, obscure and contradictory. Certainly according to the criteria of realist and well-made dramaturgy, *King John* is an awkward text. Most unsettlingly of all, the play is almost subversively cynical in political terms, and it is perhaps this most of all that prompted Tillyard (reflecting the prevailing view) to describe the play as 'uncertain' of itself.[5] Barton seemed to share this opinion; faced with the indeterminacies and contradictions of the received text, he set about fashioning a theatrical script that would reinstate the virtues of dramatic and political clarity and consistency.

Literary critics and editors have often sought clarification of these problems by referring to the play regarded either as its source or as a derivative, the anonymous two-part *The Troublesome Reign of King John*.[6] Barton followed suit. As well as his own pastiche Elizabethan verse, his version incorporated a great deal of material from *The Troublesome Reign*. This was not unprecedented: producers and directors from Garrick to Goodbody had plundered *The Troublesome Reign* in this manner.[7] Some of the imported material can be seen as having this function of resolving the lacunae in *King John*. In Barton's version, the Bastard's apparently gratuitous aggression towards the Duke of Austria (III, i) was provoked by the interpolation from *The Troublesome Reign* of Austria's class-conscious insults (*1 TR*, Scene v). The ambiguity that surrounds the attempted blinding of Arthur (IV, i), which in Shakespeare's play is inexplicably altered from the planned murder, was resolved by having Hubert read aloud the written instruction (*1 TR*, Scene xii). Barton added the Bury St Edmunds scene where the barons swear allegiance against John (*2 TR*, Scene iii), the banquet at Swinstead Abbey and John's poisoning (*2 TR*, Scene viii). But if these interpolations, and Barton's own additions, were originally intended to clarify what is confusing or ambiguous in Shakespeare's play, they soon constituted an important shift of emphasis; one which, in Barton's account of his work on the adaptation, became increasingly predominant as work on the production went on. He noted this in the programme:

Having started with very limited plans for cuts and insertions, I found that – despite myself – as I worked, and as
rehearsals progressed, new leads and possibilities emerged,
and these led me to make more textual changes than initially
envisaged.[8]

In Barton's hands, the reconstituted *King John* acquired both
metaphysical and political significance. On the former count,
Barton stretched the point about sources even further than
previous stage adaptors of the play, by using material from
John Bale's early seventeenth-century Protestant morality play
King Johan. Even so, Barton still claimed that his additions 'do
no more than develop and clarify tendencies already in the
three plays from which this version is drawn';[9] by comparison
with *The Wars of the Roses*, however, the strange hybrid that
resulted represented an unprecedented instance of textual
appropriation.

Unlike any of its sources, Barton's text had a neatly symmetrical and circular form. It began with the funeral and reading of
the will of Richard I (taken from Holinshed's *Chronicles*),
declaring the succession of King John and introducing an
injunction which was to recur throughout: 'look kindly to the
state of England'.[10] In a deliberate mirroring of the close of
Barton's *Richard II*, the burial of Richard I was immediately
followed by the elaborate ceremonial of John's coronation, in
which, to chants of 'Long live the king' and 'May the king live
forever', he was dressed in a golden cloak and mask.[11] The
ceremony and spectacle of will-reading-plus-coronation was to
be repeated several times in the course of the play. The second
will made its appearance in the revamped ii, i, with the arrival
of Prince Arthur and the French army before the walls of
Angiers. Featuring the injunction to 'look to the state of
Christendom',[12] this was read by Constance. Contesting John's
claim in favour of Arthur, the will was accompanied by a
coronation sequence which was an exact replay of the first apart
from the fact that it was conducted in French. The third will
(John's) was produced by the Bastard in the final scene, after
the death of John, and featured the injunction to 'look after the
state of England, and cherish her better than I'; this established

the succession of Prince Henry, who was duly crowned.[13] Also
included were John's second coronation (referred to in passing
in IV, ii) and the crowning of Lewis the Dauphin as King of
England by the rebel barons. The repetition was, of course,
satirical in intent, and of immediate relevance to a Britain
which in the course of 1974 saw two general elections: as one
reviewer noted, the coronation ceremony became increasingly
mechanistic and farcical, descending 'from grandeur . . . to a
weary electoral routine'.[14]

Within this neatly symmetrical framework, a sense of the
deterministic hollowness of history and power politics was
interwoven with an insistent emphasis upon human mortality.
As in *Richard II*, the notion that death makes a mockery of all
political aspirations was central to Barton's text and to the
theatrical imagery of the production. Right at the beginning of
the play, in Barton's revisions to the will of Richard I, this was
clearly spelt out:

> I pray thee to remember thine own ending, and so to live
> well, in so far as thou canst; and that thou may have no cause
> of blenching or affrightment when, in a time thou know'st
> not, or a guise thou espy not, that dark and dreadful knight,
> y-cleped Death shall visit thee, inhabit thee and consume
> thee.
>   Look to thine ending, brother John; farewell.[15]

In true morality fashion, Death was personified in this production, identified initially with the recurrent and much-expanded
part of Peter of Pomfret, and reappearing as the monk
administering poison at the Swinstead banquet, which was
staged as a parodic Last Supper, enlivened by medieval carols.
Such Christian motifs were typical of the production as a
whole. Whereas Shakespeare's *King John* differs from its
predecessors in its secular (and not notably anti-Papist) tone,
Barton's version restored the religious dimension in most
emphatic terms. Even more so than in Barton's *Richard II* in
the previous year, the production was dominated by Christian
iconography. The stage was densely populated throughout
with monks (and pretend-monks): as a chorus for John's first
coronation, as a chanting background for Constance's lament

over the loss of Arthur (II, ii), and as an all-singing, all-dancing
accompaniment to the Swinstead Abbey scenes. The rebel
barons wore cowls and swore allegiance before a shrine; John
himself mockingly adopted a penitential habit for the final act.
The image of the crucifix was similarly recurrent, from the
swords propped upright in the stage floor during the rebel
barons' choric discussion of the state of England, to the crossed
daggers held before Arthur's throat during his attempted
blinding.

In Barton's text, John's conflict with the Roman Catholic
Church was given the centrality that it enjoys in both *The
Troublesome Reign* and *King Johan* (but not in Shakespeare's
play); it was presented, however, not as a political battle but a
personal and metaphysical one. The key figure here was
Pandulph, the Papal Legate melodramatically elaborated into
monstrous and phantasmagoric dimensions. Bald-headed,
cadaverously made up and encased, as Benedict Nightingale
described it, 'in a cloth-and-metal cope much taller than
himself – leaving you with the impression of a half-opened
sarcophagus'.[16] Pandulph was a demonic figure whose
entrances were heralded by an off-key *Dies Irae*. If this figure
was meant to personify John's nemesis, the effect was also
perilously close to bathos: for Nightingale, he looked like 'Buzz
Aldrin lumbering across the moon'; while Peter Thomson saw
him as 'falling somewhere between a Morality "Death" and
King Rat in the Christmas pantomime'.[17] The uneasy wavering
between B-movie horror, metaphysical terror and farce was,
however, what the production was all about: kingship and
power politics caught up in an Absurd, Kottian vision of history
as grotesque pantomime. This was most evident in an interpolated scene, composed almost entirely by Barton, which formed
the spectacular centrepiece to the second half of the play, and
which showed John's ritual humiliation as he submitted to
Pandulph and the Catholic Church. In a grotesque rerun of the
robing and crowning rituals elsewhere in the production, John
was stripped to a Christ-style loincloth by a chorus of wailing
monks; as he handed over his crown he received a dunce's cap,
a skull and bone for orb and sceptre, and, just for laughs, a
custard pie in the face. Addressing the audience, Pandulph
held up the crown to point to the moral of the play:

Within this circle is thy wretched story.
I charge all men that sitteth here in hall,
Think well upon the history of John:
For though you live in lust and liking all,
Your flesh, as his corrupt, will fade anon:
For flesh, the soul's thin garments, is but lent
To mortal man, therefore be penitent.[18]

The point, as I understand it, is not a confirmation but rather a subversion of Christian orthodoxy, in that the vocabulary of transience is deployed not to induce penitence but to provoke existential horror. The style and tone is that of the Moralities, but the prevailing sentiment is Absurdist: here, as throughout, the Christian framework is designed to impress upon the spectator the terror of mortality in the absence of God, salvation and resurrection.

At the centre of all this was Barton's King John; in this scene, as throughout, a combination of buffoon, comic villain, post-Christian Everyman and tragic hero. At one level, this was simply the emblematic 'Bad King John' of popular myth, or, as E. H. Carr once put it, of a moralising and naively individualistic 'nursery history', wherein 'the badness of King John consisted in his greed or stupidity or ambition to play the tyrant'.[19] Barton's John made this explicit:

O England, now art thou most miserable,
And 'tis my sins that make thee miserable.[20]

As played by Emrys James, this King John was less a feudal monarch than a cross between Ionesco's Otto Berenger, Jarry's Pere Ubu and a hyperactive child. John was seen as a creature of comically simple motives and appetites, prone to temper-tantrums, switching from greed to casual ruthlessness to abject terror, frequently driven by the demands of his stomach, and clearly under the sway of a domineering mother in the shape of a handbag-wielding Queen Eleanor. Barton's text offered plenty of scope for clowning from the king, particularly in the early stages of the play. The characteristic tone was set in the first court scene, which illustrated John's selfishness and lack of responsibility by having him plan his French campaign at the same time as he insouciantly arbitrated between an increasingly exasperated Bastard and Faulconbridge. In another typical moment, the territorial bartering before the walls of Angiers (II, i) became a childish squabble, centring on John's pathetically arbitrary desire to retain the town of Volquessen:

KING JOHN.   here is my niece,
            Here in marriage with Touraine,
            Anjou, Poitiers and Maine.
KING PHILIP.   Thou dost omit
            Volquessen, John.
KING JOHN.   Volquessen too?
KING PHILIP.   Volquessen.[21]

This verbal parody of the terse exchange between John and Hubert ordering the murder of Arthur (II, iii, 75) was followed by the sight of taking a sword to a map of France and cutting it to pieces:

Lo, here I carve you out an empire, France.
But where's Volquessen?[22]

Cue for a gag sequence: John hunts frantically for the missing fragment on the map, meticulously cuts it out, hands it over. But if such sequences of political tomfoolery were reminiscent of the Marx Brothers in *Duck Soup*, the satirical presentation of John as irresponsible child also had less amusing implications. In particular, much of the humour in James's performance stemmed from John's relationship with his 'comically' domineering mother. Peter Thomson describes a typical moment:

John is badgered by the Citizen of Angiers, who thinks too quickly for him. 'Mother, a word', he says (courtesy of John Barton), and leads Elinor downstage with a confidential smile to everyone else. Now, with only the audience as witness, he mouths in a comically exaggerated stage-whisper, 'What shall I do?' It's a familiar routine which, if properly timed, produces one of those compulsory laughs which is no necessary reflection of the audience's good humour.[23]

As Thomson saw it, the joke is about John's 'Freudian ineptitude': its serious side is the clear misogynist message that the titular hero is a victim of bad mothering. The theme of dysfunctional parenting also emerged in the portrayal of Pandulph, the terrorising patriarch and emissary from the 'Holy Father', who symbolically castrates 'little Lord John' through the removal of his crown[24] – which perhaps accounted for the depth of John's fear and humiliation in the mock-coronation scene.

At heart, the satirical and political thrust of Barton's *King John* was quite simple, and broad-ranging: politics is a farcical yet destructive game, politicians both the deluded victims of history and its murderously ambitious agents. 'Nursery history' seems an appropriate term for the mode of historiographical understanding displayed in this production, for at the centre of Barton's version lay the contradictory figure of the child, viewed here as an emblem of both innocence and wanton destructiveness. If James's erratic, inconsistent, dangerous King John exemplified the latter tendency, the text also sentimentally reconstituted the roles of Princes Arthur and Henry to embody the former. Prince Arthur, especially, was transformed into a symbol of unworldly, 'apolitical' common sense and maturity, acting as a conciliatory mediator between the quarrelling monarchs in the dispute over Angiers:

> Nay, mother, peace I say,
> If it will tend to all our quietness,
> Then let my uncle keep the crown.[25]

Playing the familiar child's role of holy innocent, Prince Arthur seemed to provide a moral centre to Barton's text: his very unworldly simplicity and selflessness offering an antidote to the 'politics' of the play's adult world. If the political arena was seen to be the realm of the childish, then Barton appeared to be elegiacally celebrating the idealised qualities of the childlike both as a voice of sanity and as a means of escaping the nightmare of history. Yet this solution was equally an ideological one. The conflict that the production played out, between the childish and the childlike, between the child as angel and the child as monster, can be seen as a simple restaging of the contradictions within the liberal humanist view of human nature, wherein man is both noble and savage, superhero and beast.

The idealised child was implicated within the political discourse of Barton's text at another level, too: however cherubic and artless Prince Arthur's pronouncements appeared, it still appeared that he was innocently offering lessons in decency, common sense and compromise. Thus his role was central to the overall political project of the production. This leads us to the other significant aspect of Barton's adaptation of *King John*, which is its explicit engagement with contemporary political history. Barton stressed this in the programme:

> Our world of outward order and inner instability, of shifting ideologies and self-destructive pragmatism, is also the world of *King John*. Even the specific political issues have modern parallels, although I have never seen this emerge fully in production.[26]

The modern parallels with the Britain of 1974 are easy to trace: *King John*'s concern with questions of sovereignty and national unity had a particular resonance in the context of industrial unrest, governmental instability and deteriorating national status. At home, only a matter of weeks before the production opened in March 1974, the Conservative Prime Minister, Edward Heath, had lost a general election on the issue of 'who rules Britain'; the winter had seen the protracted coal strike which finished off Heath's government, a state of emergency, the three-day working week, power cuts, petrol rationing and accelerating inflation. Abroad, the United Kingdom was at loggerheads with the European Economic Community over levels of agricultural subsidy – a battle which was to a large extent symptomatic of more profound concerns over the loss of power and influence in the European context. In an atmosphere of crisis, as Barton wrote in the programme, *King John* spoke directly to 'this age of Brecht, Arden and Edward Bond.'[27] The implicit alignment of *King John* with this triumvirate of revolutionary drama was, for Barton and for the RSC, an unprecedentedly explicit political appropriation of a Shakespearean text. Brecht and Bond had themselves produced radical reworkings of Shakespeare: the former in the unfinished *Coriolan*, the latter in *Lear* (1971); while John Arden had offered his own quirkily subversive treatment of King John in *Left-Handed Liberty* (1965).[28] But if Brecht and Bond were aiming for subversion, interrogation and radical reconstitution, Barton's revision of Shakespeare was conducted in precisely the opposite spirit. Enough has been said already to indicate how far removed *King John* was from Brecht's, Bond's or Arden's Epic dramaturgy; and yet the production, confusing political theatre with topicality, still seemed concerned to insist upon its would-be radical credentials. The staging, described by one reviewer as 'Brechtian in the airy, as opposed to the earthy, manner',[29] self-consciously flaunted Epic mannerisms, as Peter Thomson noted:

> The lights around the acting area were displayed to the audience, and there was a practical curtain which would allow the staging of a number of front scenes to cover the scene-shifting. It was a set designed to remind us that we were in a theatre, and the actors were constantly reinforcing the point, for all the world like doctrinaire Brechtians.[30]

As in *The Wars of the Roses*, this is Epic Theatre as stylistic fetish, an apparatus within which 'modern parallels' in Barton's text could be 'hammered home one after another'.[31] The parallels certainly were emphasised in the text, nowhere more so than in Barton's revisions to the interpolated scene from *The Troublesome Reign* depicting the rebel barons' swearing of the oath against John. In a double pastiche of the 'chorus' of nobles from *Richard II*, and the Knights' speeches at the end of *Murder in the Cathedral*, Barton offered a satirical editorial on the state of the nation:

> My lords, my friends, I speak to you of England.
> This realm is rent asunder quite by faction;
> By disputation, doubts and darkling questions,
> By strife domestic, courts inquisitive,

By grevious imposts, duties, tolls and taxes,
The exchequer eats us quite; the price of goods
Soars meteor-like into the louring heavens,
Whiles that our purses dwindle and decline.[32]

It is difficult to determine exactly what level of mock-heroic
irony is intended here, but one thing is clear: this is the voice of
the 'silent majority', the put-upon middle class caught in the
crossfire between capital and labour, suffering the effects of
punitive taxation, and wondering at the managerial incompetence of those in power. In the wake of the election of Harold
Wilson's Labour government, the rhetoric might well have
struck a chord with the RSC's audiences:

             ourselves
Are plundered quite of almost all we have;
Ourselves, that set this thief upon the throne,
Ourselves, that wake and watch for England's honour
Ourselves, sans whom the very soul of state
Would fall into chaos and confusion,
Ourselves that – nay, I need not urge it more;
Only this I say, and speak to Englishmen,
That this most lovely, yet divided, isle
Must be new knit in amity and honour.[33]

So too would the solution that Barton's text sensibly proposed,
encapsulated in a repeated refrain lifted from Bales's *King
Johan*: 'look to the state of England'. Here was the production's moral, an appeal from the heart of middle England (to
trade union 'barons', perhaps) to the values of social responsibility and restraint, urging the disciplined subordination of self
to national interest, and to the ideal of national unity. For all its
references to Brecht, Bond and Arden, the ideological sympathies and class loyalties of Barton's *King John* were ultimately those of liberal, consensual, one-nation Conservatism.
Against the background of a sharp swing to the authoritarian
Right within the Conservative party, even this was an elegiac,
increasingly desperate position. Maybe Barton did not quite
believe in the possibility of negotiated unity either: the play
ended with the Bastard reciting the traditionally rousing final

lines from a book (emending 'mock' to 'shock'[34]), and then whistling derisively as he walked off.

The reviewers' response to the production was mixed. Whereas Barton's scissors-and-pastiche job on *The Wars of the Roses* had earned more or less unanimous praise, opinions were more divided on this production. On the whole Barton's efforts were praised in inverse proportion to the critic's regard for (or knowledge of) Shakespeare's play. Some saw *King John* in the same negative light as the *Henry VI* plays, and were accordingly positive about Barton's 'improvements'. Michael Billington of the *Guardian* described Barton's adaptation as 'a complex, densely textured play' that he found 'infinitely more satisfying than the published Shakespearean version'.[35] Irving Wardle concurred:

> The problem with *King John* is that it begins with a marvellous cold-blooded exposure of medieval *Realpolitik* and then proceeds to disperse the interest in rhetoric, individual destiny, and Tudor commonplaces on government. Mr Barton's efforts have gone into keeping the play on what he sees as the rails . . .[36]

One reviewer critic at least seemed blithely unaware that any such changes had taken place: referring to it as 'a totally unknown play', a clearly bemused Herbert Kretzmer of the *Daily Express* hailed the production as 'an event of pace, power and even good humour', and praised Barton for having 'steered this complicated and unlikely play with great lucidity'.[37] Others, however, expressed doubts: Robert Cushman wrote in the *Observer* that he was 'dismayed by Mr Barton's attempts to turn *King John* into a play about everything', and defended the original, which, although it was 'no masterpiece', did 'have its points: pace is one of them and humanity another'.[38] Several commentators singled out the overtly contemporary references. Whereas Michael Billington of the *Guardian* appreciated Barton's 'passionate concern for the state of the nation',[39] John Elsom in the *Listener* found the parallels 'dramatically self-defeating' in that they 'simply stressed the clichés'.[40] Benedict Nightingale, in the *New Statesman* was more forthright:

> We should be used to excessive direction by now; but this
> time the level has risen from workaday arrogance to a
> staggering hubris . . . it seems to me superfluous, to say the
> least, to start implying that the Papal Legate is a Common
> Market commissioner based in Rome, or that King John is
> really Fred Peart with a crown on, bickering with France
> about agriculture.[41]

Barton's own blank verse efforts were the occasion of much
hilarity, with many reviewers making jokes about 'King John
Barton' in response to the textual and authorial confusions that
these involved. As a consequence, much of the explicitly
contemporary material was dropped from the production when
it subsequently transferred to London, and consequently it was
better received. But there was a further issue at stake, which
was that of textual and authorial authenticity. Despite the
magnitude of the changes engineered by Barton, the play as
presented still operated under the auspices of Shakespeare. As
might be expected, the more scholarly reviews of the production attached more weight to this concern. Robert Speaight,
writing in *Shakespeare Quarterly*, denounced Barton's version
as 'a travesty of what Shakespeare wrote', and (invoking Buzz
Goodbody's 1971 production of the play) concluded that it was
'the second time in the last few years that *King John* has
tempted Stratford to impertinence'.[42] Peter Thomson, in
Shakespeare Survey, was more disturbed by the deceptiveness
of the production, pointing out that 'it cannot be *ignored* that
the audience at the Stratford theatre will assume that the *King
John* they are seeing is Shakespeare's, and that no amount of
programme notes will erase that impression.'[43] The adaptation
was also the subject of a critical article by Robert Smallwood in
Shakespeare Jahrbuch, which concluded that as 'the most
severely altered Shakespearian text ever to be delivered at the
Stratford theatre', it at least had the virtue of 'making one think
about the structure of Shakespeare's play, and await, with
greater interest, a revival of it'.[44]

Barton's declared conviction that his additions did 'no more
than develop and clarify tendencies already in the three plays
from which this version is drawn'[45] was disingenuous, not only
because it is addressed to a spectator who is likely to have little

knowledge of the originals, but also because it subtly conflates the three plays as thematically and dramatically congruent while still retaining Shakespeare as the literary proprietor. Barton's text was presented as a version of Shakespeare's play with insertions from *King Johan*, *The Troublesome Reign* and himself; it would be equally legitimate to see it as a version of *The Troublesome Reign*, or as an updated *King Johan*, or as a meditation upon all the three plays (and much else besides) by Barton. But then this would substantially alter the terms within which the production could be viewed and evaluated. Because Barton's manipulation of Shakespeare to suit his own purposes was so overt, the authority of the adaptation was severely compromised; and, unlike *The Wars of the Roses*, Barton's *King John* has been consigned to the margins of Shakespearean theatre history. And yet this bizarre exercise is significant in that it is only the logical culmination of the interventionist editorial practices established in the 1960s. However inadvertently, Barton was testing the elasticity of the Shakespeare-plus-relevance formula, as well as probing the limits of directorial licence within the traditional auspices of 'Shakespeare' itself. Perhaps also Barton's impertinence can be seen as having the consolidatory function that deviance often has, in that it effectively reinforced the legitimacy of 'straight' Shakespearean production. Perversely enough, Barton's *King John* might have performed the RSC a substantial service.

There is another sense in which the production was historically significant. It marked the end of an era of conspicuous textual interventionism in the RSC's productions; it was also deeply enmeshed within its immediate cultural and political context. Although it appeared that Barton's eclecticism, his frantic assimilation and *bricolage* of disparate dramatic discourses was verging on self-parodic or the obsessive, they embodied a specific cultural response to the situation in Britain in the early 1970s. Perhaps the invocation of *Murder in the Cathedral* was more suggestive than it might first appear. Barton's intervention can be paralleled with Eliot's modernist project in both formal and political terms, in that it aimed to effect an imaginary resolution of political and cultural fragmentation through quotation, the revival of traditional forms and the resuscitation of myth. In Eliot's reading of Joyce's *Ulysses*, for example, Homeric myth, 'in manipulating a continuous parallel between contemporaneity and antiquity . . . is simply a way of controlling, of ordering, of giving a shape and a significance to the immense panorama of futility and anarchy which is contemporary history'.[46] This seems to me to have a direct relevance to Barton's *King John*. Its very diversity in terms of form, style, genre and dramatic register – the Elizabethan history play, medieval Moralities, the Absurd, Brecht, Eliot's own drama – invokes a great tradition of English and European drama (centring upon Shakespeare and upon England) that might fulfil that mythical, consolidating function. The touchstone is literary language itself, the concrete embodiment of the Englishness that might form the basis for the reconstruction of a unified national identity, and the restitution of national sovereignty. Barton's script, an ingenious and meticulously assembled mosaic of textual fragments, strived to preserve, to ventriloquise and to mobilise, in a strangely literal and pedantic manner, the integral truth that is crystallised in each gobbet – whether this consisted of a scene, a passage, a couplet or a half-line. Even as the production opened, however, the mosaic was disintegrating. Barton has not directed a Shakespearean history for the RSC since.

Chapter Eleven

All is True? The Davies–Edgar Henry VIII (1983)

The RSC's 1983 production of *Henry VIII*, directed by Howard Davies, was another contentious production of an already troublesome play. In this instance, however, the difficulties arose out of a determined attempt to produce a theatrically and politically radical reading at odds with the dominant culture of the RSC. Although Barton's textual interventions had been controversial (nowhere more so than in the case of *King John*), they have nonetheless been conducted within the mainstream of the company's work; and, as we have seen, his occasional authorial and directorial daring has steered clear of political radicalism. Howard Davies, by contrast, was a director with an altogether different theatrical and political pedigree. Davies had joined the company in 1974, having worked mainly in radical fringe theatre; unprecedentedly for an RSC director, he had at the time no desire to direct Shakespeare, and was indeed reportedly wary of 'the RSC's "Cambridge clique", who always seemed to be quoting Shakespeare to each other'.[47] As a director based at The Other Place and as Artistic Director of the RSC's Warehouse theatre in London in the late 1970s, he worked almost exclusively on contemporary drama, notably the work of Brecht, Bond and Barker. Under Davies's direction, The Warehouse had developed a distinctive social and political identity that was a world away from the RSC's work in the larger theatres; in the words of the theatre's dramaturg, Walter Donohue, it was about 'trying to engage ourselves and our work in the social struggle that is going on at the moment'.[48]

This was relevance of a different order of political commitment to that envisaged by Peter Hall back in the 1960s, and when Davies eventually came to direct Shakespeare for the

RSC it showed. Prior to *Henry VIII*, Davies had directed two Shakespeares: a touring production of *Much Ado About Nothing* in 1980, and *Macbeth* in the main house at Stratford in 1982. In both productions Davies flouted traditional expectations. In *Much Ado* he questioned the sentimental fairy tale by subjecting the play to feminist scrutiny, as summarised by one critic: 'in this Sicilian dump the men instinctively mistrust the women, and the women have good reason to dislike the men.'[49] For another (female) reviewer, it was 'the most serious and involving production of the play' that she had seen.[50] Davies's *Macbeth* approached the play from a materialist perspective, eschewing the customary paraphernalia of black magic and metaphysical evil by playing the action under stark white light, and using Alienation effects such as the visible presence of two percussionists on stage throughout. The production had a mixed reception. Some saw it as a feminist or even Marxist reading: Victoria Radin wrote in the *Observer* that 'here . . . is Capitalism, for is not the Elizabethan age reckoned to be the dawning of it? Here then is capitalism's implacable motor, greed, and its ally, a macho, repressively patrichal [sic] . . . insensitivity to others.'[51] Elsewhere, Davies was pilloried for his iconoclasm; Richard Findlater concluded his hostile review in *Plays and Players* by asserting that Davies's attempt to demystify the play worked to 'diminish and devalue' it: 'there is a limit to "democratisation", to travestying Shakespearian texts in the name of "accessibility", and I think that the limit has been exceeded by Mr Davies.'[52] If Davies's attempt to transfer the political aesthetic of The Warehouse to main-house Shakespearean production was, in the case of *Macbeth*, asking for trouble, then a key factor in the hostile reception was the canonical centrality of the text itself: after all, a Marxist production of *Macbeth* constitutes an assault upon the very heart of the canon, and of Shakespeare. Initially at least, *Henry VIII* appears to offer safer ground for radical intervention: as a play which is often thought to be the product of a collaboration between Shakespeare and (probably) John Fletcher, and whose literary and theatrical identity and status is therefore already in dispute, it might even invite rehabilitation, reconstitution or radical revision.

The authorship question provides a useful initial point of

departure for Davies's *Henry VIII*. In an interview given just
before the production opened, Davies accounted for the
marginal status and uncertain reputation of the play by referring to its divided authorship: 'Critics think Shakespeare should
have stopped with *The Tempest*, instead of having other works
finished for him. It would have been tidier.'[53] Davies's lack of
sympathy with standard RSC textual pieties is revealed not
only in his dismissal of the usual sentimentalities about *The
Tempest* being Shakespeare's farewell to the stage, but also in
the dismissive attitude to Shakespeare himself. This is an
unusual move, and a particularly apt one in relation to this
play, its literary reputation and its theatrical history. Ever since
the play became a test case for Victorian philologers in the mid-
nineteenth century, the question of authorship has persistently
haunted the critical evaluation of it, with arguments following a
predictable division: sole authorship is seen to equate with
literary quality, and collaboration with unevenness and lack of
unity. As the editor of the Penguin edition used in the
production summarises:

> Critics who contend that Shakespeare wrote the whole play
> generally find it coherent, organically developed, and them-
> atically rewarding: those who detect a second hand . . .
> generally discover no more than a superficial unity in spirit,
> themes, structure or characterisation.[54]

For Shakespearean scholarship and criticism committed to
principles of authorial intentionality, the integrity of the canon,
and the coherence of texts, *Henry VIII* presents severe
problems. Until the start of the twentieth century, however,
such considerations appeared to carry little weight in the
theatre; indeed, in the eighteenth and nineteenth centuries
Henry VIII was a popular, frequently performed play – largely
for reasons which tend to confirm, rather than contradict, its
negative literary-critical reputation. From Colley Cibber's 1727
production through to Beerbohm Tree's in 1910, it had
provided the opportunity for royalist celebration, set-piece
crowd scenes, sumptuous pageantry and scenic spectacle; as
well as for the indulgence of a trio of star turns in the parts of
Henry, Wolsey and Katherine.[55] For more recent critics and

directors, the nineteenth-century traditions of staging *Henry VIII* embodied what might well be seen as all the worst vices of the Victorian spectacular Shakespearean theatre: sentiment, superfluous pageantry, a subordination of text to spectacle. In reaction to this, the twentieth century has seen more sceptical, ironic and playful treatments, from Terence Gray's notorious 1931 Cambridge Festival Theatre production, which was billed as 'a masque in the modern manner with the text attributed to Shakespeare and others',[56] dressed the cast as playing-cards, and was staged on a Meyerholdian set of galvanised steel which revolved madly in the final scene, sending the infant Queen Elizabeth flying into the audience; to Tyrone Guthrie's 1949 production at Stratford, which tempered an earnest celebration of the coronation of Queen Elizabeth II with a degree of flippancy.[57] The more sober approach is to assume sole Shakespearean authorship and to place it in the thematic and biographical context of the Late Romances, so that, in the words of the editor of the Arden edition, 'like *The Tempest*, it is a study in the ways in which men may be saved.'[58]

This was the perspective informing the RSC's only previous production of the play, which was directed by Trevor Nunn for the 1969 season: here it was placed alongside *Pericles* and *The Winter's Tale*. The emphasis that season was upon the positive elements of celebration and regeneration; in Nunn's view, the late plays 'reconcile the paradox of man' so that 'grace is achieved, through love'.[59] *Henry VIII* ended with what one reviewer called 'a sonorous white hippie mass',[60] as actors advanced into the auditorium chanting, as a mantra, Cranmer's prophesy of the 'Peace, plenty, love and truth' (v, iv, 47) that would attend upon the infant Elizabeth. This atmosphere of harmony could not be created without some subtle reconstitution of the text: significantly, it had to omit the final term in Cranmer's litany – terror. Furthermore, in an attempt to broaden the frame of reference, Cranmer's eulogy to the Stuart succession (41–54) was subtly emended so as to transfer Elizabeth's legacy from James I to the cast and audience:

Nor shall this peace sleep with her, but stand fixed.
Peace, plenty, love and truth,

That are servants to this chosen infant,
Shall then be ours, and like a vine grow to us.[61]

In Nunn's production, the totalitarian implications of the play's
final scene were neatly evaded in an effortless and anachronistic transition from absolutist monarchy to constitutional
democracy. Whatever conviction this belated tribute to the
Summer of Love might have carried in the Britain of the late
1960s, it was not the spirit informing Davies's production in
1983. Indeed, Davies cited this detail of Nunn's production in
his programme in order to underline the fact that terror had
been restored to his reading. As a director of Bond, perhaps he
also concurred with the dramatist's striking revisionist reading
of the play: 'the play passes deeper into the Absurd: Elizabeth,
and infant Miranda, is cradled in the red hands of a monster
and fussed over by a Queen who will shortly have her head
chopped off for sleeping with her brother. Shakespeare, in
recording contemporary history, returns to the world of Titus
Andronicus.'[62] Bond's is more than a dark reading of the play:
he is also drawing attention to the 'hidden history' of the text
and of most critical and theatrical appropriations of it – its
symptomatic silences, evasions and duplicities. Davies's stated
view was less lurid (and, it must be said, rather less compelling): *Henry VIII* was, as he put it, 'very much a modern play,
dealing with taxes, unemployment and social divisions'.[63] The
directness of the appeal to the Britain of 1983, in the year of the
post-Falklands landslide re-election of the Conservative
government, is very evident; what is more debatable was
whether the modernity Davies imputed to the play was simply a
variation on the well-worn RSC theme of Shakespeare-plus-
relevance, or a more radical form of intervention.

Certain aspects of the production suggested that Davies was
attempting something different to the usual liberal formula.
This was initially signalled by his willingness to foreground the
problems of the play's authorship, and of its textual and
historiographical status. Seemingly aware that arguments about
who wrote the play have a political as well as a literary
significance, Davies made a point of emphasising the divisions,
contradictions and indeterminacies on *Henry VIII* flyers and
production posters and the programme afforded John Fletcher

equal billing with Shakespeare. To underline the idea that this
was a modern play in the Warehouse style, the advertising
artwork for the production centred on a caricature of a grossly
fat Henry VIII surrounded by a mess of papers and ink, drawn
by radical political cartoonist Ralph Steadman (best known for
his savage caricatures of Margaret Thatcher). It was an image
strongly suggestive of violence and corruption, with black ink
taking the place of Steadman's trademark splashes of blood,
but also of both the power and the provisionality of textuality.
This reflected the bureaucratic political world of the play: texts,
writing and pieces of paper featured strongly in the production,
as 'characters clutch portfolios, take frantic notes on each
other's conversations and document their allegations';[64] it also
drew attention to *Henry VIII* itself, and the version of history it
proffered, as texts. The treatment of the Prologue and Epilogue developed this concept: the production opened with
Richard Griffiths (who played Henry) reading aloud the Prologue from a sheet of paper, and closed with him reading the
Epilogue and then throwing a bundle of papers over his
shoulder. As one reviewer wryly commented, 'the whole thing
is only a yarn, after all.'[65]

As an important part of the mediating apparatus of the
production, the programme offered some vital clues as to how
the play might be read by the spectator. Conventionally, the
typical RSC programme has a number of functions: it helps to
make sense of both text and performance in scholarly terms, in
the form of critical extracts, historical and contextual material,
and plot synopses; it locates the present production in the
context of theatre history via the inclusion of photographs of
past productions; and, as a souvenir, it provides a permanent
memento of the magic of the performance, of Stratford, and of
Shakespeare. In this instance, conversely, the programme
seemed to have been designed to challenge, rather than
confirm, the authority of Shakespeare, text and production.[66]
The artwork and graphical style sustained the notion of competing and provisional textualities, consisting of a jumble of
printed extracts and handwritten notes (ranging from
Holinshed to *Woman's Own* magazine), critical commentary
and speculative asides, and roughly sketched Steadman caricatures of the cast. The front cover, a facsimile of the title page of

the Penguin edition of the play, with 'John Fletcher' scribbled underneath 'William Shakespeare', was jokily stamped 'Prompt Copy' (positioning the spectator as prompter?); extracts from the text and from critical and historical works were presented in the form of cut-outs stuck in a scrapbook, annotated, in different handwriting, with interpretative and explanatory notes. Thus Henry's 'Sixth part of each? / A trembling contribution!' (I, ii, 94–5) is accompanied by '1/6th part = approx. 15% = rate of VAT!!'; while Wolsey's defence of his taxation policy (I, ii, 85–8) is paralleled with the Thatcherite politics of conviction:

> If we shall stand still,
> In fear our motion will be mocked or carped at,
> We should take root here where we sit,
> Or sit state-statues only.

This is annotated as a reiteration of one of Margaret Thatcher's famed slogans: 'The resolute approach – hard measures necessary, "THERE IS NO ALTERNATIVE." ' Such devices ensured that the programme provoked some critical comment; one reviewer noted that its style was an index of 'complexity', but that it was 'a wheeze rather an interpretation'.[67] In a more theoretically informed analysis, Simon Barker argues that the style of relevance it promotes is simply part of 'a seamless discourse of eternal verities' and that, moreover, it is designed to privilege Shakespeare's literary text: 'the contrast between the printed word of Shakespeare and the pencilled additions is complete; print and scrawl, text and meaning.'[68] I would suggest, however, that this very emphasis on textuality, on the constructedness of meaning (and hence 'relevance') lends itself to a different reading, in that it both offers parallels between past and present and ironises or interrogates them. As well as highlighting the affinities with Thatcher's Britain, Davies was keen to historicise the play. As he saw it, the 'social divisions' were those of the nobility, 'as they realise that they may have to share power with the new rising middle class';[69] and a socialist perspective was indicated by the lengthy extract from R. H. Tawney's *Religion and the Rise of Capitalism* (dealing with the secularisation of the Tudor state) included in the programme.[70]

Promoting Fletcher to equal status with Shakespeare's was one means of distancing the play from the institutional conservatism of the canon and authorial myth, and a way of opening up divisions and contradictions in the play itself. Davies had originally intended to develop this idea even further, inviting the playwright David Edgar in as co-director and co-author on the production:

I wanted David Edgar to work on it with me because it's a bastard script, parts of it were written by Shakespeare and parts by somebody else. I felt it was an old playwright working with a young one, and it varies from the terrible to very good. I said to David, 'Why don't you re-write the poor bits so that we can stay with the Shakespeare, but would it become a Shakespeare and Edgar play?' I didn't feel people would grieve too much because it was only *Henry VIII*.[71]

The choice of Edgar was a interesting one, given his track record: in addition to his work with Trevor Nunn and the company on the RSC's adaptation of *Nicholas Nickleby* in 1979, he had been a key figure in both fringe and mainstream political theatre of the 1970s, with work ranging from agitprop pieces written for radical theatre groups such as The General Will in the early 1970s to his major anti-Fascist play *Destiny*, written for the RSC in 1976.[72] While *Henry VIII* was running at Stratford, Edgar's epic account of post-war revolutionary socialism, *Maydays*, opened at the Barbican Theatre, amid much critical and political controversy. In this context, a 'Shakespeare and Edgar play' might have seemed like an excitingly disruptive, potentially radical proposition, a dialogue between a 'classic' and the present that might have echoed the oppositional interventions of Brecht and Bond rather than the recuperative efforts of (say) John Barton. Sadly (although perhaps unsurprisingly), as it turned out, this radical collaboration did not quite materialize, as Davies regretfully noted:

In the end, I don't think he could quite bring himself to do it. He stayed in rehearsals and was invaluable and did re-write scenes which we rehearsed, and that was very exciting, but he just felt he didn't have the courage to be that impertinent.[73]

Edgar's diffidence in the face of Shakespearean authority is in striking contrast to Barton's confident assumption of the authorial mantle, and is indicative of the affective as well as the institutional power of bardolatry. An examination of the production promptbook reveals that little of Edgar's editorial efforts survived in actual performance beyond routine and unobtrusive cuts. Nonetheless, the production did retain one piece of textual reconstitution which indicates the direction that Davies and Edgar might have taken the play had they had the courage of their initial convictions: in an important sense it went right to the heart of the play. It came in the scene of Queen Anne's coronation procession (IV, i), which has traditionally provided the opportunity for the indulgence of pageantry, spectacle and scenic illusion. In Tree's 1910 production, for example, the scene switched places with the death of Katherine (IV, ii) and the whole of the last act was cut, providing a satisfying finale to the play.[74] The spectacular tradition is not merely vacuous, of course: at the very least it has ensured that the political dimensions of the play (and the politics of the spectacle itself) have tended to disappear from view. In previous productions, packing the stage with flags and extras cheering on the royal procession has presented a mythical vision of social hierarchy, and in the totalising and harmonising discourse of the illusionist theatre, there is no space for contradiction within, or alternative perspectives upon, this picture of patriotism, order and subordination. In Davies's production (reflecting perhaps on the more recent monarchical spectacles of the Royal Silver Jubilee in 1977 and a Royal Wedding in 1981), the machinery of pageantry was opened up for critical inspection. This followed logically from a simple emendation to the speech of the First Gentleman at the beginning of the scene (l.3):

You come to take your stand here and behold
The Lady Anne pass from her coronation?

In the Davies and Edgar version this became:

You come to take your stand here and behold
The Lady Anne pass to her coronation?[75]

With the two Gentleman characterised as stewards setting out
crowd barriers, the scene that followed was played as a slightly
panicky rehearsal for the coronation procession, with robed
tailors' dummies standing in for the Court and rows of coat-
racks for the cheering crowds. At l.21 (on the Second Gentleman's 'I should have been beholding to your paper') the text
broke off, and the lengthy descriptive stage direction at l.36
meticulously delineating the 'Order of the Coronation' was
read aloud, in the form of written instructions relayed by the
Lord Chamberlain to the two Gentlemen:

LORD CHAMBERLAIN
        Trumpets
1ST GENT
        I. Trumpets sound
L. CHAMB.
        2.   two judges
2ND GENT
        Stand close, the Queen is coming.
L. CHAMB
        3.   Lord Chancellor.
        4.   Choristers singing.
             Music.
1ST GENT
        Music.[76]

The metatheatrical joke is a double-edged one: obviously
undercutting state ceremonial, it also satirises the text and the
earnest theatrical tradition that has been attendant upon it,
inverting the normative relations between text and performance, and estranging and distancing the practices of illusionistic
Shakespearean production. Even more disconcertingly, the
exposure of the mechanisms of rehearsal, and the emphasis
upon the unstable artifice of spectacle, might even extend into
the performance of *Henry VIII* within which it was ostensibly
framed: the scene was as much a reflection upon what was

occurring there and then on the stage of the Royal Shakespeare Theatre. Read symptomatically, the disruption of the discursive hierarchies of stage directions, speech headings and the spoken word suggested a critical, even deconstructive, stance that, by exposing not only the theatricality of power but also the hidden politics of theatricality, implicitly problematised the production's own claims to representational authority.

This was probably the most 'Brechtian' moment in a production which was almost universally characterised by its reviewers in terms of what one of its chroniclers has called 'that all-extinguishing epithet'.[77] In terms of staging, this *Henry VIII* drew heavily on the style and technique of the Epic Theatre: Robert Cushman of the *Observer* spoke for the majority of reviewers when he described it as 'the most thoroughgoing Brechtianisation of Shakespeare' that he had ever seen;[78] while Irving Wardle concurred in *The Times* that 'the stage is well and truly alienated'.[79] The settings were emblematic: flimsy, cut-out cartoon fragments of Tudor architecture suspended from the flies, set against a projected background of an Elizabethan Long View of the City of London, and contrasted with strikingly solid-looking pieces of furniture. According to Davies, the visual style was influenced by Holbein – not the portraiture, but the drawings; creating the lightweight, provisional, alterable feel of a sketch rather than the incontestable density of a painting. This was also reflected in the simplified period costumes, which like Holbein's drawings 'emphasised the face and hands, leaving the rest to fade away'.[80] The colour scheme, under uniformly bright lighting, was dominated by pastel yellows, grey, the deep red worn by the Churchmen and the black robes assumed by Henry and the newly powerful bureaucrats of the Tudor state in the final scenes. If all this were not enough to discourage empathy and foster scepticism and detachment, the production also featured a mobile eight-piece band in modern dress, accompanying and, more frequently, deflating the action with a brash, ostentatiously Weill-influenced score (composed by Ilona Sekacz). These pastiche elements were matched by recurrent references to Brecht's dramaturgy in the staging of certain scenes: Buckingham's final oration (II, i) sounded to Irving Wardle 'like Macheath on the gallows';[81] and Anne Bullen received her summons from Henry

(II, iii) amid a group of women folding sheets, recalling one of Brecht's suggested 'exercises for acting schools'.[82]

These self-consciously Epic mannerisms afforded the pleasures of conscious pastiche and theatrical quotation (raising once again the question of appropriation in the RSC's work); but the overall approach could also be described as Brechtian in its sustained interrogation of the traditional reading of the play, its consistent irony, and its refusal of sentimentality. This showed in the treatment of the three 'star' roles. Richard Griffiths, who played Henry, saw his character as 'an early version of Stalin, quite ruthless';[83] and the play (according to Robert Cushman) showed him 'working his passage from dependence to despotism'.[84] Gemma Jones's Katherine was an angry, imperious figure, 'rousing herself from her mortal sickness in order to berate a messenger who fails to kneel to her',[85] smiling maliciously on hearing of the death of Wolsey (IV, ii) and making 'no attempt at eye-pricking pathos'[86] during her own death scene. The casting of John Thaw (then better known for his portrayal of a cockney detective in TV's *The Sweeney* in the 1970s) as Wolsey emphasised the class divisions in the play: 'a prole persecuted by nobles',[87] this 'Ipswich working-class boy made good'[88] was as ruthless as his aristocratic antagonists. Supporting characterisations consolidated the picture of a society of opportunists. The traditionally virtuous Cranmer was cast against type in the shape of Richard O'Callaghan, an actor who (according to Benedict Nightingale in the *New Statesman*) 'has trouble *not* looking slippery, fly and mischievous';[89] David Schofield's Buckingham was 'a posturing self-justifier';[90] and even 'such apparently harmless supports as Lord Sands and the Old Lady (here, less endearingly, a middle-aged lady) are sternly placed as lecherous or envious: maggots, both of them'.[91] This was very much 'a Tudor world seen through modern eyes',[92] but, as Benedict Nightingale concluded:

> The effect is not, however, self-consciously 'Brechtian'. We aren't presented with a load of thespians knowingly sending up the characters they are playing. Rather, we're invited coolly and detachedly to contemplate the high-level wranglings and finaglings as Richard Griffiths's earnest, conscien-

tious but naive Henry receives a series of lessons in the meaning of power . . .[93]

Ultimately, however, for all its consistency of purpose and impeccably Brechtian credentials, Davies's *Henry VIII* failed to provoke the re-evaluation of the play that he might have wished to achieve. The director himself later conceded that the production had not worked, largely because he and Edgar had fought shy of the sort of radical reconstitution of the text that might have justified the Brechtian approach: 'the final result was a disappointment to me because there was a disparity between what I'd wanted to do and what I achieved.'[94] This disparity is also due, I would suggest, to uncertainty as to whether to contest the play or appropriate it; although had Davies taken the former course it would no doubt have been met with howls of outrage. Most reviewers retained their scepticism as to whether the play itself matched up to the political and theatrical claims that the production appeared to be making for it; consequently, Davies's efforts could be variously interpreted as misguided, eccentric or offensively appropriative. For Nicholas de Jongh, writing in the *Mail on Sunday*, it was 'as perverse an example of doctrinaire distortion as I can remember . . . a conservative farewell chronicle is here interpreted as a Brechtian demonstration of the wickedness of Tudor nobility, riding high on the fruits of capitalism'.[95] The *Shakespeare Survey* reviewer, similarly, saw it as 'an exercise in sustained playing against the spirit of the text . . . a perverse curiosity'.[96] The final irony, though, is that for many reviewers, the problem was not simply that Davies had set his own radicalism against Shakespeare's conservatism, but that he had dodged his responsibility to history, by avoiding a potentially more explosive confrontation with the dishonesties and evasions of the play itself. In this respect, the hidden history of the play identified by Bond seems to have crept back onto the agenda. Griffiths's identification of Henry with Stalin seems an apt one, for, as Steve Grant put it in the *Observer*, *Henry VIII* was still 'a highly selective and historically inaccurate chronicle . . . Stalin would have been proud of it'.[97] Jack Tinker in the *Daily Mail* also registered unease: surprisingly tolerant of Davies's Brechtian treatment, he still felt that the play 'remains an elaborate PR exercise on behalf of the Tudor dynasty, as remote from the realities of history as Mrs Thatcher's presidential-style Wembley rally'.[98] Even the most sympathetic review (Michael Billington's in the *Guardian*), registered a conflict between text and production:

> although Mr Davies (assisted by David Edgar) treats the piece as if it were a Tawneyesque study of the link between religion and capitalism, his approach is somewhat at odds with the play that Shakespeare (assisted by John Fletcher) actually wrote . . . I felt I had witnessed a very enjoyable production of *The Threepenny Opera* rather than Shakespeare's elaborate piece of Tudor myth-making.[99]

For Billington, the production was so intelligent, ironic and self-consciously intertextual that it seemed almost to have floated free of the play itself: here, as perhaps never before, there was a clear contradiction between Shakespeare and 'relevance', between the critical and institutional imperatives of serving the bard and modern liberal sensibilities. For an attempt at a radical intervention in the context of the RSC's main house at Stratford, this is hardly a very surprising outcome; and it need not be seen as an altogether negative one either. Even if *Henry VIII* did not emerge as the hard-hitting political study that Davies and Edgar might have hoped it to be, it was, at least able to foreground the contradictions between appropriation and contestation and within what Christopher McCullough has called 'the machinery of its own cultural production',[100] leading some to question the conventional wisdom of uncritical canonical loyalty. In the end, the fact that the production left a sense of contradiction and conflict may not be a mark of failure but a measure of the extent of its subversiveness.

Chapter Twelve

A bastard to the time: King John at The Other Place, 1988

Davies's *Henry VIII* went about as far as it was possible to go in radicalising Shakespeare on Stratford's main stage. It is this stage space, the Royal Shakespeare Theatre, that has formed the setting for all of the productions discussed so far; for our final production, Deborah Warner's *King John* in 1988, it is now necessary to move outside of the main house and into the RSC's studio theatre, The Other Place. Before examining Warner's production, however, it may be useful to consider briefly some of the history and the characteristics of The Other Place itself. Opened in 1974, The Other Place was very much the legacy of the small-scale experiments of the 1960s. Throughout the history of the company, RSC practitioners (and this includes both mainstream and more peripheral figures) have made efforts to overcome the restrictions and contradictions of large-scale, proscenium-arch Shakespearean production by setting up alternative projects outside of the company's main theatres; this has frequently been connected with attempts to link Shakespeare more closely with both contemporary experimental theatre and new writing, from the 1963–4 Theatre of Cruelty season at LAMDA to the season at The Place in 1971. During the 1960s and early 1970s, there was also Theatregoround, a semi-autonomous touring outfit which 'brought live theatre to schools, youth clubs, colleges, community centres, housing estates, and factories'.[101] Viewed as attempts to overcome the alienations of scale inherent not only in the Royal Shakespeare Theatre but also the corporate structure of the RSC, such projects can be seen to reflect diverse – and possibly contradictory – cultural and political aspirations: an avant-garde preoccupation with experiment, a desire to extend the RSC's audience base, the radical inter-

163

ventionism of theatre-in-education. For all the potentially critical force of these outreach operations, however, they nonetheless remained within the remit of Shakespeare-plus-relevance, confirming the belief that Shakespeare's natural home is among contemporary drama.

When The Other Place started operations in 1974, it was as the culmination of a miniature tradition of small-scale, alternative Shakespeare within the RSC. Interestingly, its actual origins have been subject to dispute. The official RSC version, as propounded by Terry Hands, is that the impetus behind the project was not political but pragmatic and artistic: 'simply an idea of making theatre more immediate in a circumstance which was, in terms of stage-craft, much easier to control'.[102] On the other hand, in his account of the RSC's studio spaces, Colin Chambers has emphasised the links between The Other Place (and subsequently The Warehouse) and the political fringe, and in particular the pioneering role of the director Buzz (Mary Ann) Goodbody, who was appointed as The Other Place's artistic director in 1974; this view has been echoed in Dympna Callaghan's recent study of her work.[103] Goodbody was recruited to the RSC in 1967 having been a founder of the Women's Street Theatre, and was a key figure in Theatrego-round (directing the notorious *King John*, discussed above); in the early 1970s she acted as an assistant director to John Barton and Trevor Nunn. An active feminist and Communist, Good-body's commitments shaped the political character of the early work at The Other Place. Crucially, she believed that 'Shake-speare . . . is saying all the time that politics is people, and people politics';[104] for her, The Other Place was a dream of democratic, accessible and popular classical theatre, with low seat prices for low-budget, stripped-down and hard-hitting productions which placed a strong emphasis on political relev-ance and immediacy. Thus her 1974 production of *King Lear* (retitled *Lear*, after Bond), which was designed with school audiences in mind, began with an interpolated prologue on homelessness in contemporary Britain, and emphasised the violence, brutality and oppression; while the treatment of the relationship between Lear and the daughters seemed to focus on issues of familial sexual abuse. In her *Hamlet* of the following year, the main concern was the limits of personal activism, together with a compelling (and prescient) preoccupation with suicide and female madness. In political terms, however, the productions were open to diverse appropriations; for Goodbody, in intention at least, the personal was political, but the modernity and stylistic simplicity of productions such as these could as easily lend them to an apolitical reading, so that *Hamlet* could be commended for its 'Strindbergian intensity' and 'existential imaginings'.[105] Following Goodbody's suicide in 1975, the drift towards 'chamber classic' productions of Shakespeare became more pronounced; and from Nunn's celebrated *Macbeth* in 1976 to his *Othello* in 1989, for all their inventive minimalism in theatrical terms, they frequently confirmed conservative readings of the plays themselves – which might seem to endorse Hands's view.

This was partly due to the contradictory nature of The Other Place itself when considered, like the main-house theatre, as an institutional and physical space. In both theatrical and political terms, The Other Place has been beset by the rhetoric of authenticity and immediacy, and this has inevitably shaped the ways in which its productions have been read. In the 1960s underground theatre (transformed, in the 1970s, into the 'fringe'), the intense and disruptive intimacy of the physical and communicative relationship between performers and audience imbued politics with an environmental dimension, and vice versa: direct contact and intervention seemed to offer a radical disruption of the elitism and distance of the traditional theatre apparatus. As Graham White has recently put it: 'the end was premised on the wish to replace "art" with life, contemplation with involvement, separation with integration, polemic with action.'[106] At its inception, The Other Place appeared to embody some of these characteristics, while suggesting others. For the initial short run in 1973, it was, as Chambers puts it, a 'leaking hut . . . with puddles on the floor and an out-of-tune piano', and this rudimentary quality was preserved: 'benches without backs were put in to seat 180, leaving a playing area of from eighteen to twenty yards.'[107] A few cosmetic improvements were made for the 1974 opening, but the theatre retained its rough-edged character:

The Other Place was painted black, the wooden flooring put

in . . . in front and to the sides is the gallery seating –
wooden, with hard backs and folding seats . . . Downstairs
on the right are the toilets – though a Portaloo had to be used
at first – and, beyond them, the auditorium, which then leads
straight back to the outside world.[108]

With its hard seating reminiscent of a Methodist chapel, its
leaking roof and its Portaloo, and its vital link with the world
outside, this was a theatre space which offered a sufficient
degree of physical discomfort to demand both high-minded
seriousness and virtuous commitment from audience and performers alike. In such a context, and with a repertoire of
modern plays dominated by the likes of Brecht and Bond, it is
not hard to see how an atmosphere of nonconformist radicalism
was fostered in the early years of the mid-1970s. At the same
time, this being the RSC, it could also seem that the Shakespeare work that was put on within this space was tending to
confirm rather than disrupt traditional truths. As Peter Holland
points out, the intimacy of scale of the studio setting for
Shakespeare, when compared with the non-illusionist Elizabethan public playhouse, tends to naturalise and domesticate
the drama. Whereas the public theatres 'encouraged a rapid
and almost vertiginous oscillation between general and particular, between human and abstract',

> 'Studio Shakespeare' cannot do this. It brings the actor close
> to the audience – satisfyingly so for many, unnervingly so for
> some . . . But all this concentration on the actor and the
> essential theatricality of performance allows no room for
> many of the ways in which the plays aim to disturb the
> audience.[109]

The intense proximity of RSC-style studio Shakespeare elim-
inates distance and with it some of the strangeness and
otherness of the plays; quite simply, 'the domesticity of scale
drastically limits the range of the means of expression.'[110]
Although Holland doesn't say so, this often results in the
embourgeoisement of Shakespeare's drama, a focus on character and interpersonal relationships at the expense of the
social and political dimension. To this may be added the

essentialising tendency of the RSC's small-scale work: there has been a powerful sense in which the intimate conditions and stripped-down approach of the poor theatre have been seen to invite direct access to the texts' timeless, universal and *essential* identity. Thus was *Macbeth*, typically, seen as 'a demonstration, without prevarication or elaboration, of the eternal struggle between good and evil'.[111] Like Lear's hovel, the draughty shed of The Other Place offered a space for an encounter with Shakespeare's naked, unaccommodated humanity; bereft of the decorative delights of ornate period costumes and elaborate scenery, the productions in The Other Place had tougher pleasures to offer.

Whether Shakespeare at The Other Place took the form of a redefinition of a canonically central play (such as Goodbody's *Hamlet* and *Lear*, Nunn's *Macbeth* and *Othello* and Adrian Noble's *Antony and Cleopatra* in 1982), or a low-risk production of a peripheral or marginal text (examples being Ron Daniels's *Pericles* in 1979 and *Timon of Athens* in 1980), it has generally tended to favour naturalistic intensity over a more epic style. In itself, this tendency raises a question of genre. Shakespearean tragedy has thrived in The Other Place, but Shakespearean comedy has not, possibly because the studio space chillingly lacks the romance and glamour of the main house. The history plays have proved problematic for different reasons. To date, there have been only four productions of history plays in The Other Place: Barry Kyle's *Richard III* in 1975, Deborah Warner's *King John* in 1988, Sam Mendes's *Richard III* in 1992 and, a real curiosity, John Barton and Barry Kyle's production of John Ford's Stuart history *Perkin Warbeck* in 1975 (to these may also be added the Theatregoround productions of *King John* in 1970, and of *Richard II* and *Henry V* in 1971; and a touring production of both parts of *Henry IV* in 1981). As we have seen, stage traditions of producing the histories reveal remarkable convergences between institutional status, genre and theatrical space: within the RSC especially, the theatrical vocabulary of history production has been of a spectacular scale commensurate with the plays' cultural status. It has, however, proved difficult to rescore what are seen as operatic or symphonic works for the chamber setting: when they are displaced from such prestigious frameworks as the

Royal Shakespeare Theatre, Shakespeare's histories (and, indeed, those of other Elizabethan and Jacobean writers) can sometimes emerge as more contradictory and unsettling texts. The 1975 productions of *Perkin Warbeck* and *Richard III*, for example, have been described as ' "main house" affair[s] crammed into The Other Place';[112] upon closer inspection, the interest of the productions lies in their determination to evade the implications of the theatrical and cultural space they occupied. Barton and Kyle's *Perkin Warbeck* was, in the verdict of Michael Coveney in the *Financial Times*, 'a vivid job of reclamation that both complements and extends Mr Barton's work on Shakespeare's histories'.[113] The staging utilised a chessboard motif, with the floor covered in black and white square tiles and the opposing factions costumed in black and white. For anyone baffled by the historical background, helpful contextual material was also a strong feature: 'Wall hangings present family trees, a map of the battle of Bosworth, portraits of Henry and of the early Stuart kings, lit up and pointed out by Henry to explain the feudal complexities of the background.'[114] Faced with the indeterminacies of a non-canonical, non-Shakespearean history, Barton characteristically resituated the play within a quasi-Shakespearean paradigm of order and lineage; this treatment effectively drew *Perkin Warbeck* into the orbit of the director's main-house Shakespearean histories. Not surprisingly, the expository approach appeared to stifle the play; as one reviewer concluded, it was 'a pity that the two directors of the production did not see fit to play it up with the gusto suggested by the text'.[115] But while *Perkin Warbeck* may have been diligent but dull, the same season's *Richard III*, directed by Barry Kyle and with Ian Richardson in the title role, was more adventurous. This production's ruling idea was an invocation of both Peter Weiss's *Marat-Sade* and Peter Nichols's satire on the state of the nation, *The National Health*: bandages, straitjackets and hospital beds, staged with a pervasive sense of tawdry shabbiness, seemed to locate the action in a ward in a psychiatric hospital. Eric Shorter of the *Daily Telegraph* interpreted the institutional setting as a suggestion that 'all the world's a hospital or lunatic asylum and all the men and women in it merely aspects of some disease or other'; he concluded that the production provided 'an interesting and quirky evening of echoes from other thinkers than Shakespeare – Brecht, Peter Weiss, Peter Brook and so on'.[116] Striking as it was, the self-conscious experimentation of this production didn't seem to add up to very much, nor to say anything particularly about *Richard III* itself.

Deborah Warner's 1988 production of *King John* was an altogether different matter. Presented in the same season as the *Plantagenets* cycle in the main house, this was not the marginal event that it might otherwise have been. Warner had joined the RSC in the previous year, after seven years of running her own small-scale touring company, Kick Theatre, which had received much acclaim for its minimalist ensemble productions of Shakespeare. Warner's already formidable reputation as a Shakespearean director was further enhanced by her production of *Titus Andronicus* in the RSC's Swan Theatre in 1987; the combination of Warner's direction and the theatre space transformed an undervalued, notoriously difficult play into a theatrical experience of brutal power, savage comedy and, most challengingly of all, extraordinary strangeness. Whereas previous Stratford productions of this play had tended either to envelop it in mystificatory ritual or to camp up its violent excesses for cheap laughs, Warner's production brought a gendered political perspective to the cruelty and violence, while simultaneously recognising its otherness as a text. It is this recognition of difference alongside relevance that accounted for the complexity as well as the intensity of Warner's work; it is what differentiates it from RSC norms. This stemmed in part from a textual fundamentalism which contrasts tellingly with the appropriative pragmatism which is characteristic of the RSC. Whereas the espousal of loyalty to Shakespeare usually goes along with surreptitious editorial revisionism, Warner has made it a point of principle not to cut, emend or adapt the text, particularly when that text confronts the tenets of realism:

> I feel if you do reach a dead-end, then, as a director, it is your fault. It's no good thinking, oh, well, it's an early play, not one of his best, it's not my fault. I happen to find it hard to believe that this particular author is ever at fault.[117]

This approach may well reflect an unnervingly rigorous form of bardolatry; paradoxically, however, it may have radical implications, since it means that the more bizarre, unsettling and contradictory elements in the plays themselves cannot be wished away, disguised or silently erased.

This rigorous consistency was the key to Warner's *Titus*; it also underpinned her *King John*. Whereas John Barton had attempted to resolve the 'problems' of the play by rewriting it in terms of his own liberal humanist agenda, Warner was prepared to allow the difficulties to work themselves out in performance:

> I think that Shakespeare was actually experimenting when he wrote it and after doing so he changed how he worked . . . it has very real technical problems . . . If I was pushed, I would be tempted to say it was an Elizabethan black comedy about politics, perhaps an Elizabethan *Ubu Roi*, but I didn't set out with any of these ideas firmly fixed because that's not how I work.[118]

Warner's policy of respect for the text was consistent with her view of the directorial role, which again was rather different from the one which has been fostered by the RSC. Warner has made a point of distancing herself from the idea of the director as manipulator exerting sole rights of ownership over a production, as the author of the production's concept, and as the privileged interpreter of the play: 'I think a director's role is to create the right environment and then step out of it for as long as possible and hope the actors will feel confident and brave enough to try to experiment.'[119] The desired result is a collective rather than an individual vision of the play:

> I'm against directors forcing their own stamp onto a production rather than the stamp of the whole company. With a cast of ten . . . and a director, you've got eleven people's ideas making up a show. And it's essential that you have eleven people's ideas, because it's going to be much better than one director's idea, however brilliant that director is.[120]

Again, this genuine commitment to the principles of ensemble theatre might well be at odds with the prevailing RSC culture (and, indeed, with the political culture of 1980s Britain), but it recaptures some of the original egalitarian spirit of The Other Place. In the case of *King John*, so too did the production's style of staging and performance: as Paul Taylor of the *Independent* put it, it had Warner's 'distinctive look . . . of still having one foot in the rehearsal room'.[121] To this end, the props and costumes formed an eclectic, unruly and anachronistic ragbag of styles and periods, ranging from medieval chainmail to First World War greatcoats, and from the lion's skin 'complete with huge yawning head'[122] sported by Limoges to stockbroker-fashion suits and striped shirts. King John himself, played by Nicholas Woodeson, was a diminutive comic figure in an oversized trenchcoat and tin helmet, carrying the crown on a chain suspended from his belt. The only significant items of scenery in an otherwise empty acting space were plain wooden chairs and the aluminium ladders which are the trademark of Warner's productions, manoeuvred by the actors to form trestle tables or to suggest walls, prison bars and, indeed, 'virtually everything'.[123] As Nicholas Woodeson pointed out, this style matched the experimental and contradictory nature of the text, which suggested 'Beethoven writing like Mozart':

> what is the function of history in the history plays? Shakespeare's plays are full of anachronisms: cannon, flags and clocks when none would have existed. Period realism is irrelevant. History is an ingredient, with popular myth, politics and spectacle in creative dramatic 'history' . . . In responding with some anachronisms of our own, we have discovered a tough political drama.[124]

In this context, as in *Titus*, moments of violence and horror were presented with shocking literalness, as one reviewer recorded:

> A severed head in a sack is smashed wetly down on the floor, leaving an ugly little puddle. Preparing to put out Arthur's eyes, Hubert experiments with tongs and pincers while burning coals are toted on in a hideously ordinary-looking

bucket; pathetically defenceless in his schoolboy dressing-gown, the youngster is held down by two helpers in black plastic butcher's aprons.[125]

In the anachronistic context of the production, the immediacy and simplicity is stylistically very close to the dramaturgy of Edward Bond, in particular the nightmare world of *Lear*, where 'the anachronisms are for the horrible moments in a dream when you know it's a dream but can't help being afraid.'[126] The acting was an equally disconcerting mixture of tones and styles, moving between psychological naturalism and caricature. Nicholas Woodeson's John, for example, was both a comic grotesque and a quasi-tragic figure, 'a cross between a despotic petulant toddler and a glazedly smiling psychotic',[127] and 'a brilliant study in kingly insecurity'.[128] Robert Demeger's Hubert similarly switched from caricature to character as the action progressed: appearing first on the walls of Angiers with the stereotypical French beret, baguette, moustache and silly accent, he later 'sheds the comedy to convey the moral revulsion of the ordinary man caught up in state brutality'.[129]

As in Warner's previous work, one of the notable features of the production was the way in which scenic minimalism allowed space for extremes of emotion, cartoon-style violence and energetic physicality. Accompanied by a raucous percussive score, kings and nobles wrestled each other to the floor, hurled ladders at each other, and, as if straining against the domesticity of scale of the studio theatre, 'hurtle on and off stage and burst through the back exit of the Other Place as though the venue itself, like the characters, can hardly contain its febrile, pointless energy'.[130] But while most reviewers concurred with the view that these brutal fun and games offered enthralling entertainment, there were few who attributed the production any profounder significance; as Charles Osborne put it in the *Daily Telegraph*, it was a production which 'engagingly matches the play's lack of complexity'.[131] Conversely, a number read the energetic rehearsal-room style as constituting an interpretative emphasis, and possibly a commentary upon the play itself. As Nicholas de Jongh recorded in the *Guardian*:

She interprets the Kings of England and France as if their

grand wars were no more than games and pageants, and they themselves a cross between perpetual adolescents and amateur actors caught up in village hall theatricals.[132]

Thus the Battle of Angiers appeared to this critic as 'a playground brawl, a fancy dress battle'. It is this metadramatic dimension, I would suggest, that was the most subversive aspect of the production's style: in the context of the RSC, and especially against the background of *The Plantagenets*, perhaps the real butt of its satire was less the historical world of the play than the dominant modes of Shakespearean history play production. In this respect the production drew attention to what may be a basic element of these plays' appeal for both actors and audience: the boyishly simple desire to dress up, charge around on stage and wave large swords. Referring to what he perceived as its 'female derision', Irving Wardle wrote in *The Times* that in this production 'politics emerges as a lethally stupid boy's game':[133] its ferocious brawling and stomping seemed to be implicated in a vision of masculinity as both comically infantile and frighteningly destructive. Once again, as in Goodbody's and Barton's productions, there was an emphasis on childishness and immaturity, with Woodeson's King John 'an arresting study in protracted adolescence',[134] who ended the play 'wrapped in a blanket and dumped on the floor, an undignified bundle, his bare, faintly bluish feet sticking out, pathetically vulnerable',[135] regressing 'virtually back to babyhood . . . as he passes away almost imperceptibly, it is as though we are witnessing a cot death'.[136] In this production, in marked contrast to the previous ones, the avoidance of cliché and sentimentality ensured that the image of John as a child in rapid regression was first playfully engaging and then harrowing, rather than merely ludicrous.

Lacking the seductive glamour of RSC main-stage Shakespeare, this *King John* was not a comfortable experience, but its austere energy nonetheless afforded it a powerfully visceral appeal. Its most radical (and hence most controversial) element, however, was its treatment of the Bastard (played by David Morissey). This role, of course, presents what is in the traditional reading another of the play's critical and theatrical 'problems': in particular, how to effect the transition from a

bruisingly sardonic outsider to patriotic spokesman and moral
centre of the play. In this production the problem disappeared
because Morissey's Bastard remained a thuggishly unsympath-
etic figure throughout. Rather than growing in moral and
political stature, he was 'big and gangling, earringed and
unshaven . . . a rumbustious bully, doubling up his half brother
with a blow to the stomach, ribbing King John, slapping Queen
Eleanor on the shoulders'.[137] Here was the relevance and
immediacy of the production: wrapped in an English flag for
the battle of Angiers, this Bastard was a strikingly contemporary figure. Variously described as 'a demi-bearded soccer
hooligan',[138] 'a football supporter with his blood up: a style that
he keeps up even over Arthur's corpse',[139] 'a swaggering
bovver boy',[140] 'a Scouse nationalist spoiling for trouble'[141] and
'a National Front yobbo';[142] he was an appallingly literal and
consistent embodiment of the nationalist triumphalism
inscribed in his final words (v, vii, 116–18):

> Come the three corners of the world in arms,
> And we shall mock them. Nought shall make us rue,
> If England to itself do rest but true.

This Bastard's patriotism, stripped (like the play as a whole)
of the veneer of respectability, was simply another manifesta-
tion of the prevailing cult of masculinity; his bullying and his
xenophobic outbursts, like the fascist sympathies and murderous behaviour of some English football fans, merely the logical
culmination of the official nationalism which, at the end of the
1980s, was enjoying a resurgence in the form of virulent
opposition to European federalism. Unsurprisingly, a number
of reviewers, mainly in the right-wing press, resisted the
implications of this reading by making allegations about distortion or appropriation of Shakespeare. Charles Osborne wrote
in the *Daily Telegraph* that the Bastard was 'apparently
misunderstood by the director';[143] John Gross concluded in the
Sunday Telegraph that it was 'hard to tell from this performance why Faulconbridge is such an interesting character';[144]
while Milton Shulman of the *Evening Standard* simply wrote
that Morissey 'irritated me behaving like a boastful hippie',
although 'the Dauphin of Ralph Fiennes indicated that not all

dignity had evaporated from medieval warfare'.[145] But it was difficult to make these charges stick because, as Robert Small-wood concluded in his *Shakespeare Quarterly* review, this oppositional reading staked its authority on its firm and consistent grounding in the text, and so 'the challenge it presents cannot easily be dismissed, even if it leaves the play seeming a meaner, a bleaker thing than it did (and, perhaps, after all, than it is)'.[146] In *King John*, Warner and her cast had finally made the RSC and its audiences face up to the contradiction between Shakespearean history as patriotic myth and the brutal social and political realities of post-imperial Britain. What was so startling about this production was that it achieved this through commitment, clarity and consistency of purpose rather than mockery and defensive irony; and so it demonstrated the paradoxical possibilities of staging Shakespeare uncut and unadapted in order to subvert tradition rather than confirm it. Whether or not this could be said to be authorised by Shakespeare (and perhaps Warner might have claimed that it could) is, perhaps, ultimately a moot point: in the end, it was the authority of the production that mattered rather than that of Shakespeare. As Brecht never tired of pointing out, the proof of the pudding is in the eating.

Conclusion

This history began in 1963 with *The Wars of the Roses*, a production conceived amidst optimism about the possibilities of large-scale, publicly funded and academically informed Shakespearean theatre, and addressed to a nation which seemed to many to be on the verge of radical economic and social change. It ends in 1988, with the diametrically opposed productions of *The Plantagenets* and *King John*, the former a momentous event which recalled the triumph of twenty-five years earlier and which staged the lavish spectacle of a conservative history, the latter a studio-scale experiment on a shoestring budget which fiercely interrogated the theatrical and political values promoted on the RSC's main stage. Both of these productions were presented to a Britain which, while still entertaining fantasies of its own pre-eminence as a world power, was in truth beset by unemployment, poverty and inequality, subordinate to the military interests of the United States, and in a condition of possibly terminal economic decline. Whereas in 1964 the case for the subsidised Shakespearean theatre seemed, at least temporarily, to have been won, the RSC was never again to enjoy the level of state support that produced *The Wars of the Roses*. By the time of *The Plantagenets*, like so many of the products of the welfarist political consensus of the post-war period, the RSC had become a casualty of the Thatcherite project of reversing the liberalising social, economic and cultural policies of the previous three decades: at the end of the 1980s, the company could only look to a precarious future with trepidation. From the vantage point of the RSC, the prospects were bleak indeed, with the promise of the reign of Thatcherism in perpetuity, further erosion of the company's economic and cultural base, yet more compromises to its original liberal aims, and the banishment of radicalism, innovation and experiment into smaller and more marginal spaces.

It is tempting to break off this history at this point, not least because the fortuitous juxtaposition of *The Plantagenets* and *King John* provides such a suggestive image of the two nations of rich and poor Shakespearean theatre. And yet, of course, history does not stop in such a convenient fashion, and neither does the RSC's involvement in the histories. The next time Shakespeare's England appeared on the main stage at Stratford, however, it did so in an altogether darker, shabbier and less reassuring form. In 1990 the company mounted its first production of *Richard II* since the Barry Kyle-directed version of 1986, which had acted as a romantic star vehicle for Jeremy Irons, and which had anticipated the splendours of *The Plantagenets* with its colourful Garden of England settings straight out of a medieval Book of Hours. The 1990 production, directed by Ron Daniels, was a brutal, almost monochromatic reading, taking place in front of concrete walls, and staged, according to Robert Smallwood in his *Shakespeare Quarterly* review, 'on a slag heap, a smoldering dump for toxic chemicals, a terrible image of the ruin and decay to which Richard's rule has brought England'; a mirror of contemporary social reality which was itself cynically framed by 'a white plastic false proscenium of the kind popular with totalitarian regimes'.[1] This picture of decay and oppression, making no concession to traditional elegiac lyricism, offered a far more disconcerting vision of Britain as a post-industrial wasteland than the glittering pageants of previous seasons; but perhaps the most interesting aspect of this staging was that it provided evidence of the RSC looking beyond the nationalist introversion of its preoccupation with England to a European context, as 'Romania in late 1989 kept wafting back into one's imagination'.[2] This *Richard II* was followed a year later by Adrian Noble's production of the two parts of *Henry IV* for the 1991 season, which marked the director's accession as sole Artistic Director of the RSC. While this production was 'a necessary piece of self-assertion by the new regime',[3] it was an event on an altogether more modest scale than previous cycles; in contrast to the postmodernist pyrotechnics of the same director's *Henry*

V and *The Plantagenets*, it was a subdued, bleak reading. Dominated by Robert Stephens's depressive, seriously alcoholic Falstaff, its most striking feature was its almost carnivalesque emphasis upon the low-life side of the plays, set against the austerity and sterility of power politics. Most recently, in 1992, the RSC mounted a small-scale touring production of *Richard III*. Directed by Sam Mendes, this was staged in much the same intensely physical, anachronistic and eclectic style as Deborah Warner's *King John*: it had the effect of liberating the play from the grip of both Antony Sher's one-man histrionics and the deterministic machinery of *The Plantagenets* cycle. The central emblem of this lucid and challengingly contradictory production was the crown itself, 'a thin, flat, tall, gold circle cut into a series of points, halfway between a proper crown and a comic hat out of a Christmas cracker'.[4] Half-joking, half-serious, it seems an appropriately ambivalent emblem of the vicious tragi-comedy of British political life in the early 1990s.

Throughout this book I have argued that Shakespearean theatre production is far more thoroughly and directly implicated in contemporary history than most of those involved in its production, mediation and reception would care to admit. While it has long been recognised that Shakespeare's plays in performance will inevitably resonate with the conflicts and concerns of the present, it has equally been held that behind the localised, ephemeral nuances of relevance, theatre production can – and indeed should – still reproduce the eternal, universal and transhistorical truths that are inalienably present in the texts themselves. This humanist view of modern Shakespearean theatre practice thus makes a distinction between the text's permanence and its response to reproduction and appropriation. As Ralph Berry formulated it in 1981 in his seminal work of production criticism, *Changing Styles in Shakespeare*, this distinction operates in terms of 'the capacity of a given society, in its day, to recognize the permanent truths that are coded into a Shakespeare text'.[5] Those forms of production criticism and theatre history which adopt this perspective may be generously responsive to incursions of social and political relevance which afford a Shakespearean production anything from a fashionable piquancy (David Warner's student scarf in *Hamlet*) to a compelling urgency (echoes of the Falklands War in *Henry V*), but ultimately they will be more interested in how it handles the real matter of the eternal verities (the problem of evil in *Macbeth*, the problem of order in the histories). Here lies the crucial methodological and theoretical difference between humanist and materialist theatre criticisms. Rejecting the idealist and essentialist separation of depth and surface, and the concomitant distinction between the unchanging Shakespearean text and the history of its theatrical inscriptions, materialist theatre criticism (and practice) maintains that the apparently 'permanent truths' ascribed to the Shakespeare text and delivered in performance are as much the immediate product of the history in which it is embedded as its contemporary accretions. For materialist criticism, all of the elements of Shakespearean production, its sceneography, lighting and costume, the bodies and gestures of the performers, and even the Shakespeare text itself which has been reproduced from words on the page as sound and movement, originate and remain within social reality; as a communicative process and as a social event, Shakespearean performance is a contingent (and unfinished) dialogue between gendered subjects in history, and between themselves and their real conditions of existence. It is in this sense that Shakespearean performance is political, irretrievably enmeshed in relations of power and resistance, oppression and desire.

Once this view is accepted, it becomes clear that the distinction between Shakespeare and relevance – which has been so fundamental to the RSC, paradoxically as the condition of their symbiosis – is a purely ideological one: those elements which we choose to attribute to Shakespeare are simply the conflicts of the present in a different guise. This ideological stratagem of the humanist theatre can also be approached from a psychoanalytic perspective, as a process of displacement, whereby Shakespeare takes on that which cannot be owned or resolved in political reality. To perform or to watch Shakespeare is to participate in a kind of cultural dreamwork, in which the mutation of contemporary history into the cyclical narratives, heroes and villains of Shakespeare's England enacts both collective fantasies of wish-fulfilment and, more traumatically, the compulsion to repeat. In this endlessly revisited and reshaped fantasy zone of Shakespeare's England, the terrors and complexities of the postmodern state can be reduced to recognisable, simple and more ordered patterns of individual motives and actions; it also provides the possibility of the resolution of the contradictions of the present. The brutal and cynical versions of history may be as much part of this process as the heroic and idealised ones: the function, and the immense appeal, of both lies in their capacity to render history simple.

By repeatedly reanimating Shakespeare's histories to almost unbroken acclaim, the RSC may be seen to have played an important ideological role in the political and cultural history of post-war Britain. This role, however, needs to be put in perspective. The prestigious cultural profile of the RSC as Shakespeare's representatives, and the detailed and extensive attention that has been paid to its productions in the media and in subsequent accounts (such as this one), have ensured that the company and its work has continued to maintain a powerful and influential cultural position; but it is strangely dispro-portionate to the actual numbers of spectators who attend the productions themselves. Paradoxically, the RSC's work may be more significant in its subsequent narrative and mythical inscriptions than in its enactment as theatre. Even in the heady early days of the 1960s, and certainly in the 1990s, the live Shakespearean theatre was and is a minority pursuit, and a dwindling one at that. At the beginning, Peter Hall wanted the RSC to restore the status of the classical theatre, partly in response to the challenge posed by the more populist media of cinema and television, and struggled to secure the public funding to achieve this. In this he was only partially successful, and ever since the RSC has been haunted by its own elitism, the threat of extinction, and, worst of all, its own marginality and irrelevance. Looking back at the productions discussed in this book in the light of this, it may be that they contain another elegiac and metadramatic dimension as yet undisclosed: they trace the passing of the English theatre as much as that of England itself. Hall's desire to revitalise Shakespeare in the theatre can be seen in a wider critical context: a similar wish also fuelled the increasingly vociferous insistence by stage-centred critics upon the live theatre as the realm of the authentically Shakespearean; an insistence which has paralleled the waning fortunes of the theatre medium itself. Hall wanted to institute a popular revolution in the classical theatre, drawing in the paperback-buying masses but also those whom he saw as the agents of social change, the youthful, educated middle class; by the 1990s, had Hall's thinking theatregoer chosen to visit the Royal Shakespeare Theatre at all, they would have found themselves sitting alongside not only the culture-lovers and earnest students and professors of literature, but also coach parties of bored and disruptive schoolchildren, tourists whose grasp of English might well leave them completely baffled at what was happening on stage, and executives on corporate hospitality tickets, dozing drunkenly through the entire performance. Notwithstanding all the rich and complex critical narratives that are woven around the Royal Shakespeare Company's reproduction of Shakespeare's plays, these are the real theatrical conditions within which their politics are constructed, negotiated and contested. How, when and to what effect these conditions change, and consequently what happens to Shakespeare's histories next, will be a matter for all of us, in history, to determine.

Notes

Introduction

1. Quoted in Michael Coveney, 'Terry Hands, Adrian Noble and Peter Hall, masters of the RSC, talk theatre', *Observer*, 28 June 1992.
2. Peter Saccio, *Shakespeare's English Kings: History, Chronicle and Drama* (Oxford: Oxford University Press, 1977), p. 4.
3. See Nicola J. Watson, 'Kemble, Scott, and the Mantle of the Bard', in Jean I. Marsden (ed.), *The Appropriation of Shakespeare: Post-Renaissance Reconstructions of the Works and the Myth* (Hemel Hempstead: Harvester Wheatsheaf, 1991), pp. 73–92. For an account of the cultural reproduction of Shakespeare's history see Graham Holderness, *Shakespeare Recycled: The Making of Historical Drama* (Hemel Hempstead: Harvester Wheatsheaf, 1992).

Part I: Performing Histories

1. See David Addenbrooke, *The Royal Shakespeare Company: The Peter Hall Years* (London: William Kimber, 1974), and Sally Beaumann, *The Royal Shakespeare Company: A History of Ten Decades* (Oxford: Oxford University Press, 1982).
2. Alan Sinfield, 'Royal Shakespeare: theatre and the making of ideology', in Jonathan Dollimore and Alan Sinfield (eds), *Political Shakespeare: New Essays in Cultural Materialism* (Manchester: Manchester University Press, 1985), pp. 158–81. See also Sinfield, 'The theatre and its audiences', in Sinfield (ed.), *Society and Literature 1945–1970* (London: Methuen, 1983), pp. 173–98; and Sinfield, *Literature, Politics and Culture in Postwar Britain* (Oxford: Blackwell, 1989), pp. 232–52.
3. Sinfield, 'Royal Shakespeare', p. 159.
4. Peter Hall, 'Avoiding a method', in Royal Shakespeare Company, *Crucial Years* (London: Max Reinhardt, 1963), p. 14.

5. Peter Hall, 'Shakespeare and the modern director', in John Goodwin (ed.), *Royal Shakespeare Theatre Company 1960–1963* (London: Max Reinhardt, 1964), p. 46.

6. Quoted in Michael Coveney, 'Terry Hands, Adrian Noble and Peter Hall, masters of the RSC talk theatre', *Observer*, 28 June 1992.

7. Quoted in Peter Ansorge, 'Director in interview: Trevor Nunn', *Plays and Players*, September 1970.

8. Ronald Bryden, *Observer*, 12 October 1969.

9. Ansorge, 'Director in interview'.

10. Peter Brook, *The Empty Space* (Harmondsworth: Penguin, 1968), pp. 53–4.

11. Quoted in Addenbrooke, *Royal Shakespeare Company*, p. 174.

12. See Catherine Itzin, *Stages in the Revolution: Political Theatre in Britain Since 1968* (London: Methuen, 1980), pp. 152–60.

13. See Colin Chambers, *Other Spaces: New Theatre and the RSC* (London: Methuen, 1980); Peter Holland, 'The RSC and Studio Shakespeare', *Essays in Criticism*, 32 (1982), pp. 205–18; and Dympna Callaghan, 'Buzz Goodbody: directing for change', in Jean I. Marsden (ed.), *The Appropriation of Shakespeare Post-Renaissance Reconstructions of the Works and Myth* (Hemel Hempstead: Harvester Wheatsheaf, 1991) pp. 163–81.

14. Herbert Kretzmer, *Daily Express*, 9 April 1975.

15. Norman Marshall, *The Other Theatre* (London: John Lehmann, 1947), p. 175.

16. See J. L. Styan, *The Shakespeare Revolution: Criticism and Performance in the Twentieth Century* (Cambridge: Cambridge University Press, 1977), pp. 47–159; and Robert Speaight, *William Poel and the Elizabethan Revival* (London: Heinemann, 1954).

17. William Bridges-Adams, *Observer*, 8 January 1928, quoted in Beaumann, *Royal Shakespeare Company*, pp. 112–13.

18. *Ibid.*, p. 111.

19. Addenbrooke, *Royal Shakespeare Company*, p. 44.

20. Quoted in J. C. Trewin, *Shakespeare on the English Stage, 1900–1964* (London: Barrie and Rockliff, 1964), p. 249.

21. Tyrone Guthrie, *A Life in the Theatre* (London: Hamish Hamilton, 1959), pp. 191–2.

22. Bertolt Brecht, 'A short organum for the theatre', in John Willett (ed.), *Brecht on Theatre* (London: Methuen, 1964), p. 189.

23. Keir Elam, *The Semiotics of Theatre and Drama* (London: Methuen, 1980), p. 8.

24. Karl Marx, 'The fetishism of commodities', in David McLellan (ed.), *Karl Marx: Selected Writings* (Oxford: Oxford University Press, 1977), pp. 435–6.
25. Catherine Belsey, *The Subject of Tragedy: Identity and difference in Renaissance drama* (London: Methuen, 1985), pp. 24–5.
26. *Ibid.*, pp. 25–6.
27. See Marvin and Ruth Thomson, 'Performance criticism from Granville-Barker to Bernard Beckerman and beyond', in Marvin and Ruth Thomson (eds), *Shakespeare and the Sense of Performance* (London and Toronto: Associated University Presses, 1989), pp. 13–23.
28. For a deconstructive critique of performance criticism's claims to authenticity, see W. B. Worthen, 'Deeper meanings and theatrical technique: the rhetoric of performance criticism', *Shakespeare Quarterly*, 40 (1989), pp. 441–55.
29. David A. Samuelson, 'Preface', in Philip C. McGuire and David A. Samuelson (eds), *Shakespeare: The Theatrical Dimension* (New York: AMS Press, 1979), p. xiii.
30. See for example G. Wilson Knight, *Shakespearian Production* (Harmondsworth: Penguin, 1949); Gordon Crosse, *Shakespearean Playgoing 1890–1952* (London: A. R. Mowbray, 1953); A. C. Sprague, *Shakespearean Players and Performances* (London: A. & C. Black, 1954); and Margaret Webster, *Shakespeare Today* (London: Dent, 1957).
31. Marvin Rosenberg, *The Masks of Othello* (Berkeley: University of California Press, 1961). This was followed by *The Masks of King Lear* (Berkeley: University of California Press, 1971); *The Masks of Macbeth* (Berkeley: University of California Press, 1978); and *The Masks of Hamlet* (Newark: University of Delaware Press, 1993).
32. A. C. Sprague, *Shakespeare's Histories: Plays for the Stage* (London: Society for Theatre Research, 1964).
33. John Russell Brown, *Shakespeare's Plays in Performance* (London: Edward Arnold, 1966).
34. See for example John Russell Brown, 'The study and practice of Shakespeare production', *Shakespeare Survey 18* (1965), pp. 58–69; and 'English criticism of Shakespeare performances today', *Deutsche Shakespeare-Gesellschaft West Jahrbuch 1967*, pp. 163–74; Stanley Wells, 'Shakespeare's text and the modern stage', *Deutsche Shakespeare-Gesellschaft West Jahrbuch 1967*, pp. 175–93; Gareth Lloyd Evans, 'Shakespeare, the twentieth century and "Behaviourism"', *Shakespeare Survey 20* (1967), pp. 133–42; and Robert Weimann, 'Shakespeare on the modern stage:

past significance and present meaning', *Shakespeare Survey 20* (1967), pp. 113–20.

35. Richard David, 'Actors and scholars: a view of Shakespeare in the modern theatre', *Shakespeare Survey 12* (1959), pp. 76–87.
36. For a survey of published and unpublished research on the RSC, see Lennart Nyberg, *The Shakespearean Ideal: Shakespeare Production and the Modern Theatre in Britain* (Uppsala: Acta Universitatis Upsaliensis, 1988), pp. 16–23.
37. See Walter Cohen, 'Political criticism of Shakespeare' and Don E. Wayne, 'Power, politics and the Shakespearean text: recent criticism in England and the United States', in Jean E. Howard and Marion F. O'Connor (eds), *Shakespeare Reproduced: The Text in Ideology and History* (London: Methuen, 1987), pp. 18–46; pp. 47–67.
38. See for example Alfred Harbage, *Conceptions of Shakespeare* (Cambridge, Mass.: Harvard University Press, 1966); and Morris Weitz, *'Hamlet' and the Philosophy of Literary Criticism* (Chicago: University of Chicago Press, 1965).
39. See Arnold Kettle (ed.), *Shakespeare in a Changing World* (London: Lawrence and Wishart, 1964); and Terence Eagleton, *Shakespeare and Society* (London: Chatto and Windus, 1967).
40. Jan Kott, *Shakespeare our Contemporary*, trans. Boleslaw Taborski, 2nd edn (London: Methuen, 1967).
41. Peter Hall, 'Introduction', in John Barton and Peter Hall, *The Wars of the Roses* (London: BBC Books, 1970), p. ix.
42. Sally Beaumann (ed.), *The Royal Shakespeare Company's Centenary Production of Henry V* (Oxford: Pergamon Press, 1976).
43. Stanley Wells, *Royal Shakespeare: Four Major Productions at Stratford-upon-Avon* (Manchester: Manchester University Press, 1977).
44. Richard David, *Shakespeare in the Theatre* (Cambridge: Cambridge University Press, 1978).
45. See Stanley Wells, 'Director's Shakespeare', *Deutsche Shakespeare-Gesellschaft West Jahrbuch 1976*, pp. 79–99; Robert Speaight, 'Truth and relevance in Shakespeare production', in David Bevington and Jay L. Halio (eds), *Shakespeare: Pattern of Excelling Nature* (Newark: University of Delaware Press, 1976), pp. 183–9; and Helen Gardner, 'Shakespeare in the directors' theatre', in *In Defence of the Imagination* (Oxford: The Clarendon Press, 1982), pp. 55–81.
46. John Russell Brown, *Free Shakespeare* (London: Heinemann, 1974), p. 112. In some respects, Brown's argument for an anti-

authoritarian, performance-centred pedagogy poses important, challenging questions for the practices of professional scholarship that are still unanswered. At the very least, a materialist performance-based approach offers scope for radical engagement and intervention in Shakespeare that is group-based rather than individualistic, physical as well as intellectual, conducted through dialogue rather than relying upon the oracular authority of the lecturer. Such an approach has the potential to be more potently subversive than current radical approaches still caught up with traditional literary-based pedagogies. For a politicised approach to performance-centred pedagogy, see Simon Shepherd, 'Acting against bardom: some utopian thoughts on workshops', in Lesley Aers and Nigel Wheale (eds), *Shakespeare in the Changing Curriculum* (London: Routledge, 1991), pp. 88–107.

47. David Selbourne, 'Brook's *Dream*', in *Culture and Agitation: Theatre Documents* (London: Action Books, 1972), p. 17. See also his *The Making of 'A Midsummer Night's Dream'* (London: Methuen, 1982).

48. Quoted in the *Sunday Times*, 28 March 1976.

49. Styan, *Shakespeare Revolution*, p. 1.

50. *Ibid.*, p. 46.

51. *Ibid.*, p. 234.

52. Kiernan Ryan, *Shakespeare* (Hemel Hempstead: Harvester Wheatsheaf, 1989), pp. 1–2.

53. See John Drakakis, 'Introduction', in *Alternative Shakespeares* (London: Methuen, 1985), pp. 1–25.

54. Quoted in Coveney, 'Masters of the RSC', *Observer*, 28 June 1992.

55. Styan, *Shakespeare Revolution*, p. 237.

56. Ralph Berry, *Changing Styles in Shakespeare* (London: Allen and Unwin, 1981), pp. 1–2.

57. J. L. Styan, *Shakespeare in Performance: All's Well that Ends Well* (Manchester: Manchester University Press, 1984).

58. Sara Eaton, 'Defacing the feminine in Renaissance tragedy', in Valerie Wayne (ed.), *The Matter of Difference: Materialist Feminist Criticism of Shakespeare* (Hemel Hempstead: Harvester Wheatsheaf, 1991), p. 182.

59. Berry, *Changing Styles*, p. 15.

60. Alexander Leggatt, *Shakespeare in Performance: King Lear* (Manchester: Manchester University Press, 1991), p. 15.

61. Belsey, *Subject of Tragedy*, p. 53.

62. Susan Sontag, *On Photography* (Harmondsworth: Penguin, 1977), pp. 9–16.
63. Styan, *Shakespeare Revolution*, p. 8.

Part II: Cycles

1. Bernard Levin, *Sunday Times*, 24 April 1978.
2. See E. M. W. Tillyard, *Shakespeare's History Plays* (London: Chatto and Windus, 1944); and Lily B. Campbell, *Shakespeare's Histories: Mirrors of Elizabethan Policy* (San Marino, Calif.: Huntingdon Library, 1947).
3. See John Dover Wilson and T. C. Worsley, *Shakespeare's Histories at Stratford 1951* (London: Max Reinhardt, 1952); Richard David, 'Shakespeare's history plays: epic or drama?', *Shakespeare Survey 6* (1953), pp. 129–39; Graham Holderness, *Shakespeare Recycled: The Making of Historical Drama* (Hemel Hempstead: Harvester Wheatsheaf, 1992), pp. 211–20; and Scott McMillin, *Shakespeare in Performance: Henry IV, Part One* (Manchester: Manchester University Press, 1991), pp. 35–51.
4. See David Addenbrooke, *The Royal Shakespeare Company: The Peter Hall Years* (London: William Kimber, 1974), pp. 126–9; Sally Beaumann, *The Royal Shakespeare Company: A History of Ten Decades* (Oxford: Oxford University Press, 1982), pp. 267–72.
5. Continuing attention is ensured partly because the production was televised by the BBC and its script has passed into print: see John Barton and Peter Hall, *The Wars of the Roses* (London: BBC Books, 1970). Within the growing body of writing documenting productions of the histories, the cycle crops up in Ralph Berry, *Changing Styles in Shakespeare* (London: Allen and Unwin, 1981); T. F. Wharton, *Text and Performance: Henry the Fourth Parts 1 and 2* (Basingstoke: Macmillan, 1983); Julie Hankey (ed.), *Plays in Performance: Richard III*, 2nd edn (Bristol: Bristol Classical Press, 1988); Hugh M. Richmond, *Shakespeare in Performance: King Richard III* (Manchester: Manchester University Press, 1989); and Scott McMillin, *Shakespeare in Performance: Henry IV, Part One* (Manchester: Manchester University Press, 1991). For recent editions of the plays which take account of the cycle, see Michael Hattaway (ed.), *The New Cambridge Shakespeare: The First Part of King Henry VI* (Cambridge: Cambridge University Press, 1991); *The New Cambridge Shakespeare: The Second Part of King Henry VI*

(Cambridge: Cambridge University Press, 1992); and *The New Cambridge Shakespeare: The Third Part of King Henry VI* (Cambridge: Cambridge University Press, 1993).

6. *The Times*, 16 April 1964.
7. Ronald Bryden, *New Statesman*, 24 April 1964.
8. Robert Speaight, 'Shakespeare in Britain', *Shakespeare Quarterly*, 15 (1964), p. 387.
9. Gareth Lloyd Evans, 'Shakespeare, the twentieth century and "Behaviourism" ', *Shakespeare Survey 20* (1967), p. 139.
10. Charles Marowitz, *Confessions of a Counterfeit Critic* (London: Methuen, 1973), p. 81.
11. *The Times*, 21 August 1963.
12. Bryden, *New Statesman*, 24 April 1964.
13. Quoted in Michael Coveney, 'Terry Hands, Adrian Noble and Peter Hall, masters of the RSC talk theatre', *Observer*, 28 June 1992.
14. Quoted in Frank Cox, 'Towards a theatre of ritual: an interview with Peter Hall', *Plays and Players*, May 1964.
15. Kenneth Tynan, *Observer*, 2 September 1956.
16. See Christopher J. McCullough, 'From Brecht to Brechtian: estrangement and appropriation', in Graham Holderness (ed.), *The Politics of Theatre and Drama* (London: Macmillan, 1992), pp. 120–33.
17. J. C. Trewin, *Birmingham Post*, 16 April 1964.
18. Bernard Levin, *Daily Mail*, 18 July 1963.
19. John Bury, 'The set', in Barton and Hall, *Wars of the Roses*, p. 236.
20. Speaight, 'Shakespeare in Britain', p. 381.
21. Barton and Hall, *Wars of the Roses*, p. x.
22. *Ibid.*, p. xii.
23. See Jan Kott, *Shakespeare Our Contemporary*, trans. Boleslaw Taborski, 2nd edn (London: Methuen, 1967), pp. 3–46.
24. See Alan Sinfield, 'Royal Shakespeare: theatre and the making of ideology', in Jonathan Dollimore and Alan Sinfield (eds), *Political Shakespeare: New Essays in Cultural Materialism* (Manchester: Manchester University Press, 1985); and Jonathan Dollimore and Alan Sinfield, 'History and ideology: the instance of *Henry V*', in John Drakakis (ed.) *Alternative Shakespeares* (London: Methuen, 1985), pp. 206–27.
25. Bryden, *New Statesman*, 24 April 1964.
26. Gerald Fay, *Guardian*, 21 August 1963.
27. Bryden, *New Statesman*, 24 April 1964.
28. L. C. Knights, *Drama and Society in the Age of Jonson* (London:

Chatto and Windus, 1937). See also Francis Mulhern, *The Moment of 'Scrutiny'* (London: New Left Books, 1979).

29. Bryden, *New Statesman*, 24 April 1964.
30. Harold Hobson, *Sunday Times*, 21 July 1963.
31. Robert Speaight, 'Shakespeare in Britain', *Shakespeare Quarterly*, 14 (1963), p. 431.
32. John Russell Brown, 'Three kinds of Shakespeare: 1964 productions at London, Stratford-upon-Avon and Edinburgh', *Shakespeare Survey 18* (1965), p. 149.
33. See Alan Sinfield, 'The theatre and its audiences' in Sinfield (ed.), *Society and Literature 1945–1970* (London: Methuen, 1983), pp. 184–8.
34. Ronald Bryden, 'According to Kott', *Spectator*, 19 February 1965.
35. See Sinfield, 'Royal Shakespeare'; Christopher McCullough, 'The Cambridge connection: towards a materialist theatre practice', in Graham Holderness (ed.), *The Shakespeare Myth* (Manchester: Manchester University Press, 1988), pp. 112–21.
36. For detailed discussions of Barton's adaptation, see Barbara Hodgon, '*The Wars of the Roses*: scholarship speaks on the stage', *Deutsche Shakespeare-Gesellschaft West Jahrbuch 1972*, pp. 170–84; and G. K. Hunter, 'The Royal Shakespeare Company plays *Henry VI*', *Renaissance Drama*, 9 (1978), pp. 91–108.
37. Barton and Hall, *Wars of the Roses*, p. vii.
38. *Ibid.*, p. xiv.
39. *Ibid.*, p. xi.
40. *Ibid.*, p. xviii.
41. *Ibid.*, p. 77.
42. *Ibid.*, p. xviii.
43. *Ibid.*, p. xxiv.
44. *Ibid.*, p. 14.
45. *Ibid.*, p. x.
46. Frank Cox, *Plays and Players*, October 1964.
47. *The Times*, 24 August 1964.
48. See Michael L. Greenwald, *Directions by Indirections: John Barton of the Royal Shakespeare Company* (Newark: University of Delaware Press, 1986).
49. Quoted in Addenbrooke, *Royal Shakespeare Company*, p. 182.
50. Quoted in Ronald Hayman, 'Terry Hands', in *Playback* (London: Davis-Poynter, 1973), p. 89.
51. Quoted in Lucy Hughes-Hallet, 'The Geometry of Necessity', *NOW!*, 31 October 1980.
52. Irving Wardle, *The Times*, 25 March 1975.

53. John Elsom, *The Listener*, 3 July 1975.
54. *Ibid.*
55. Irving Wardle, *The Times*, 24 April 1975.
56. W. Stephen Gilbert, *Plays and Players*, July 1975.
57. Quoted in Christopher McCullough, 'Terry Hands interview', in Holderness (ed.), *Shakespeare Myth*, p. 123.
58. Sally Beaumann (ed.), *The Royal Shakespeare Company's Centenary Production of Henry V* (Oxford: Pergamon Press, 1976), p. 16.
59. Quoted in Beaumann, *Royal Shakespeare Company*, p. 339.
60. Quoted in Homer D. Swander, 'The rediscovery of *Henry VI*', *Shakespeare Quarterly*, 29 (1978), p. 149.
61. *Ibid.*, p. 149.
62. Hunter, 'The RSC plays *Henry VI*', p. 105.
63. David Daniell, 'Opening up the text: Shakespeare's *Henry VI* plays in performance', in James Redmond (ed.), *Themes in Drama 1: Drama and Society* (Cambridge: Cambridge University Press, 1979), p. 252.
64. Quoted in Swander, 'Rediscovery', p. 150.
65. *Ibid.*, pp. 149–50.
66. *Ibid.*, p. 150.
67. Sally Emerson, *Plays and Players*, September 1977.
68. Irving Wardle, *The Times*, 15 July 1977.
69. Benedict Nightingale, *New Statesman*, 22 July 1977.
70. Bernard Levin, *Sunday Times*, 24 April 1978.
71. Quoted in 'Terry Hands in interview on Henry VI', in Simon Trussler (ed.), *Royal Shakespeare Company 1978* (Stratford: RSC/TQ Publications, 1979), p. 57.
72. *Ibid.*, p. 57.
73. Michael Coveney, *Financial Times*, 14 July 1977.
74. Daniell, 'Opening up the text', p. 266.
75. Levin, *Sunday Times*, 24 April 1978.
76. Colin Chambers, *Morning Star*, 14 March 1978.
77. Dick Hebdige, *Subculture: The Meaning of Style* (London: Methuen, 1979), p. 27.
78. Quoted in McCullough, 'Terry Hands interview', p. 124.
79. Michael Billington, 'The RSC betrayal', *Guardian*, 13 February 1990.
80. Quoted in Coveney, 'Masters of the RSC', *Observer*, 28 June 1992.
81. Robert Smallwood, '*Henry IV, Parts 1 and 2* at the Barbican Centre', *Critical Quarterly*, 25 (1983), p. 15.
82. Michael Coveney, *Financial Times*, 11 June 1982.

83. Michael Billington, *Guardian*, 11 June 1982.

84. Smallwood, '*Henry IV, Parts 1 and 2*', p. 15.

85. Billington, *Guardian*, 11 June 1982.

86. Wharton, *Henry IV*, pp. 49–51.

87. Nicholas Shrimpton, 'Shakespeare performances in Stratford-upon-Avon and London, 1981–2', *Shakespeare Survey 36* (1983), p. 153.

88. Benedict Nightingale, *New Statesman*, 18 June 1982.

89. *Ibid.*

90. See Donald Horne, *The Great Museum: The Re-presentation of History* (London: Verso, 1984); and Robert Hewison, *The Heritage Industry: Britain in a Climate of Decline* (London: Methuen, 1987).

91. See Simon Reade, *Cheek by Jowl: Ten Years of Celebration* (Bath: Absolute Classics, 1991).

92. See Isobel Armstrong, 'Thatcher's Shakespeare?', *Textual Practice*, 3 (1989), pp. 1–14; Michael Bogdanov and Michael Pennington, *The English Shakespeare Company: The Story of 'The Wars of the Roses', 1986–1989* (London: Nick Hern Books, 1990); Lois Potter, 'Recycling the early histories: "The Wars of the Roses" and "The Plantagenets" ', *Shakespeare Survey 43* (1991), pp. 171–81; Andrew Jarvis and Stephen Phillips, 'Telling the story: Shakespeare's histories in performance', *New Theatre Quarterly*, no. 23 (1990), pp. 207–14; and McMillin, *Henry IV, Part One*, pp. 106–22.

93. William Shakespeare, *The Plantagenets* (London: Faber and Faber, 1989).

94. *Ibid.*, p. xii.

95. *Ibid.*, p. xii.

96. Quoted in Neil Taylor, 'Room at the top', *Plays International*, March 1988.

97. *Plantagenets*, p. xiii.

98. *Ibid.*, p. x.

99. Robert Gore Langdon, 'The Plantagenets', *Plays and Players*, October 1988.

100. Charles Wood, *Tumbledown* (Harmondsworth: Penguin, 1987).

101. *Plantagenets*, p. xii.

102. *Ibid.*, p. xiii.

103. *Ibid.*, p. xiv.

104. *Ibid.*, p. xv.

105. *Ibid.*, p. xv.

106. Richmond, *Shakespeare in Performance: King Richard III*, p. 19.

107. *Plantagenets*, p. xii.
108. Quoted in Langdon, 'The Plantagenets'.
109. *Plantagenets*, pp. xii–xiii.
110. *Plantagenets*, p. 85.
111. Paul Taylor, *Independent*, 24 October 1988.
112. Christopher Edwards, *Spectator*, 5 November 1988.
113. Michael Ratcliffe, *Observer*, 30 October 1988.
114. The portrayal of Margaret irresistibly reminds me of the
    sympathetic representation of her namesake in Ian Curteis's
    unproduced, right-wing television drama-documentary, *The
    Falklands Play* (London: Hutchinson, 1987). I am thinking in
    particular of the parallel between this scene and her reaction to
    the sinking of the *HMS Sheffield* as it is portrayed in Curteis's
    play:

    > NOTT (quietly): The *Sheffield*'s been hit. We think by an
    > Exocet. There may be a lot of casualties.

    > *The PM says nothing. Her hands clench and unclench. She
    > arches her head back and the tears silently flood down her face.*

    See Derek Paget, 'Oh what a lovely post-modern war: drama
    and the Falklands', in Holderness (ed.), *Politics of Theatre and
    Drama*, pp. 154–79.
115. *Plantagenets*, p. x.
116. *Ibid.*, p. x.
117. *Ibid.*, p. xi.
118. *Ibid.*, p. 43.
119. Ratcliffe, *Observer*, 30 October 1988.
120. *Plantagenets*, p. xv.
121. Charles Osborne, *Daily Telegraph*, 24 October 1988.
122. Lyn Gardner, *City Limits*, 10 November 1988.

Part III: Heroes and Villains

1. See Timothy O'Brien, 'Designing a Shakespeare play: *Richard
   II*', *Deutsche Shakespeare-Gesellschaft West Jahrbuch 1974*, pp.
   111–20; James Stredder, 'John Barton's production of *Richard II*
   at Stratford-on-Avon, 1973', *Deutsche Shakespeare-Gesellschaft
   West Jahrbuch 1976*, pp. 23–42; Stanley Wells, *Royal Shakespeare: Four Major Productions at Stratford-upon-Avon* (Manchester: Manchester University Press, 1977); Richard David,
   Shakespeare in the Theatre (Cambridge: Cambridge University

Press, 1978); Miriam Gilbert, '*Richard II* at Stratford: role-playing as metaphor', in Philip C. McGuire and David A. Samuelson (eds), *Shakespeare: The Theatrical Dimension* (New York: AMS Press, 1979), pp. 85–101; Helen Gardner, 'Shakespeare in the directors' theatre', in *In Defence of the Imagination* (Oxford: Clarendon Press, 1982); Michael L. Greenwald, *Directions by Indirections: John Barton of the Royal Shakespeare Company* (Newark: University of Delaware Press, 1986); Malcolm Page, *Text and Performance: Richard II* (London: Macmillan, 1987); Liisa Hakola, *In One Person Many People: The Image of the King in Three RSC Productions of William Shakespeare's King Richard II* (Helsinki: Suomalainen Tiedeakatemia, 1988); and Margaret Shewring, *Shakespeare in Performance: Richard II* (Manchester: Manchester University Press, 1993).

2. O'Brien, 'Designing a Shakespeare play', pp. 114–18.
3. Ernst H. Kantorowicz, *The King's Two Bodies* (Princeton: Princeton University Press, 1957). See also Marie Axton, *The Queen's Two Bodies: Drama and the Elizabethan Succession* (London: Royal Historical Society, 1977).
4. Anne Barton, 'The king's two bodies', RSC Programme for *Richard II*, 1973, p. 13.
5. *Ibid.*, p. 14.
6. Anne Righter (later Barton), *Shakespeare and the Idea of the Play* (London: Chatto and Windus, 1962; reprinted Harmondsworth: Penguin, 1967).
7. See James L. Winny, *The Player King: A Theme of Shakespeare's Histories* (London: Chatto and Windus, 1968); James L. Calderwood, *Shakespearean Metadrama* (Minneapolis: University of Minnesota Press, 1971); and *Metadrama in Shakespeare's Henriad* (Berkeley: University of California Press, 1979).
8. Robert Speaight, 'The Stratford-upon-Avon season', *Shakespeare Quarterly*, 24 (1973), p. 400.
9. John Elsom, *The Listener*, 19 April 1973.
10. Benedict Nightingale, *New Statesman*, 20 April 1973.
11. Wells, *Royal Shakespeare*, p. 65.
12. Peter Hall, 'Shakespeare and the modern director', in John Goodwin (ed.), *Royal Shakespeare Theatre Company 1960–63* (London: Max Reinhardt, 1964), p. 41.
13. Quoted in Stredder, 'Barton's *Richard II*', p. 29.
14. See for example Peter Ansorge, *Plays and Players*, June 1973.
15. Peter Thomson, 'Shakespeare straight and crooked: a review of

the 1973 season at Stratford', *Shakespeare Survey 27* (1974), p. 146.

16. Ansorge, *Plays and Players*, June 1973.
17. Gilbert, '*Richard II* at Stratford', p. 87.
18. Hakola, *In One Person*, p. 87.
19. Stredder, 'Barton's *Richard II*', p. 30.
20. Roland Barthes, 'The death of the author', in Stephen Heath (ed.) *Image – Music – Text* (Glasgow: Fontana, 1977), p. 147.
21. Anne Barton, 'The king's two bodies', p. 14.
22. Speaight, 'The Stratford-upon-Avon season', p. 400.
23. Benedict Nightingale, *New Statesman*, 20 April 1973.
24. Ansorge, *Plays and Players*, June 1973.
25. Nightingale, *New Statesman*, 20 April 1973.
26. Quoted in Eileen Totten, 'A pair of kings: Richard Pasco and Ian Richardson in interview', *Plays and Players*, June 1973, p. 28.
27. *Ibid.*, p. 28.
28. John Barton, *Playing Shakespeare* (London: Methuen, 1984), p. 45.
29. Nightingale, *New Statesman*, 20 April 1973.
30. Thomson, 'Shakespeare straight and crooked', p. 152.
31. Ansorge, *Plays and Players*, June 1973.
32. Gilbert, '*Richard II* at Stratford', p. 91.
33. This was not unique to this production: during the twentieth century, productions of *Richard II* have frequently set Richard against Bolingbroke in terms of their implied sexualities. The tradition seems to have been established in 1899 by F. R. Benson's rather Wildean portrait of 'the capable and faithful artist in the same skin as the incapable and unfaithful king . . . a typical, a consummate artist' (C. E. Montague, 'F. R. Benson's *Richard II*', in Jeanne T. Newlin (ed.), *Richard II: Critical Essays*, New York and London: Garland, 1984, p. 108). Camp lyricism was also the keynote of the performances by John Gielgud at the Old Vic and Queen's theatre in the 1930s, and by Michael Redgrave at Stratford in 1951. In the wake of legislation partially decriminalising gay sex in Britain, and in the context of the post-Stonewall politicisation of the gay community, Ian McKellan played the king in the 1968 Prospect Theatre production alongside Marlowe's *Edward II*; see Michael Billington, *The Modern Actor* (London: Hamish Hamilton, 1973); and Page, *Richard II*.
34. Wells, *Royal Shakespeare*, p. 80.
35. David, *Shakespeare in the Theatre*, p. 170.

36. Alan Sinfield, *Literature, Politics and Culture in Postwar Britain* (Oxford: Blackwell, 1989), p. 279.

37. John Elsom, *Listener*, 19 April 1973.

38. See Sally Beaumann (ed.), *The Royal Shakespeare Company's Centenary Production of Henry V* (Oxford: Pergamon Press, 1976) and *The Royal Shakespeare Company: A History of Ten Decades* (Oxford: Oxford University Press, 1982), pp. 325–9.

39. Peter Roberts, *Plays and Players*, August 1964.

40. Gareth Lloyd Evans, 'Shakespeare, the twentieth century and "Behaviourism" ', *Shakespeare Survey 20* (1967), p. 139.

41. Ronald Bryden, *New Statesman*, 12 June 1964.

42. John Arden, letter to the *New Statesman*, 19 June 1964.

43. Trevor Nunn, 'Introduction' in Beaumann (ed.), *RSC Henry V*, p. 6.

44. Charles Lewsen, *The Times*, 9 April 1975.

45. Harold Hobson, *Sunday Times*, 13 April 1975.

46. Herbert Kretzmer, *Daily Express*, 9 April 1975.

47. W. Stephen Gilbert, *Plays and Players*, June 1975.

48. Benedict Nightingale, *New Statesman*, 18 April 1975.

49. Beaumann, *Royal Shakespeare Company*, p. 326.

50. Ronald Bryden, *RSC Henry V*, p. 247.

51. Hands, *RSC Henry V*, p. 16.

52. *Ibid.*, p. 31.

53. Peter Brook, *The Empty Space* (Harmondsworth: Penguin, 1968), p. 109.

54. Hands, *RSC Henry V*, p. 31.

55. Lewsen, *The Times*, 9 April 1975.

56. Hands, *RSC Henry V*, p. 31.

57. *Ibid.*, p. 32.

58. *Ibid.*, p. 159.

59. *Ibid.*, p. 21.

60. Nightingale, *New Statesman*, 18 April 1975.

61. Kretzmer, *Daily Express*, 9 April 1975.

62. Lewsen, *The Times*, 9 April 1975.

63. Kenneth Hurren, *Spectator*, 19 April 1975.

64. Nightingale, *New Statesman*, 18 April 1975.

65. The production's debt to Olivier's film was considerable. The music (composed by Guy Woolfenden) was an obvious pastiche of William Walton's score; and the device of moving progressively into an illusionistic mode can be seen as a reworking of Olivier's device of starting the action in the Globe Theatre. Tracing the influence of Olivier's version on later stage productions, Anthony Davies suggests that Hands 'tried to achieve the

spatial effects of the film in a different way . . . by suggesting a movement from one level of reality to another within the theatre' (*Filming Shakespeare's Plays: The Adaptations of Laurence Olivier, Orson Welles, Peter Brook and Akira Kurosawa*, Cambridge: Cambridge University Press, 1988, p. 26.).

66. David, *Shakespeare in the Theatre*, p. 213.
67. Irving Wardle, *The Times*, 21 January 1976.
68. Hobson, *Sunday Times*, 13 April 1975.
69. Hands, *RSC Henry V*, p. 15.
70. *Ibid.*, p. 54.
71. Nightingale, *New Statesman*, 18 April 1975.
72. Hobson, *Sunday Times*, 13 April 1975.
73. Hands, *RSC Henry V*, p. 25.
74. Nightingale, *New Statesman*, 18 April 1975.
75. Wardle, *The Times*, 21 January 1976.
76. Hobson, *Sunday Times*, 13 April 1975.
77. Hands, *RSC Henry V*, p. 15.
78. Ralph Berry, *Changing Styles in Shakespeare* (London: Allen and Unwin, 1981), p. 78.
79. Graham Holderness, *Shakespeare Recycled: The Making of Historical Drama* (Hemel Hempstead: Harvester Wheatsheaf, 1992), p. 201.
80. Nicholas Shrimpton, 'Shakespeare performances in Stratford-upon-Avon and London, 1983–4', *Shakespeare Survey 38* (1985), p. 204.
81. Holderness, *Shakespeare Recycled*, p. 192.
82. Michael Ratcliffe, *Observer*, 1 April 1984.
83. Kenneth Hurren, *Mail on Sunday*, 1 April 1984.
84. Sheridan Morley, *Punch*, 29 May 1984.
85. Michael Billington, *Guardian*, 28 March 1984.
86. See Holderness, *Shakespeare Recycled*, pp 190–210; Peter Donaldson, 'Taking on Shakespeare: Kenneth Branagh's *Henry V*', *Shakespeare Quarterly*, 42 (1991), pp. 60–71; Chris Fitter, 'A tale of two Branaghs: *Henry V*, ideology, and the Mekong Agincourt', in Ivo Kamps (ed.), *Shakespeare Left and Right* (New York and London: Routledge, 1991), pp. 259–70.
87. See Kenneth Branagh, *Beginning* (London: Chatto and Windus, 1989). See also Curteis Breight, 'Branagh and the prince, or a "royal fellowship of death" ', *Critical Quarterly*, 33 (1991), pp. 95–111.
88. Kenneth Branagh, 'Henry V', in Russell Jackson and Robert Smallwood (eds), *Players of Shakespeare 2* (Cambridge: Cambridge University Press, 1988), p. 98.

89. *Ibid.*, p. 98.
90. Michael Billington, *Guardian*, 28 March 1984.
91. John Barber, *Daily Telegraph*, 29 March 1984.
92. Ratcliffe, *Observer*, 1 April 1984.
93. Hurren, *Mail on Sunday*, 1 April 1984.
94. Rosemary Say, *Sunday Telegraph*, 1 April 1984.
95. Jack Tinker, *Daily Mail*, 29 March 1984.
96. Paul Allen, *New Statesman*, 6 April 1984.
97. Ratcliffe, *Observer*, 1 April 1984.
98. Clive Hirschorn, *Sunday Express*, 19 May 1985.
99. Beatrix Campbell, *Iron Ladies: Why do Women Vote Tory?* (London: Virago, 1987), p. 233.
100. Quoted in Robert Gore Langton 'Romancing the Stage', *Plays and Players*, April 1986.
101. Shrimpton, 'Shakespeare performances in Stratford-upon-Avon and London, 1983–4', p. 207.
102. Michael Billington, *Guardian*, 20 June 1984.
103. Robert Hewison, *The Heritage Industry: Britain in a Climate of Decline* (London: Methuen, 1987), p. 9.
104. Antony Sher, *Year of the King* (London: Methuen, 1986). See also Julie Hankey (ed.), *Plays in Performance: Richard III*, 2nd edn (Bristol: Bristol Classical Press, 1988); Richmond, *Shakespeare in Performance: King Richard III* (Manchester: Manchester University Press, 1989); R. Chris Hassell, Jr, 'Context and charisma: The Sher–Alexander *Richard III* and its reviewers', *Shakespeare Quarterly*, 36 (1985), pp. 630–43; and S. P. Cerasano, 'Churls just wanna have fun: reviewing *Richard III*', *Shakespeare Quarterly*, 36 (1985), pp. 618–29.
105. Sher, *Year of the King*, p. 18.
106. *Ibid.*, p. 27.
107. *Ibid.*, p. 28.
108. *Ibid.*, p. 28.
109. *Ibid.*, p. 38.
110. *Ibid.*, p. 117.
111. *Ibid.*, p. 130.
112. Roger Warren, 'Shakespeare at Stratford-upon-Avon', *Shakespeare Quarterly*, 36 (1985), p. 83.
113. Michael Billington, *Guardian*, 20 June 1984.
114. Cerasano, 'Reviewing *Richard III*', p. 627.
115. *Ibid.*, p. 628.
116. Jack Tinker, *Daily Mail*, 21 June 1984.
117. Eric Shorter, *Daily Telegraph*, 21 June 1984.
118. Billington, *Guardian*, 20 June 1984.

119. Sher's superhuman energy and virtuosity can be seen to mark the apotheosis of a heroic tradition in modern Shakespearean acting, which subdues both spectators and fellow-performers to a state of abject subservience; as such, it represents the condition of stardom to which the majority of Shakespearean performers aspire. For a fierce critique of the 'terroristic' excesses of modern Shakespearean acting, see Martin Buzacott, *The Death of the Actor: Shakespeare on Page and Stage* (London: Routledge, 1991).
120. Hassell, 'Context and charisma', p. 642.
121. Michael Coveney, *Financial Times*, 1 May 1985.
122. Suzie Mackenzie, *Time Out*, 9 May 1985.
123. Carole Woddis, *City Limits*, 10 May 1985.
124. Coveney, *Financial Times*, 1 May 1985.
125. Eric Shorter, *Daily Telegraph*, 21 June 1984.
126. Michael Ratcliffe, *Observer*, 24 June 1984.
127. Deborah Cameron and Elizabeth Frazer, *The Lust to Kill: A Feminist Investigation of Sexual Murder* (London: Polity Press, 1987), p. 163.
128. See Cameron and Frazer, *The Lust to Kill*; and Nicole Ward Jouve, *The Streetcleaner: The Yorkshire Ripper Case on Trial* (London: Marion Boyars, 1986).
129. See Gordon Burn, *Somebody's Husband, Somebody's Son: The Story of the Yorkshire Ripper* (London: Heinemann, 1984).
130. Sher, *Year of the King*, p. 209.
131. *Ibid.*, p. 209.
132. Ward Jouve, *The Streetcleaner*. p. 35.
133. Cameron and Frazer, *Lust to Kill*, p. 166.
134. Sher, *Year of the King*, p. 130.

Part IV: Shakespeare Bastardised

1. See Muriel St Clare Byrne, 'The Shakespeare seasons at the Old Vic, 1956–7, and Stratford-upon-Avon, 1957', *Shakespeare Quarterly*, 8 (1957), pp. 482–5.
2. Colin Chambers, *Other Spaces: New Theatre and the RSC* (London: Methuen, 1980), p. 28.
3. Peter Thomson, 'A necessary theatre: the Royal Shakespeare Company Season 1970 reviewed', *Shakespeare Survey 24* (1971), p. 117.
4. See 'The modern theatre is the epic theatre', in John Willett (ed.), *Brecht on Theatre* (London: Methuen, 1964), pp. 33–42.
5. E. M. W. Tillyard, *Shakespeare's History Plays* (London: Chatto and Windus, 1944), pp. 221–39; see also E. A. J. Honigman

(ed.), *The Arden Shakespeare: King John* (London: Methuen, 1954), pp. lix–lxxiii.

6. Anon, *The Troublesome Reign of King John* (1591), in G. R. Bullough (ed.), *Narrative and Dramatic Sources of Shakespeare*, vol. 4 (London: Routledge & Kegan Paul, 1960).

7. On the stage history of *King John*, See A. R. Braunmiller (ed.), *The Oxford Shakespeare: The Life and Death of King John* (Oxford; Oxford University Press, 1989), pp. 79–93; and L. A. Beaurline (ed.), *The New Cambridge Shakespeare: King John* (Cambridge: Cambridge University Press, 1990), pp. 1–23.

8. John Barton, RSC Programme for *King John*, 1974.

9. *Ibid.*.

10. RSC Promptbook for *King John*, 1974, p. 1.

11. *Ibid.*, p. 3.

12. *Ibid.*, p. 14.

13. *Ibid.*, p. 111.

14. Irving Wardle, *The Times*, 21 March 1974.

15. *King John* Promptbook, p. 2.

16. Benedict Nightingale, *New Statesman*, 29 March 1974.

17. Peter Thomson, 'The smallest season: the Royal Shakespeare Company at Stratford, 1974', *Shakespeare Survey 28* (1975), p. 138.

18. *King John* Promptbook, p. 81.

19. E. H. Carr, *What is History?* (Harmondsworth: Penguin, 1964), p. 45.

20. *King John* Promptbook, p. 82.

21. *Ibid.*, p. 30.

22. *Ibid.*, p. 30.

23. Thomson, 'The smallest season', p. 138.

24. *King John* Promptbook, p. 80.

25. *Ibid.*, p. 25.

26. Barton, *King John* Programme.

27. *Ibid.*

28. Brecht's *Coriolan* is found in John Willett and Ralph Mannheim (eds), Bertolt Brecht: *Collected Plays*, vol.9 (New York: Vintage Books, 1973); see also 'Study of the first scene of Shakespeare's Coriolanus', in Willett (ed.), *Brecht on Theatre*, pp. 252–65. Edward Bond's *Lear* (London: Methuen, 1972) was first performed at the Royal Court in 1971; Arden's *Left-Handed Liberty* (London: Methuen, 1965) was performed at the Mermaid Theatre in 1965. For discussions of modern reconstitutions of Shakespeare, see Ruby Cohn, *Modern Shakespeare Offshoots* (Princeton: Princeton University Press, 1977); Michael Scott,

Shakespeare and the Modern Dramatist (London: Macmillan, 1988); and Alan Sinfield, 'Making space: appropriation and confrontation in recent British plays', in Graham Holderness (ed.), *The Shakespeare Myth* (Manchester: Manchester University Press, 1988), pp. 128–44.

29. Robert Cushman, *Observer*, 24 March 1974.
30. Thomson, 'The smallest season', p. 138.
31. Garry O'Connor, *Plays and Players*, May 1974.
32. *King John* Promptbook, p. 85.
33. *Ibid.*, p. 85.
34. *Ibid.*, p. 112.
35. Michael Billington, *Guardian*, 21 March 1974.
36. Irving Wardle, *The Times*, 10 January 1975.
37. Herbert Kretzmer, *Daily Express*, 21 March 1974.
38. Cushman, *Observer*, 24 March 1974.
39. Billington, *Guardian*, 21 March 1974.
40. John Elsom, *Listener*, 28 March 1974.
41. Nightingale, *New Statesman*, 29 March 1974.
42. Robert Speaight, 'Shakespeare in Britain', *Shakespeare Quarterly*, 25 (1974), p. 389.
43. Thomson, 'The smallest season', p. 138.
44. R. L. Smallwood, 'Shakespeare unbalanced: the Royal Shakespeare Company's *King John*, 1974–5', *Deutsche Shakespeare-Gesellschaft West Jahrbuch 1976*, pp. 98–9.
45. Barton, *King John* Programme.
46. T. S. Eliot, '*Ulysses*, Order and Myth', in Frank Kermode (ed.), *Selected Prose of T. S. Eliot* (London: Faber and Faber, 1975), p. 177.
47. Chambers, *Other Spaces.*, pp. 47–8.
48. Walter Donohue (ed.), *The Warehouse: A Writer's Theatre*, Dartington Theatre Papers, 3rd series, no. 8 (1979), p. 6.
49. Benedict Nightingale, *New Statesman*, 11 January 1980.
50. Clare Colvin, *Evening News*, 4 January 1980.
51. Victoria Radin, *Observer*, 4 April 1982.
52. Richard Findlater, *Plays and Players*, May 1982.
53. Quoted in Christopher Warman, '*Henry VIII* makes a rare and risky appearance', *The Times*, 11 June 1983.
54. A. R. Humphreys (ed.), *The New Penguin Shakespeare: King Henry VIII* (Harmondsworth: Penguin, 1971), p. 19.
55. See John Margeson (ed.), *The New Cambridge Shakespeare: King Henry VIII* (Cambridge: Cambridge University Press, 1990), pp. 48–59.

56. Robert Speaight, *Shakespeare on the Stage* (London: Collins, 1973), p. 163.
57. For accounts of Terence Gray's production, see J. L. Styan, *The Shakespeare Revolution: Criticism and Performance in the Twentieth Century* (Cambridge: Cambridge University Press, 1977), pp. 152–3; and Norman Marshall, *The Other Theatre* (London: John Lehmann, 1977), pp. 53–71; on Tyrone Guthrie's, see Muriel St Clare Byrne, 'A Stratford production: *Henry VIII*', *Shakespeare Survey 3* (1950), pp. 120–9.
58. R. A. Foakes (ed.), *The Arden Shakespeare: King Henry VIII* (London: Methuen, 1957), p. lxi.
59. Trevor Nunn, RSC Programme for *Henry VIII*, 1969.
60. Ronald Bryden, *Observer*, 12 October 1969.
61. RSC Promptbook for *Henry VIII*, 1969, p. 141.
62. Edward Bond, *Plays: Two* (London: Methuen, 1978), p. xi.
63. Quoted in Warman, '*Henry VIII*', *The Times*, 11 June 1983.
64. David Starkey, 'Duff King Hal', *History Today*, November 1983.
65. B. A. Young, *Financial Times*, 13 September 1984.
66. RSC Programme for *Henry VIII*, 1983.
67. Starkey, 'Duff King Hal'.
68. Simon Barker, 'Images of the sixteenth and seventeenth centuries as a history of the present', in Francis Barker *et al.* (eds), *Literature, Politics and Theory* (London: Methuen, 1986), p. 186.
69. Quoted in Warman, '*Henry VIII*', *The Times*, 11 June 1983.
70. R. H. Tawney, *Religion and the Rise of Capitalism* (Harmondsworth: Penguin, 1960).
71. Quoted in Judith Cook, *Directors' Theatre* (London: Hodder and Stoughton, 1989), p. 77.
72. David Edgar's *Destiny* (London: Methuen, 1976) was first staged at the RSC's Other Place in 1976.
73. Quoted in Cook, *Directors' Theatre*, p. 77.
74. See A. C. Sprague, *Shakespeare's Histories: Plays for the Stage* (London: Society for Theatre Research, 1964), p. 148.
75. RSC Promptbook for *Henry VIII*, 1983, p. 140.
76. *Ibid.*, p. 141.
77. Simon Trussler (ed.), *Royal Shakespeare Company 1983/84* (Stratford: RSC Publications, 1984), p. 19.
78. Robert Cushman, *Observer*, 19 June 1983.
79. Irving Wardle, *The Times*, 16 June 1983.
80. Warman, '*Henry VIII*', *The Times*, 11 June 1983.
81. Wardle, *The Times*, 16 June 1983.

82. See 'Exercises for acting schools' in Willett (ed.), *Brecht on Theatre*, p. 129.
83. Quoted in Christopher Warman, 'A massive majesty for the monster', *The Times*, 8 September 1983.
84. Cushman, *Observer*, 19 June 1983.
85. Francis King, *Sunday Telegraph*, 19 June 1983.
86. Roger Warren, 'Shakespeare in Stratford-upon-Avon and London, 1983', *Shakespeare Quarterly*, 34 (1983), p. 453.
87. Cushman, *Observer*, 19 June 1983.
88. Michael Billington, *Guardian*, 12 September 1984.
89. Benedict Nightingale, *New Statesman*, 24 June 1983.
90. Michael Billington, *Guardian*, 16 June 1983.
91. Cushman, *Observer*, 19 June 1983.
92. Warren, 'Shakespeare in Stratford-upon-Avon', p. 453.
93. Nightingale, *New Statesman*, 24 June 1983.
94. Quoted in Cook, *Directors' Theatre*, p. 77.
95. Nicholas de Jongh, *Mail on Sunday*, 19 June 1983.
96. Nicholas Shrimpton, 'Shakespeare performances in Stratford-upon-Avon and London, 1982–3', *Shakespeare Survey 37* (1984), pp. 171–2.
97. Steve Grant, *Observer*, 16 September 1984.
98. Jack Tinker, *Daily Mail*, 16 June 1983.
99. Billington, *Guardian*, 16 June 1983.
100. Christopher J. McCullough, 'From Brecht to Brechtian', in Graham Holderness (ed.), *The Politics of Theatre and Drama* (London: Macmillan, 1991), p. 129.
101. Chambers, *Other Spaces*, p. 22.
102. Quoted in Christopher J. McCullough, 'Terry Hands interview', in Holderness (ed.), *The Shakespeare Myth*, pp. 125–6.
103. Dympna Callaghan, 'Buzz Goodbody: directing for change', in Jean I. Marsden (ed.), *The Appropriation of Shakespeare: Post-Renaissance Reconstructions of the Works and Myth* (Hemel Hempstead: Harvester Wheatsheaf, 1991), pp. 163–81.
104. Quoted in the *Daily Telegraph*, 13 July 1973.
105. Michael Coveney, *Financial Times*, 19 May 1975.
106. Graham White, 'Direct action, dramatic action: theatre and situationist theory', *New Theatre Quarterly*, 36 (1993), p. 331.
107. Chambers, *Other Spaces*, p. 25.
108. *Ibid.*, p. 38.
109. Peter Holland, 'The RSC and Studio Shakespeare', *Essays in Criticism*, 32 (1982), p. 215.
110. *Ibid.*, p. 217.
111. Gareth Lloyd Evans, 'The RSC's *King Lear* and *Macbeth*',

Shakespeare Quarterly, 28 (1977), p. 194. For an extended discussion of Nunn's production, see John Turner, *Macbeth* (Buckingham: Open University Press, 1992).

112. Chambers, *Other Spaces*, p. 42.
113. Michael Coveney, *Financial Times*, 9 August 1975.
114. Keith Brace, *Birmingham Post*, 8 August 1975.
115. Eric Shorter, *Daily Telegraph*, 8 August 1975.
116. Eric Shorter, *Daily Telegraph*, 9 October 1975.
117. Quoted in Cook, *Directors' Theatre*, p. 105.
118. *Ibid.*, p. 104.
119. *Ibid.*, p. 102.
120. Quoted in Debbie Wolfe, 'Alive and kicking', *Drama*, no. 158 (1985).
121. Paul Taylor, *Independent*, 12 May 1988.
122. Jim Hiley, *Listener*, 19 May 1988.
123. Taylor, *Independent*, 12 May 1988.
124. Nicholas Woodeson, 'Troublesome John', *Guardian*, 10 May 1988.
125. Peter Kemp, *Independent*, 4 May 1989.
126. Edward Bond, 'Postcard to William Gaskill', quoted in Gregory Dark, 'Production Casebook No. 5: Edward Bond's 'Lear' at the Royal Court', *Theatre Quarterly*, 5 (1972), p. 22.
127. Taylor, *Independent*, 12 May 1988.
128. Michael Billington, *Guardian*, 12 May 1988.
129. *Ibid.*
130. Taylor, *Independent*, 12 May 1988.
131. Charles Osborne, *Daily Telegraph*, 30 May 1988.
132. Nicholas de Jongh, *Guardian*, 4 May 1989.
133. Irving Wardle, *The Times*, 12 May 1988.
134. de Jongh, *Guardian*, 4 May 1989.
135. Robert Smallwood, 'Shakespeare at Stratford-upon-Avon, 1988', *Shakespeare Quarterly*, 40 (1989), p. 93.
136. Taylor, *Independent*, 12 May 1988.
137. Smallwood, 'Shakespeare at Stratford', p. 93.
138. Hiley, *Listener*, 19 May 1988.
139. Wardle, *The Times*, 12 May 1988.
140. Kemp, *Independent*, 4 May 1989.
141. Michael Coveney, *Financial Times*, 12 May 1988.
142. Stanley Wells, 'Shakespeare performances in London and Stratford-upon-Avon, 1987–8', *Shakespeare Survey 42* (1990), p. 139.
143. Osborne, *Daily Telegraph*, 30 May 1988.
144. John Gross, *Sunday Telegraph*, 7 May 1989.

145. Milton Shulman, *Evening Standard*, 3 May 1989.
146. Smallwood, 'Shakespeare at Stratford', p. 94.

Conclusion

1. Robert Smallwood, 'Shakespeare at Stratford-upon-Avon, 1990', *Shakespeare Quarterly*, 42 (1991), p. 355.
2. *Ibid.*, p. 355.
3. Robert Smallwood, 'Shakespeare at Stratford-upon-Avon, 1991', *Shakespeare Quarterly*, 43 (1992), p. 341.
4. Robert Smallwood, 'Shakespeare at Stratford-upon-Avon, 1992', *Shakespeare Quarterly*, 44 (1993), p. 361.
5. Ralph Berry, *Changing Styles in Shakespeare* (London: Allen and Unwin, 1981), p. 2.

Bibliography

Addenbrooke, David, *The Royal Shakespeare Company: The Peter Hall Years* (London: William Kimber, 1974).

Arden, John, *Left-Handed Liberty* (London: Methuen, 1965).

Armstrong, Isobel, 'Thatcher's Shakespeare?', *Textual Practice*, 3 (1989), pp. 1–14.

Axton, Marie, *The Queen's Two Bodies: Drama and the Elizabethan Succession* (London: Royal Historical Society, 1977).

Barker, Francis, Peter Hulme and Margaret Iverson (eds), *Uses of History: Marxism, Postmodernism and the Renaissance* (Manchester: Manchester University Press, 1991).

Barker, Simon, 'Images of the sixteenth and seventeenth centuries as a history of the present', in Francis Barker, Peter Hulme, Margaret Iverson and Diana Loxley (eds), *Literature, Politics and Theory: Papers from the Essex Conference, 1976–84* (London: Methuen, 1986).

Barthes, Roland, 'The death of the author', in Stephen Heath (ed.), *Image – Music – Text* (Glasgow: Fontana, 1977).

Barton, John, *Playing Shakespeare* (London: Methuen, 1984).

Barton, John and Peter Hall, *The Wars of the Roses* (London: BBC Books, 1970).

Beaumann, Sally, *The Royal Shakespeare Company: A History of Ten Decades* (Oxford: Oxford University Press, 1982).

Beaumann, Sally (ed.), *The Royal Shakespeare Company's Centenary Production of Henry V* (Oxford: Pergamon Press, 1976).

Beaurline, L. A. (ed.), *The New Cambridge Shakespeare: King John* (Cambridge: Cambridge University Press, 1990).

Belsey, Catherine, *Critical Practice* (London: Methuen, 1980).

Belsey, Catherine, *The Subject of Tragedy: Identity and Difference in Renaissance Drama* (London: Methuen, 1985).

Berry, Cicely, *Voice and the Actor* (London: Harrap, 1973).

Berry, Cicely, *The Actor and his Text* (London: Harrap, 1987).

Berry, Ralph, *On Directing Shakespeare* (London: Croom Helm, 1977).

Berry, Ralph, *Changing Styles in Shakespeare* (London: Allen and Unwin, 1981).

Berry, Ralph, 'The reviewer as historian', *Shakespeare Quarterly*, 36 (1985), pp. 594–7.

Berry, Ralph, *Shakespeare in Performance* (London: Macmillan, 1993).

Bevington, David (ed.), *The Oxford Shakespeare: Henry IV, Part 1* (Oxford: The Clarendon Press, 1987).

Billington, Michael, *The Modern Actor* (London: Hamish Hamilton, 1973).

Bogdanov, Michael and Michael Pennington, *The English Shakespeare Company: The Story of 'The Wars of the Roses', 1986–1989* (London: Nick Hern Books, 1990).

Bond, Edward, *Plays: Two* (London: Methuen, 1978).

Branagh, Kenneth, *Beginning* (London: Chatto and Windus, 1989).

Braunmiller, A. R. (ed.), *The Oxford Shakespeare: The Life and Death of King John* (Oxford: Oxford University Press, 1989).

Breight, Curtis, 'Branagh and the prince, or a "royal fellowship of death" ', *Critical Quarterly*, 33 (1991), pp. 95–111.

Brockbank, Philip (ed.), *Players of Shakespeare: Essays in Shakespearean Performance* (Cambridge: Cambridge University Press, 1985).

Brook, Peter, *The Empty Space* (Harmondsworth: Penguin, 1968).

Brown, John Russell, 'The study and practice of Shakespeare production', *Shakespeare Survey 18* (1965), pp. 58–69.

Brown, John Russell, 'Three kinds of Shakespeare: 1964 productions at London, Stratford-upon-Avon and Edinburgh', *Shakespeare Survey 18* (1965), pp. 147–55.

Brown, John Russell, *Shakespeare's Plays in Performance* (London: Edward Arnold, 1966).

Brown, John Russell, 'English criticism of Shakespeare today', *Deutsche Shakespeare-Gesellschaft West Jahrbuch 1967*, pp. 175–93.

Brown, John Russell, *Free Shakespeare* (London: Heinemann, 1974).

Bullough, G. R. (ed.), *Narrative and Dramatic Sources of Shakespeare*, vols 3 & 4 (London: Routledge & Kegan Paul, 1960).

Burden, Dennis, 'Shakespeare's history plays: 1952–1983', *Shakespeare Survey 38* (1985), pp. 1–18.

Burn, Gordon, *Somebody's Husband, Somebody's Son: The Story of the Yorkshire Ripper* (London: Heinemann, 1986).

Buzacott, Martin, *The Death of the Actor: Shakespeare on Page and Stage* (London: Routledge, 1991).

Byrne, Muriel St Clare, 'A Stratford production: *Henry VIII*', *Shakespeare Survey 3* (1950), pp. 120–9.

Byrne, Muriel St Clare, 'The Shakespeare seasons at the Old Vic, 1956–7, and Stratford-upon-Avon, 1957', *Shakespeare Quarterly*, 8 (1957), pp. 482–5.

Calderwood, James L., *Shakespearean Metadrama* (Minneapolis: University of Minnesota Press, 1971).

Calderwood, James L., *Metadrama in Shakespeare's Henriad* (Berkeley: University of California Press, 1979).

Cameron, Deborah and Elizabeth Frazer, *The Lust to Kill: A Feminist Investigation of Sexual Murder* (London: Polity Press, 1987).

Campbell, Beatrix, *Iron Ladies: Why do Women Vote Tory?* (London: Virago, 1987).

Campbell, Lily B., *Shakespeare's Histories: Mirrors of Elizabethan Policy* (San Marino, Calif.: Huntingdon Library, 1947).

Cerasano, S. P., 'Churls just wanna have fun: reviewing *Richard III*', *Shakespeare Quarterly*, 36 (1985), pp. 118–29.

Chambers, Colin, *Other Spaces: New Theatre and the RSC* (London: Methuen, 1980).

Cohn, Ruby, *Modern Shakespeare Offshoots* (Princeton: Princeton University Press, 1977).

Cook, Judith, *Shakespeare's Players* (London: Harrap, 1983).

Cook, Judith, *Directors' Theatre* (London: Hodder and Stoughton, 1989).

Crosse, Gordon, *Shakespearean Playgoing 1890–1952* (London: A. R. Mowbray, 1953).

Curteis, Ian, *The Falklands Play* (London: Hutchinson, 1987).

Daniell, David, 'Opening up the text: Shakespeare's *Henry VI* plays in performance', in James Redmond (ed.), *Themes in Drama 1: Drama and Society* (Cambridge: Cambridge University Press, 1979).

Dark, Gregory, 'Production Casebook No. 5: Edward Bond's "Lear" at the Royal Court', *Theatre Quarterly*, no. 5 (1972), pp. 20–31.

David, Richard, 'Shakespeare's history plays: epic or drama?', *Shakespeare Survey 6* (1953), pp. 129–39.

David, Richard, 'Actors and scholars: a view of Shakespeare in the modern theatre', *Shakespeare Survey 12* (1959), pp. 76–87.

David, Richard, *Shakespeare in the Theatre* (Cambridge: Cambridge University Press, 1978).

Davies, Anthony, *Filming Shakespeare's Plays* (Cambridge: Cambridge University Press, 1988).

Dessen, Alan, 'Shakespeare's scripts and the modern director', *Shakespeare Survey 36* (1983), pp. 57–64.

Dessen, Alan, 'Reviewing Shakespeare for the record', *Shakespeare Quarterly*, 36 (1985), pp. 602–8.

Dollimore, Jonathan, *Radical Tragedy: Religion, Ideology and Power in the Drama of Shakespeare and His Contemporaries*, 2nd edn (Hemel Hempstead: Harvester Wheatsheaf, 1989).

Dollimore, Jonathan and Alan Sinfield (eds), *Political Shakespeare: New Essays in Cultural Materialism* (Manchester: Manchester University Press, 1985).

Donaldson, Peter, 'Taking on Shakespeare: Kenneth Branagh's *Henry V*', *Shakespeare Quarterly*, 42 (1991), pp. 60–71

Donohue, Walter (ed.), *The Warehouse: A Writer's Theatre*, Dartington Theatre Papers, 3rd series, no. 8 (1979).

Drakakis, John (ed.), *Alternative Shakespeares* (London: Methuen, 1985).

Eagleton, Terence, *Shakespeare and Society* (London: Chatto and Windus, 1967).

Eagleton, Terry, *William Shakespeare* (Oxford: Blackwell, 1986).

Elam, Keir, *The Semiotics of Theatre and Drama* (London: Methuen, 1980).

Elsom, John, *Postwar British Theatre* (London: Routledge & Kegan Paul, 1976).

Elsom, John (ed.), *Is Shakespeare Still Our Contemporary?* (London: Routledge, 1989).

Elsom, John, *Cold War Theatre* (London: Routledge, 1991).

Evans, Malcolm, *Signifying Nothing: Truth's True Contents in Shakespeare's Text* (Hemel Hempstead: Harvester Wheatsheaf, 1986).

Fitter, Chris, 'A tale of two Branaghs: *Henry V*, ideology, and the Mekong Agincourt', in Ivo Kamps (ed.), *Shakespeare Left and Right* (New York and London: Routledge, 1991).

Foakes, R. A. (ed.), *The Arden Shakespeare: King Henry the Eighth*, 3rd edn (London: Methuen, 1957).

Ford, John, *The Chronicle History of Perkin Warbeck: A Strange Truth*, ed. Peter Ure, The Revels Plays (Oxford: Oxford University Press, 1968).

Foster, Hal (ed.), *Postmodern Culture* (London: Pluto Press, 1985).

Gardner, Helen, 'Shakespeare in the directors' theatre', in *In Defence of the Imagination: The Charles Eliot Norton Lectures 1979–1980* (Oxford: The Clarendon Press, 1982).

Gilbert, Miriam, 'Re-viewing the play', *Shakespeare Quarterly*, 36 (1985), pp. 609–17.

Goodwin, John (ed.), *Royal Shakespeare Company 1960–63* (London: Max Reinhardt, 1964).

Greenwald, Michael L., *Directions by Indirections: John Barton of the Royal Shakespeare Company* (Newark: University of Delaware Press, 1986).

Gurr, Andrew (ed.), *The New Cambridge Shakespeare: King Henry V* (Cambridge: Cambridge University Press, 1992).

Guthrie, Tyrone, *A Life in the Theatre* (London: Hamish Hamilton, 1959).

Hakola, Liisa, *In One Person Many People: The Image of the King in Three RSC Productions of William Shakespeare's King Richard II* (Helsinki: Suomalainen Tiedeakatemia, 1988).

Hakola, Liisa, 'Not only a question of money: Shakespeare and the ego decade', *New Theatre Quarterly*, no. 33 (1993), pp. 37–43.

Hammond, Anthony (ed.), *The Arden Shakespeare: King Richard III* (London: Methuen, 1981).

Hankey, Julie (ed.), *Plays in Performance: Richard III*, 2nd edn (Bristol: Bristol Classical Press, 1988).

Happe, Peter (ed.), *Four Morality Plays* (Harmondsworth: Penguin, 1979).

Harbage, Alfred, *Conceptions of Shakespeare* (Cambridge, Mass.: Harvard University Press, 1966).

Harlock, Peter (ed.), *Royal Shakespeare Company 1985/86 1986/87* (Stratford: RSC Publications, 1987).

Hassell, R. Chris, Jr, 'Context and charisma: the Sher–Alexander *Richard III* and its reviewers', *Shakespeare Quarterly*, 36 (1985), pp. 630–43.

Hattaway, Michael (ed.), *The New Cambridge Shakespeare: The First Part of King Henry VI* (Cambridge: Cambridge University Press, 1991).

Hattaway, Michael (ed.), *The New Cambridge Shakespeare: The Second Part of King Henry VI* (Cambridge: Cambridge University Press, 1992)

Hattaway, Michael (ed.), *The New Cambridge Shakespeare: The Third Part of King Henry VI* (Cambridge: Cambridge University Press, 1993).

Hawkes, Terence, *That Shakespeherian Rag: Essays on a Critical Process* (London: Methuen, 1986).

Hawkes, Terence, *Meaning by Shakespeare* (London: Routledge, 1992).

Hayman, Ronald, *Playback* (London: Davis-Poynter, 1973).

Hebdige, Dick, *Subculture: The Meaning of Style* (London: Methuen, 1979).

Hewison, Robert, *Too Much: Art and Society in the Sixties 1960–75* (London: Methuen, 1986).

Hewison, Robert, *The Heritage Industry: Britain in a Climate of Decline* (London: Methuen, 1987).

Hewison, Robert, *In Anger: Culture in the Cold War 1945–60*, 2nd edn (London: Methuen, 1988).

Hodgon, Barbara, '*The Wars of the Roses*: scholarship speaks on the stage', *Deutsche Shakespeare-Gesellschaft West Jahrbuch 1972*, pp. 170–84.

Hodgon, Barbara, *Shakespeare in Performance: Henry IV, Part II* (Manchester: Manchester University Press, 1993).

Holderness, Graham, 'The albatross and the swan: two productions at Stratford', *New Theatre Quarterly*, no. 14 (1988), pp. 152–8.

Holderness, Graham (ed.), *The Shakespeare Myth* (Manchester: Manchester University Press, 1988).

Holderness, Graham, Nick Potter and John Turner, *Shakespeare: the Play of History* (London: Macmillan, 1988).

Holderness, Graham (ed.), *The Politics of Theatre and Drama* (London: Macmillan, 1991).

Holderness, Graham, *Shakespeare Recycled: The Making of Historical Drama* (Hemel Hempstead: Harvester Wheatsheaf, 1992).

Holderness, Graham (ed.), *Shakespeare's History Plays: a New Casebook* (London: Macmillan, 1992).

Holland, Peter, 'The RSC and studio Shakespeare', *Essays in Criticism*, 32 (1982), pp. 205–18.

Honigman, E. A. J. (ed.), *The Arden Shakespeare: King John*, 4th edn (London: Methuen, 1954).

Honigman, E. A. J. (ed.), *The New Penguin Shakespeare: King Richard the Third* (Harmondsworth: Penguin, 1968).

Horne, Donald, *The Great Museum: The Re-presentation of History* (London: Verso, 1984).

Howard, Jean E. and Marion F. O'Connor (eds), *Shakespeare Reproduced: The Text in History and Ideology* (London: Methuen, 1987).

Humphreys, A. R. (ed.), *The Arden Shakespeare: The First Part of King Henry IV*, 6th edn (London: Methuen, 1960).

Humphreys, A. R. (ed.), *The Arden Shakespeare: The Second Part of King Henry IV* (London: Methuen, 1966).

Humphreys, A. R. (ed.), *The New Penguin Shakespeare: Henry V* (Harmondsworth: Penguin, 1968).

Humphreys, A. R. (ed.), *The New Penguin Shakespeare: King Henry VIII* (Harmondsworth: Penguin, 1971).

Hunter, G. K., 'The Royal Shakespeare Company plays *Henry VI*', *Renaissance Drama*, 9 (1978), pp. 91–108.

Itzin, Catherine, *Stages in the Revolution: Political Theatre in Britain Since 1968* (London: Methuen, 1980).

Jackson, Sir Barry, 'On producing *Henry VI*', *Shakespeare Survey 6* (1953), pp. 49–52.

Jackson, Russell and Robert Smallwood (eds), *Players of Shakespeare 2: Further Essays in Shakespearean Performance* (Cambridge: Cambridge University Press, 1988).

Jarvis, Andrew and Stephen Phillips, 'Telling the story: Shakespeare's histories in performance', *New Theatre Quarterly*, no. 23 (1990), pp. 207–14.

Jouve, Nicole Ward, *The Streetcleaner: The Yorkshire Ripper Case on Trial* (London: Marion Boyars, 1988).

Kantorowicz, Ernst H., *The King's Two Bodies* (Princeton: Princeton University Press, 1957).

Kermode, Frank (ed.), *Selected Prose of T. S. Eliot* (London: Faber and Faber, 1975).

Kettle, Arnold (ed.), *Shakespeare in a Changing World* (London: Lawrence and Wishart, 1964).

Knight, G. Wilson, *Shakespearian Production* (Harmondsworth: Penguin, 1949).

Knights, L. C., *Drama and Society in the Age of Jonson* (London: Chatto and Windus, 1937).

Kott, Jan, *Shakespeare Our Contemporary*, trans. Boleslaw Taborski, 2nd edn (London: Methuen, 1967).

Leavis, F. R., *The Common Pursuit* (Harmondsworth: Penguin, 1962).

Leggatt, Alexander, *Shakespeare in Performance: King Lear* (Manchester: Manchester University Press, 1991).

Lloyd Evans, Gareth, 'Shakespeare, the twentieth century and "Behaviourism" ', *Shakespeare Survey 20* (1967), pp. 133–42.

Lloyd Evans, Gareth, 'The RSC's *King Lear* and *Macbeth*', *Shakespeare Quarterly*, 28 (1977), pp. 190–4.

McGuire, Philip C. and David A. Samuelson (eds), *Shakespeare: The Theatrical Dimension* (New York: AMS Press, 1979).

McLellan, David (ed.), *Karl Marx: Selected Writings* (Oxford: Oxford University Press, 1977).

McMillin, Scott, *Shakespeare in Performance: Henry IV, Part One* (Manchester: Manchester University Press, 1991).

Margeson, John (ed.), *The New Cambridge Shakespeare: King Henry VIII* (Cambridge: Cambridge University Press, 1990).

Marowitz, Charles and Simon Trussler (eds), *Theatre at Work* (London: Methuen, 1967).

Marowitz, Charles, *Confessions of a Counterfeit Critic* (London: Methuen, 1973).

Marowitz, Charles, *Recycling Shakespeare* (London: Macmillan, 1991).

Marsden, Jean I. (ed.), *The Appropriation of Shakespeare: Post-Renaissance Reconstructions of the Works and Myth* (Hemel Hempstead: Harvester Wheatsheaf, 1991).

Marshall, Norman, *The Other Theatre* (London: John Lehmann, 1947).

Marshall, Norman, *The Producer and the Play* (London: Davis-Poynter, 1975).

Mazer, Cary M., 'Shakespeare, the reviewer and the theatre historian', *Shakespeare Quarterly*, 36 (1985), pp. 648–61.

Mulhern, Francis, *The Moment of 'Scrutiny'* (London: New Left Books, 1979).

Mullin, Michael, *Theatre at Stratford-upon-Avon: A Catalogue-Index to Productions of the Shakespeare Memorial/Royal Shakespeare Theatre, 1879–1978* (Westport, Conn.: Greenwood Press, 1980).

Nairn, Tom, *The Enchanted Glass: Britain and its Monarchy* (London: Radius, 1988).

Newlin, Jeanne T. (ed.), *Richard II: Critical Essays* (New York and London: Garland, 1984).

Nyberg, Lennart, *The Shakespearean Ideal: Shakespeare Production and the Modern Theatre in Britain* (Uppsala: Acta Universitatis Upsaliensis, 1988).

O'Brien, Timothy, 'Designing a Shakespeare play: *Richard II*', *Deutsche Shakespeare-Gesellschaft West Jahrbuch 1974*, pp. 111–20.

Page, Malcolm, *Text and Performance: Richard II* (London: Macmillan, 1987).

Potter, Lois, 'Recycling the early histories: "The Wars of the Roses" and "The Plantagenets" ', *Shakespeare Survey 43* (1991), pp. 171–81.

Quinn, Michael, 'Celebrity and the semiotics of acting', *New Theatre Quarterly*, no. 22 (1990), pp. 154–61.

Rackin, Phyllis, *Stages of History: Shakespeare's English Chronicles* (London: Routledge, 1991).

Reade, Simon, *Cheek by Jowl: Ten Years of Celebration* (Bath: Absolute Classics, 1991).

Richmond, Hugh M., *Shakespeare in Performance: King Richard III* (Manchester: Manchester University Press, 1989).

Righter, Anne, *Shakespeare and the Idea of the Play* (London: Chatto and Windus, 1962).

Rissik, Andrew, 'Playing Shakespeare false: a critique of the "Stratford Voice" ', *New Theatre Quarterly*, no. 1 (1985), pp. 227–30.

Rosenberg, Marvin, *The Masks of Othello* (Berkeley: University of California Press, 1961).

Rosenberg, Marvin, *The Masks of King Lear* (Berkeley: University of California Press, 1971).

Rosenberg, Marvin, *The Masks of Macbeth* (Berkeley: University of California Press, 1978).

Rosenberg, Marvin, *The Masks of Hamlet* (Newark: University of Delaware Press, 1993).

Royal Shakespeare Company, *Crucial Years of the RSC* (London: Max Reinhardt, 1963).

Rutter, Carol, *Clamorous Voices: Shakespeare's Women Today*, ed. Faith Evans (London: The Women's Press, 1988).

Ryan, Kiernan, *Shakespeare* (Hemel Hempstead: Harvester Wheatsheaf, 1989).

Saccio, Peter, *Shakespeare's English Kings: History, Chronicle and Drama* (Oxford: Oxford University Press, 1977).

Sanders, Norman, 'The popularity of Shakespeare: an examination of the Royal Shakespeare Theatre's repertory', *Shakespeare Survey 16* (1966), pp. 18–29.

Scott, Michael, *Renaissance Drama and a Modern Audience* (London: Macmillan, 1982).

Scott, Michael, *Shakespeare and the Modern Dramatist* (London: Macmillan, 1988).

Selbourne, David, 'Brook's *Dream*', in *Culture and Agitation: Theatre Documents* (London: Action Books, 1972).

Selbourne, David, *The Making of 'A Midsummer Night's Dream'* (London: Methuen, 1982).

Shakespeare, William, *The Plantagenets* (London: Faber and Faber, 1989).

Shepherd, Simon, 'Acting against bardom: some utopian thoughts on workshops', in Lesley Aers and Nigel Wheale (eds), *Shakespeare in the Changing Curriculum* (London: Routledge, 1991).

Sher, Antony, *Year of the King* (London: Methuen, 1986).

Shewring, Margaret, *Shakespeare in Performance: King Richard II* (Manchester: Manchester University Press, 1993).

Sinfield, Alan, '*King Lear* versus *Lear* at Stratford', *Critical Quarterly*, 24 (1982), pp. 5–14.

Sinfield, Alan (ed.), *Society and Literature 1945–1970* (London: Methuen, 1983).

Sinfield, Alan, *Literature, Politics and Culture in Postwar Britain* (Oxford: Blackwell, 1989).

Sked, Alan and Chris Cook, *Post-War Britain: A Political History*, 4th edn (Harmondsworth: Penguin, 1993).

Smallwood, Robert, 'Shakespeare unbalanced: the Royal Shakespeare Company's *King John*, 1974–5', *Deutsche Shakespeare-Gesellschaft West Jahrbuch 1976*, pp. 23–42.

Smallwood, Robert, '*Henry IV, Parts 1 and 2* at the Barbican Theatre', *Critical Quarterly*, 25 (1983), pp. 15–20.

Smallwood, Robert, 'Shakespeare at Stratford-upon-Avon, 1988', *Shakespeare Quarterly*, 40 (1989), pp. 83–94.

Smallwood, Robert, 'Shakespeare at Stratford-upon-Avon, 1990', *Shakespeare Quarterly*, 42 (1991), pp. 345–59.

Smallwood, Robert, 'Shakespeare at Stratford-upon-Avon, 1991', *Shakespeare Quarterly*, 43 (1992), pp. 341–56.

Smallwood, Robert, 'Shakespeare at Stratford-upon-Avon, 1992', *Shakespeare Quarterly*, 44 (1993), pp. 343–62.

Sontag, Susan, *On Photography* (Harmondsworth: Penguin, 1977).

Speaight, Robert, *William Poel and the Elizabethan Revival* (London: Heinemann, 1954).

Speaight, Robert, 'Shakespeare in Britain', *Shakespeare Quarterly*, 14 (1963), pp. 419–32.

Speaight, Robert, 'Shakespeare in Britain', *Shakespeare Quarterly*, 15 (1964), pp. 377–89.

Speaight, Robert, 'Shakespeare in Britain', *Shakespeare Quarterly*, 24 (1973), pp. 400–5.

Speaight, Robert, *Shakespeare on the Stage* (London: Collins, 1973).

Speaight, Robert, 'Shakespeare in Britain', *Shakespeare Quarterly*, 25 (1974), pp. 389–98.

Speaight, Robert, 'Shakespeare in Britain', *Shakespeare Quarterly*, 27 (1976), pp. 15–23.

Speaight, Robert, 'Truth and relevance in Shakespeare production', in David Bevington and Jay L. Halio (eds), *Shakespeare: Pattern of Excelling Nature* (Newark: University of Delaware Press, 1976).

Sprague, A. C., *Shakespearean Players and Performances* (London: A. & C. Black, 1954).

Sprague, A. C., *Shakespeare's Histories: Plays for the Stage* (London: Society for Theatre Research, 1964).

Sprague, A. C. and J. C. Trewin, *Shakespeare's Plays Today: Customs and Conventions of the Stage* (London: Sidgwick and Jackson, 1970).

Stredder, James, 'John Barton's production of *Richard II* at Stratford-on-Avon, 1973', *Deutsche Shakespeare-Gesellschaft West Jahrbuch 1976*, pp. 23–42.

Styan, J. L., *The Shakespeare Revolution: Criticism and Performance in the Twentieth Century* (Cambridge: Cambridge University Press, 1977).

Styan, J. L., *Shakespeare in Performance: All's Well that Ends Well* (Manchester: Manchester University Press, 1984).

Swander, Homer D., 'The rediscovery of *Henry VI*', *Shakespeare Quarterly*, 29 (1978), pp. 146–63.

Tawney, R. H., *Religion and the Rise of Capitalism* (Harmondsworth: Penguin, 1960).

Taylor, Gary, *Moment by Moment by Shakespeare* (London: Macmillan, 1985).

Taylor, Gary, *Reinventing Shakespeare: A Cultural History from the Restoration to the Present* (London: The Hogarth Press, 1990).

Tennenhouse, Leonard, *Power on Display: The Politics of Shakespeare's Genres* (London: Methuen, 1986).

Thompson, Marvin and Ruth Thompson (eds), *Shakespeare and the Sense of Performance* (London and Toronto: Associated University Presses, 1989).

Thomson, Peter, 'A necessary theatre: the Royal Shakespeare Company season 1970 reviewed', *Shakespeare Survey 24* (1971), pp. 117–26.

Thomson, Peter, 'Shakespeare straight and crooked: A review of the 1973 season at Stratford', *Shakespeare Survey 27* (1974), pp. 143–54.

Thomson, Peter, 'The smallest season: the Royal Shakespeare Company at Stratford in 1974', *Shakespeare Survey 28* (1975), pp. 137–48.

Thomson, Peter, 'Towards a poor Shakespeare: the Royal Shakespeare Company at Stratford in 1975', *Shakespeare Survey 29* (1976), pp. 151–6.

Tillyard, E. M. W., *The Elizabethan World Picture* (London: Chatto and Windus, 1943).

Tillyard, E. M. W., *Shakespeare's History Plays* (London: Chatto and Windus, 1944).

Trewin, J. C., *Shakespeare on the English Stage 1900–1964* (London: Barrie and Rockliff, 1964).

Trewin, J. C., 'Shakespeare in Britain', *Shakespeare Quarterly*, 29 (1978), pp. 212–21.

Trussler, Simon (ed.), *Royal Shakespeare Company 1978* (London: RSC/TQ Publications, 1979).

Trussler, Simon (ed.), *Royal Shakespeare Company 1979/80* (Stratford: RSC Publications, 1980).

Trussler, Simon (ed.), *Royal Shakespeare Company 1980/81* (Stratford: RSC Publications, 1981).

Trussler, Simon (ed.), *Royal Shakespeare Company 1982/83* (Stratford: RSC Publications, 1983).

Trussler, Simon (ed.), *Royal Shakespeare Company 1983/84* (Stratford: RSC Publications, 1984).

Trussler, Simon (ed.), *Royal Shakespeare Company 1984/85* (Stratford: RSC Publications, 1985).

Turner, John, *Macbeth* (Buckingham: Open University Press, 1992).

Warren, Roger, 'Theory and practice: Stratford 1976', *Shakespeare Survey 30* (1977), pp. 169–79.

Warren, Roger, 'Comedies and histories at two Stratfords, 1977', *Shakespeare Survey 31* (1978), pp. 141–53.

Warren, Roger, 'Shakespeare in Stratford-on-Avon and London, 1982', *Shakespeare Quarterly*, 34 (1983), pp. 79–83.

Warren, Roger, 'Shakespeare in Stratford-on-Avon and London, 1983', *Shakespeare Quarterly*, 34 (1983), pp. 449–56.

Watson, Donald G., *Shakespeare's Early History Plays: Politics at Play on the Elizabethan Stage.* (London: Macmillan, 1990).

Wayne, Valerie (ed.), *The Matter of Difference: Materialist Feminist Criticism of Shakespeare* (Hemel Hempstead: Harvester Wheatsheaf, 1991).

Webster, Margaret, *Shakespeare Today* (London: Dent, 1957).

Weimann, Robert, 'Shakespeare on the modern stage: past significance and present meaning', *Shakespeare Survey 20* (1967), pp. 113–20.

Weitz, Morris, *'Hamlet' and the Philosophy of Literary Criticism* (Chicago: University of Chicago Press, 1965).

Wells, Stanley (ed.), *The New Penguin Shakespeare: King Richard II* (Harmondsworth: Penguin, 1969).

Wells, Stanley, 'Director's Shakespeare', *Deutsche Shakespeare-Gesellschaft West Jahrbuch 1976*, pp. 79–99.

Wells, Stanley, *Royal Shakespeare: Four Major Productions at Stratford-upon-Avon* (Manchester: Manchester University Press, 1977).

Wells, Stanley, 'Shakespeare performances in London and Stratford-upon-Avon, 1987–8', *Shakespeare Survey 42* (1990), pp. 129–48.

Wharton, T. F., *Text and Performance: Henry the Fourth Parts 1 and 2* (London: Macmillan, 1983).

White, Graham, 'Direct action, dramatic action: theatre and situationist theory', *New Theatre Quarterly*, no. 36 (1993), pp. 239–40.

Willett, John (ed.), *Brecht on Theatre* (London: Methuen, 1964).

Willett, John and Ralph Mannheim (eds), *Bertolt Brecht: Collected Plays*, vol. 9 (New York: Vintage Books, 1973).

Wilson, John Dover and T. C. Worsley, *Shakespeare's Histories at Stratford, 1951* (London: Max Reinhardt, 1952).

Winny, James L., *The Player King: A Theme of Shakespeare's Histories* (London: Chatto and Windus, 1968).

Wood, Charles, *Tumbledown* (Harmondsworth: Penguin, 1987).

Worthen, W. B., 'Deeper meanings and theatrical technique: the rhetoric of performance criticism', *Shakespeare Quarterly*, 40 (1989), pp. 441–55.

Index

Ackland, Joss, 75
Addenbrooke, David, 18, 27
Aldrin, Buzz, 138
Alexander, Bill, 6, 11, 122–30
Alien, 125
Allied Irish Bank, 77
Ansorge, Peter, 97, 101
Arden, John, 106–7, 142
   Left-Handed Liberty, 143
Arts Council, 42, 52, 106

Bale, John
   King Johan, 136, 138, 144, 147
Barker, Howard, 134, 149
Barker, Simon, 155
Barthes, Roland, 98
Barton, Anne (née Righter), 92, 93, 98
Barton, John, 1, 6, 11, 13, 22, 27, 28,
   39, 41–58, 60, 66, 70, 79, 81, 85,
   86, 91–104, 108, 111, 133–48, 149,
   164, 168, 170, 173
Beaumann, Sally, 27, 108
Beckett, Samuel, 12, 32, 49, 64,
   Krapp's Last Tape, 32
Beethoven, 171
Belsey, Catherine, 20, 32
Benson, F. R., 39, 43
Berliner Ensemble, 12, 45
Berry, Ralph, 30, 32, 115, 178
Billington, Michael, 73, 75, 127, 145,
   162
Birmingham Repertory Theatre, 66, 81
Boadicea, 121
Bogdanov, Michael, 77, 85
Bond, Edward, 55, 134, 142, 149, 153,
   165, 166,
   Lear, 143, 165
Bradbrook, M. C., 29

Bradley, A. C., 29
Branagh, Kenneth, 6, 77, 116, 118–21,
   122, 127
Brando, Marlon, 125
Brecht, Bertolt, 6, 19, 28, 45–6, 53, 55,
   61, 96, 112, 117, 135, 142–3,
   159–61, 166, 169, 175
   Coriolan, 143
   Threepenny Opera, The, 162
Brenton, Howard, 134
Breughel, 46
Bridges-Adams, William, 17
Brook, Peter, 13, 14, 15, 28, 50, 51, 64,
   102, 108–9, 169
Brown, John Russell, 23, 27–8
Bryden, Ronald, 44, 50, 108
Burn, Gordon, 129
Bury, John, 52, 75

Callaghan, Dympna, 164
Callaghan, James, 16
Cambridge Festival Theatre, 152
Campbell, Beatrix, 121
Cameron, Deborah, 128–30
Carr, E. H., 139
Carroll, Lewis, 134
Cerasano, S. P., 126
Chambers, Colin, 27, 70, 134, 164,
   165–6
Chariots of Fire, 86
Charles, Prince, 119
Cheek by Jowl, 77
Chkhivadze, Ramaz, 124
Churchill, Winston, 121
Cibber, Colley, 151
Coveney, Michael, 1, 168
Cox, Frank, 55–6
Crowley, Bob, 77, 85, 87

Cushman, Robert, 145, 159, 160

Daniels, Ron, 167, 177
David, Richard, 24, 27, 29–30
Davies, Howard, 6, 149–62, 163
de Jongh, Nicholas, 161
Demeger, Robert, 172
Dickens, Charles, 75
  Nicholas Nickleby, 74–5, 76, 80, 156
Donellan, Declan, 77
Donohue, Walter, 149
Dormandy, Simon, 86
Downie, Penny, 82–3
Dudley, William, 122

Eaton, Sara, 31
Edgar, David, 156–7, 161, 162
  Destiny, 156
  Maydays, 156
Elam, Keir, 19
Eliot, T. S., 57, 147–8,
  Murder in the Cathedral, 143, 147
Elsom, John, 95, 103, 145
English Shakespeare Company, 77

Farrah, 108, 109, 117
Festival of Britain, 39
Fiennes, Ralph, 174
Findlater, Richard, 150
Fletcher, John, 150, 153–4, 162
Ford, John
  Perkin Warbeck, 167, 168
Ford, Julia, 84
Frazer, Elizabeth, 128–30
Fry, Christopher, 57

Gardner, Lyn, 86
Garrick, David, 135
General Will, The, 156
Gielgud, John, 43, 99
Gilbert, Miriam, 97, 101
Gilbert, W. Stephen, 107
Godfather, The, 125
Goodbody, Buzz, 15, 134, 135, 146, 164–5, 167, 173
Granville-Barker, Harley, 28
Gray, Terence, 152
Greenwald, Michael, 57
Gregson, Edward, 86
Griffiths, Richard, 154, 160

Gross, John, 174
Grotowski, Jerzy, 15
Guthrie, Tyrone, 19, 28, 152

Hack, Keith, 134
Hair, 14
Hakola, Liisa, 97
Hall, Peter, 1, 11, 12, 14, 18, 24, 27, 39, 41–58, 61, 66–7, 70, 79, 85, 86, 95, 102, 149, 180–1
Hands, Terry, 1, 6, 11, 16, 29, 60–71, 73, 78, 91, 105–16
Heath, Edward, 15, 62, 103, 134, 142
Hewison, Robert, 123
Hitler, Adolf, 122
Hobson, Harold, 49, 107
Hogarth, William, 75
Hogg, Quintin, 13, 44
Holbein, Hans, 159
Holderness, Graham, 117, 118
Holinshed, 136, 154
Holland, Peter, 166
Holm, Ian, 43, 44, 106, 124
Howard, Alan, 6, 11, 62, 67, 68–9, 105, 111, 114–15, 119
Hunchback of Notre Dame, The, 125
Hunter, G. K., 66–7

Ionesco, Eugene, 49, 139
Irons, Jeremy, 177
Irving, Henry, 28

James, Emrys, 62, 66, 109, 111, 139–41
Jarry, Alfred, 139
  Ubu Roi, 170
Jaws, 125
Jones, Gemma, 160
Jouve, Nicole Ward, 129
Joyce, James
  Ulysses, 147–8

Kantorowicz, E. H., 92
Kemble, John, 4
Kick Theatre, 169
Knights, L. C., 48
Kott, Jan, 5, 13, 22, 26, 40, 47, 50–1, 61, 104, 122, 123, 138
Kretzmer, Herbert, 145
Kyle, Barry, 134, 167, 177

Lacan, Jacques, 20
LAMDA, 13, 50, 163
Laughton, Charles, 124
Leavis, F. R., 5, 22, 40, 48, 50
Leggatt, Alexander, 32
Les Miserables, 73
Lesser, Anton, 67, 85
Levin, Bernard, 37, 70
Lewsen, Charles, 107
Lord Chamberlain, 50, 97

Macmillan, Harold, 13, 44
McCullough, Christopher, 50, 162
McDiarmid, Ian, 117
Marlowe Society, 57
Marowitz, Charles, 55
Marx Brothers, 140
Marx, Karl, 19
Mason, Brewster, 62
Mendes, Sam, 167, 178
Meyerhold, Vsevolod, 152
Mikael, Ludmila, 109
Milne, A. A., 134
Moiseiwitsch, Tanya, 46
Morissey, David, 173–4
Mozart, 171
Mulvey, Laura, 31
Murphy, Gerald, 75–6

Napier, John, 74
National Theatre, 15, 42, 52, 55, 73
Nichols, Peter
    National Health, The, 168
Nightingale, Benedict, 95, 99, 107, 112,
    138, 145–6, 160–1
Nilsen, Dennis, 129
Nixon, Richard, 134
Noble, Adrian, 1, 6, 16, 77, 78–87,
    116–21, 122, 167, 177–8
Nunn, Trevor, 13, 14, 16, 28, 61, 72–7,
    107, 152–3, 164, 167

O'Brien, Timothy, 91
O'Callaghan, Richard, 160
Olivier, Laurence, 67, 113, 124–5
Orwell, George, 122
Osborne, Charles, 172, 174
Osborne, John, 45

Palace Theatre, 73

Pasco, Richard, 6, 91, 93, 98–102
Peart, Fred, 146
Pennington, Michael, 85, 128
Philip, Prince, 107
Pinter, Harold, 44, 49
Place, The, 15, 163
Planche, J. R., 4
Plantagenets, The, 1, 2, 6, 78–87, 169,
    173, 176, 178
Poel, William, 17, 22, 28, 29
Profumo, John, 44
Pryce, Jonathan, 124

Quayle, Anthony, 39, 40
Queen Elizabeth II, 152

Radin, Victoria, 150
Ratcliffe, Michael, 85, 128
Reinhardt, Max, 17
Renaissance Theatre Company, 77
Richardson, Ian, 6, 91, 93, 98–102, 168
Richmond, Hugh, 81
Righter, Anne *see* Barton, Anne
Romans, The, 14
Rosenberg, Marvin, 23
Royal Insurance, 16
Ryan, Kiernan, 28
Rylands, George, 57

Saccio, Peter, 4
Saint-Denis, Michel, 13
Samuelson, David, 23
Schofield, David, 160
Seale, Douglas, 66
Sekacz, Ilona, 159
Selbourne, David, 28
Sex Pistols, 70
Shakespeare Birthplace Trust, 25
Shakespeare, William
    All's Well that Ends Well, 30, 77
    Antony and Cleopatra, 14, 167
    Coriolanus, 14
    Cymbeline, 134
    Hamlet, 13, 54, 102, 164–5, 167, 178
    Henry IV plays, 5, 6, 11, 43, 46, 49,
        60–4, 72–7, 99, 105, 167, 177
    Henry V, 1, 4, 5, 39, 43, 60, 63, 65,
        77, 105–21, 167, 177–8, 179
    Henry VI plays, 6, 11, 27, 37, 39, 41,
        52–5, 65–71, 109

Shakespeare, William (*continued*)
  Henry VIII, 2, 4, 6, 11, 14, 133, 149–62, 163
  Julius Caesar, 14
  King John, 2, 4, 6, 11, 133–48, 163, 164, 169–75, 167, 177, 178
  King Lear, 13, 32, 50, 77, 164, 167
  Macbeth, 150, 165, 179
  Measure for Measure, 134
  Merry Wives of Windsor, The, 6, 60, 65
  Midsummer Night's Dream, A, 14, 28, 64, 102, 108
  Much Ado about Nothing, 150
  Othello, 165, 167
  Pericles, 152, 167
  Richard II, 6, 11, 28, 39, 43, 47, 85, 91–104, 108, 111, 136, 137, 167, 177
  Richard III, 6, 11, 39, 41, 47, 50, 81, 85, 91, 122–30, 167, 168–9, 178
  Taming of the Shrew, The, 57
  Tempest, The, 152
  Timon of Athens, 167
  Titus Andronicus, 14, 169, 170, 171
  Troilus and Cressida, 13
  Twelfth Night, 134
  Winter's Tale, The, 14, 152
Sher, Antony, 6, 11, 123–30, 178
Shorter, Eric, 127, 168
Shulman, Milton, 174
Sinfield, Alan, 12, 50, 103
Smallwood, Robert, 146, 175
Sontag, Susan, 32
Speaight, Robert, 94, 146
Sprague, A. C., 23
Stalin, Joseph, 160, 161
Stanislavsky, Constantin, 66–7, 69, 100, 125
Stardust, Alvin, 111
Star Wars, 86
Steadman, Ralph, 154
Stephens, Robert, 178
Stewart, Patrick, 75
Stredder, James, 97
Strindberg, August, 125, 165
Styan, J. L., 28–9, 30, 33

Sutcliffe, Peter, 129–30
Sweeney, The, 160

Tawney, R. H., 155
Taylor, Paul, 171
Thatcher, Margaret, 15, 16, 73, 77, 116, 119, 121, 126, 154, 155, 162, 176, 177
Thaw, John, 160
Theatregoround, 15, 112, 134, 163, 164
Thomson, Peter, 96–7, 101, 134, 138, 140–1, 143, 146
Tillyard, E. M. W., 5, 22, 38, 40, 47–8, 50, 80, 86, 96, 104, 135
Tinker, Jack, 126–7, 161–2
Troublesome Reign of King John, The, 135–8, 143, 147
Tree, Beerbohm, 151, 157
Tynan, Kenneth, 45, 46

US, 13, 50

Wagner, Richard, 41
Wardle, Irving, 145, 159, 173
Warner, David, 45, 47, 49, 54, 178
Warner, Deborah, 6, 163, 169–75, 178
Wars of the Roses, The, (English Stage Company), 77, 85
Wars of the Roses, The (RSC), 2, 5, 11, 13, 14, 39, 40, 41–59, 60, 61, 63, 66, 75, 78, 81, 91, 102–3, 106, 136, 143, 145, 147, 176
Weill, Kurt, 159
Weiss, Peter
  Marat/Sade, 50, 168–9
Wells, Stanley, 27, 95, 101
Wesker, Arnold, 45
White, Graham, 165
Williams, Clifford, 42
Wilson, Harold, 13, 48, 103, 144
Wilson, John Dover, 40
Woman's Own, 154
Women's Street Theatre, 164
Wood, Charles
  Tumbledown, 80
Woodeson, Nicholas, 171, 172, 173
Woolfenden, Guy, 74